Penguin Handbooks
The Penguin Book of Dogs

Roger Caras has been in the vanguard of nature conservation in the United States for many years. He is well known for his appearances on television and for his radio broadcasts, and has lectured to colleges, universities and other organizations. He is the author of over forty books on nature, the environment and companion animals, including *Antarctica: Land of Frozen Time, Last Chance on Earth, Death as a Way of Life, Venomous Animals in the World, The Private Lives of Animals* and *Dangerous to Man* (Pelican), as well as several books for children. A Fellow of the Royal Society of Arts, he has also been on the board of several conservation organizations.

Michael Findlay was born in Ayr in 1942. He qualified at Glasgow University in 1966. Since then he has been in practice as a small animal veterinary surgeon. He appears frequently on radio and television and is press spokesman for the British Small Animal Veterinary Association. He is also interested in zoological animals, cat shows and breeding, and dog obedience clubs, and was a founder member of a D.O.C. while at college and ultimately became its president. For the past eleven years he has been one of the Honorary Veterinary Surgeons to Cruft's Dog Show and is also a member of the Kennel Club in London.

THE PENGUIN BOOK OF

DOGS

ROGER CARAS
AND MICHAEL FINDLAY

PENGUIN BOOKS

Penguin Books Ltd, Harmondsworth, Middlesex, England
Penguin Books, 40 West 23rd Street, New York, New York 10010, U.S.A.
Penguin Books Australia Ltd, Ringwood, Victoria, Australia
Penguin Books Canada Ltd, 2801 John Street, Markham, Ontario, Canada L3R 1B4
Penguin Books (N.Z.) Ltd, 182–190 Wairau Road, Auckland 10, New Zealand

This book originated as *The Roger Caras Dog Book*,
published in the U.S.A. by Holt, Rinehart and Winston
and simultaneously in Canada by Holt, Rinehart and Winston of Canada,
Limited, 1980
This amended edition published in Penguin Books 1983

All the photographs reproduced in this book are by Alton Anderson, with
the exception of those that appear on the following pages:

Marc Henrie, A.S.C.: 39, 41, 61, 73, 79, 81, 83, 85, 87, 99, 101 (Long-coated Chihuahua),
103, 107 (Smooth Collie), 111 (Long-haired and Wire-haired Dachshund), 119, 127, 129,
131, 133, 137 (Smooth Fox Terrier), 149, 151, 155, 159, 161, 163, 169 (Hungarian Wire-
haired Vizsla), 183, 189, 201, 203, 205, 209, 215, 221, 223, 225, 231, 241, 243, 255, 257,
263, 287, 303, 325, 331; Anne Roslin-Williams: 55, 97, 109, 249, 329; Animals
Unlimited: 121, 219; Panther Photographic International: 143, 293, 327; Animal
Photography Ltd: 173, 195, 223.

Typeset by CCC, printed and bound in Great Britain by William Clowes (Beccles) Limited,
Beccles and London
Set in Clowes Dante

To Mum and Dad
and
to 'Blacksam of Selborne'

Contents

Preface

In many ways, it is invidious to base a dog book on that of Roger Caras, a well-respected and famous American author, and his photographer, Alton Anderson. But I have tried in *The Penguin Book of Dogs* to produce the most comprehensive and up-to-date text possible on the thoroughbred (or pure-bred, as they would say west of the Atlantic) dog.

With great help from the Kennel Club, I have listed (subject to the usual limitations of publishing deadlines) alphabetically all breeds registrable (and therefore recognized) by the U.K. Kennel Club; some breeds are so 'rare' numerically that show standards do not exist. Undoubtedly, by the time you read this, new breeds will have been recognized because of importation of dogs; standards will change as a result of selective breeding, and some breeds may even have disappeared – partly as a reflection of evolutionary progress and partly as a result of dog-buyers' foibles and of supply and demand.

The Penguin Book of Dogs is hopefully aimed as a guide to would-be purchasers of the pedigree animal, and also as a reasonably priced reference book for caninophiles, such as vets, kennel-owners, pet-shop proprietors, journalists, schools and libraries. In production of the final text, I have spoken to countless breeders, judges and renowned pundits of the many breeds; it is therefore, I trust, an authoritative work, for the breed-by-breed comments are gleaned from the experts.

A few words of explanation are necessary where there may appear to be omissions in the text. The discrepancy in text lengths in some breeds reflects the amount of information available to the author. Breeds with short descriptions are invariably very rare in numbers – in some cases they may be 'extinct' in Britain, and little is known therefore about the specific characteristics. Where minimum height or weight is unstated, this is because no precise standards have (as yet) been set for the breed. Breed popularity reflects the most recent Kennel Club figures available for the numbers of dogs of the breed registered – only the top forty breeds have been given to show the most popular varieties. 'Rare' breeds may be absent from the U.K. or have so few dogs registered that they are very uncommon. Please note, however, that 'rare breed' is also defined by the Kennel Club as a variety which has not yet been awarded Championship show status. 'Moderate' popularity denotes breeds not in the top forty numerically, but still enjoying a frequency in excess of the rare breeds. N.S.G. denotes that there are no breed standards available at time of writing.

A large number of photographs have been supplied for this book by Marc Henrie, an exceptional animal photographer, with whom I have had the pleasure of working for many years. In addition to supplying visuals of the rarer breeds, he has furnished pictures of breeds which in Europe and America commonly sport cropped ears; such dogs quite rightly may not be shown in the U.K.

My grateful thanks are due to my long-suffering secretary, Patricia Stephens, to the Kennel Club, and in particular to Bill Edmond, to my veterinary colleagues for their kind advice and to the many experts and enthusiasts of all the various breeds; their guidance, help and patience are, I hope, fully acknowledged in the publication of this book.

Michael A. Findlay
February 1982

Useful Addresses

ANIMAL HEALTH TRUST, Lanwades Hall, Kennett, Newmarket, Suffolk CB8 7PN.

BREED CLUBS
BREED COUNCILS
BREED RESCUE CLUBS
} As Officers change frequently, contact KENNEL CLUB (see below).

BRITISH SMALL ANIMAL VETERINARY ASSOCIATION, 5 St George's Terrace, Cheltenham, Gloucestershire GL50 3PT.

BRITISH VETERINARY ASSOCIATION, 7 Mansfield Street, London W1M 0AT.

DOG TRAINING WEEKLY, 7 Greenwich South Street, London SE10 8BR.

DOG WORLD, Clergy House, The Churchyard, Ashford, Kent TN23 1QW.

KENNEL CLUB, 1 Clarges Street, Piccadilly, London W1Y 8AB. Telephone: (01) 493 6651.

MINISTRY OF AGRICULTURE, FISHERIES AND FOOD, Hook Rise South, Tolworth, Surbiton, Surrey KT6 7NF.

NATIONAL CANINE DEFENCE LEAGUE, 10 Seymour Street, London W1H 5WB.

NATIONAL DOG OWNERS' ASSOCIATION, 39–41 North Road, London N7 9DP.

NATIONAL SAVE OUR PETS ASSOCIATION, 85 Sylvan Avenue, Timperley, Altrincham, Cheshire WA15 6AD.

OUR DOGS, Oxford Road, Station Approach, Manchester M60 1SX.

PEOPLE'S DISPENSARY FOR SICK ANIMALS, P.D.S.A. House, South Street, Dorking, Surrey RH4 2LB.

PET HEALTH COUNCIL, Gwynne Hart & Associates Ltd, Walter House, 418–22 Strand, London WC2R 0PL.

PRO DOGS, Arden House, Holt Wood, Aylesford, Kent ME20 7QH.

ROYAL COLLEGE OF VETERINARY SURGEONS, 32 Belgrave Square,
London SW1X 8QP.

ROYAL SOCIETY FOR THE PREVENTION OF CRUELTY TO ANIMALS,
The Manor House, Horsham, Sussex RH12 1HG.

SELECTADOG, Pedigree Petfoods Education Centre, National Office,
Waltham-on-the-Wolds, Melton Mowbray, Leicestershire LE14 4RS.

Group Classification of U.K. Kennel Club Registrable Breeds

SPORTING BREEDS

Hound Group

AFGHAN HOUNDS

BASENJIS

BASSET HOUNDS

BEAGLES

BLOODHOUNDS

BORZOIS

DACHSBRACKES

DACHSHUNDS (LONG-HAIRED)

DACHSHUNDS (SMOOTH-HAIRED)

DACHSHUNDS (WIRE-HAIRED)

DACHSHUNDS (MINIATURE
   LONG-HAIRED)

DACHSHUNDS (MINIATURE
   SMOOTH-HAIRED)

DACHSHUNDS (MINIATURE
   WIRE-HAIRED)

DEERHOUNDS

ELKHOUNDS

FINNISH SPITZ

FOXHOUNDS

GREYHOUNDS

HAMILTON STOVARES

IBIZAN HOUNDS

IRISH WOLFHOUNDS

OTTERHOUNDS

PETIT BASSETS GRIFFONS VENDEEN

PHARAOH HOUNDS

PORTUGUESE WARREN HOUNDS

RHODESIAN RIDGEBACKS

SALUKIS

SLOUGHIS

SWISS LAUFHUNDS (JURA)

WHIPPETS

Gun-dog Group

BRITTANY SPANIELS

DRENTSE PARTRIDGE DOGS

ENGLISH SETTERS

GERMAN LONG-HAIRED POINTERS

GERMAN SHORT-HAIRED POINTERS

GERMAN WIRE-HAIRED POINTERS

GORDON SETTERS

HUNGARIAN VIZSLAS

HUNGARIAN WIRE-HAIRED
   VIZSLAS

IRISH SETTERS

ITALIAN SPINONES

LARGE MUNSTERLANDERS

POINTERS

POINTING WHITE-HAIRED
   GRIFFONS

RETRIEVERS (CHESAPEAKE BAY)

RETRIEVERS (CURLY-COATED)

RETRIEVERS (FLAT-COATED)

RETRIEVERS (GOLDEN)

RETRIEVERS (LABRADOR)

SETTERS, RED-AND-WHITE

SMALL MUNSTERLANDERS

SPANIELS (AMERICAN COCKER)

SPANIELS (CLUMBER)

SPANIELS (COCKER)

SPANIELS (ENGLISH SPRINGER)
SPANIELS (FIELD)
SPANIELS (IRISH WATER)
SPANIELS (SUSSEX)
SPANIELS (WELSH SPRINGER)
WEIMARANERS

Working Group

ALASKAN MALAMUTES
ANATOLIAN (KARABASH) DOGS
AUSTRALIAN CATTLE DOGS
   (KELPIES)
BEARDED COLLIES
BEAUCERONS
BELGIAN SHEPHERD DOGS
   (GROENENDAELS)
BELGIAN SHEPHERD DOGS
   (LAEKENOIS)
BELGIAN SHEPHERD DOGS
   (MALINOIS)
BELGIAN SHEPHERD DOGS
   (TERVUERENS)
BERNESE MOUNTAIN DOGS
BORDER COLLIES
BOUVIERS DES FLANDRES
BOXERS
BRIARDS
BULLMASTIFFS
COLLIES (ROUGH)
COLLIES (SMOOTH)
DOBERMANS
ESKIMO DOGS
ESTRELA MOUNTAIN DOGS
GERMAN SHEPHERD DOGS
   (ALSATIANS)
GREAT DANES
HOVAWART
HUNGARIAN KUVASZ
HUNGARIAN PULIS
KOMONDORS

LANCASHIRE HEELERS
MAREMMA SHEEPDOGS
MASTIFFS
NEAPOLITAN MASTIFFS
NEWFOUNDLANDS
NORWEGIAN BUHUNDS
OLD ENGLISH SHEEPDOGS
POLISH SHEEPDOGS
PORTUGUESE WATER DOGS
PYRENEAN MOUNTAIN DOGS
ROTTWEILERS
SAINT BERNARDS
SAMOYEDS
SHETLAND SHEEPDOGS
SIBERIAN HUSKIES
SWEDISH VALLHUNDS
TIBETAN MASTIFFS
WELSH CORGIS (CARDIGAN)
WELSH CORGIS (PEMBROKE)

Terrier Group

AIREDALE TERRIERS
AUSTRALIAN TERRIERS
BEDLINGTON TERRIERS
BORDER TERRIERS
BULL TERRIERS
BULL TERRIERS (MINIATURE)
CAIRN TERRIERS
DANDIE DINMONT TERRIERS
FOX TERRIERS (SMOOTH)
FOX TERRIERS (WIRE)
GLEN OF IMAAL TERRIERS
IRISH TERRIERS
KERRY BLUE TERRIERS
LAKELAND TERRIERS
MANCHESTER TERRIERS
NORFOLK TERRIERS
NORWICH TERRIERS
SCOTTISH TERRIERS

SEALYHAM TERRIERS
SKYE TERRIERS
SOFT-COATED WHEATEN TERRIERS

STAFFORDSHIRE BULL TERRIERS
WELSH TERRIERS
WEST HIGHLAND WHITE TERRIERS

NON-SPORTING BREEDS

Utility Group

BOSTON TERRIERS
BULLDOGS
CANAAN DOGS
CHOW CHOWS
DALMATIANS
FRENCH BULLDOGS
GIANT SCHNAUZERS
ICELAND DOGS
JAPANESE AKITAS
JAPANESE SPITZ
KEESHONDS
LEONBERGERS
LHASA APSOS
MEXICAN HAIRLESS
MINIATURE SCHNAUZERS
POODLES (MINIATURE)
POODLES (STANDARD)
POODLES (TOY)
SCHIPPERKES
SCHNAUZERS
SHAR-PEIS
SHIH TZUS
TIBETAN SPANIELS
TIBETAN TERRIERS

Toy Group

AFFENPINSCHERS
AUSTRALIAN SILKY TERRIERS
BICHONS FRISES
CAVALIER KING CHARLES
   SPANIELS
CHIHUAHUAS (LONG COAT)
CHIHUAHUAS (SMOOTH COAT)
CHINESE CRESTED DOGS
ENGLISH TOY TERRIERS
   (BLACK AND TAN)
GRIFFONS BRUXELLOIS
ITALIAN GREYHOUNDS
JAPANESE CHINS
KING CHARLES SPANIELS
LOWCHENS
MALTESE
MINIATURE PINSCHERS
PAPILLONS
PEKINGESES
POMERANIANS
PUGS
YORKSHIRE TERRIERS

Introduction

1 DOES A DOG DESERVE ME?

This brief section of *The Penguin Book of Dogs* is aimed at the caring, thinking, responsible owner. It summarizes the practical considerations, commitments and pitfalls of dog ownership – often gone into in much depth and detail in large books dealing with various aspects of the pet dog. The author's intention is to focus some thought on the practicability of pet-dog owning, in the hope that some patently unsuited owners will decide against acquiring a dog or puppy as a companion, plaything or status symbol. It is by abrogating responsibilities of this nature that a minority of people gets the vast majority of caring and thinking owners a bad name.

A dog needs food, comfort, sleep, exercise and company.

(i) *Food* – costs money but prepared foods (e.g. canned plus meal) are entirely satisfactory, cheapest and best. *But* the larger or more active the dog, the more food it will require (for an 'average' size dog, e.g. a thirty-pound adult Cocker Spaniel with moderate exercise requirements, allow, say, one can of food plus ten ounces of biscuit meal per day).

Misguidedly, some owners, particularly of small breeds, allow themselves to be bullied into feeding expensive cuts of fresh meat, albeit in smaller quantities (a fifteen-pound terrier requires, say, seven ounces of rump steak plus four ounces of rice per day). This situation should not arise if animals are reared correctly on accepted dog-foods from puppyhood.

(ii) *Comfort* – the vast majority of dogs live in the house as a member of the family. However, it is essential that there is adequate room for a full-grown dog and the family in the day rooms, and sufficient space for the dog's own bed at night.

Providing it is accustomed to it from the start, it is, of course, perfectly acceptable for an outdoor kennel to be used. This should be properly draught-proofed and insulated, and adequate bedding supplied during the winter.

(iii) *Sleep* – as with all animals, sleep is essential for battery recharging and, especially with puppies and children, supervision may be required to ensure enough rest periods. Dogs should be trained to use their own beds – whatever form they may take – from the very beginning. Provided it is quietly situated, draught-free and of adequate size, no special comments need be made about design preference.

(iv) *Exercise* – all dogs require exercise; their needs vary, and not always in proportion to the size of the dog. For example, a Great Dane will get by with moderate exercise – often considerably less than a terrier. A fair guide is given by the origin of the breeds: working dogs like collies, terriers and gun-dogs crave unlimited exercise as adults, whereas primary guard-dog strains and toys cope well with shorter and less frequent walks. It is possible to *over-exercise* growing puppies, so breeder and veterinary advice should be sought if in doubt.

(v) *Company* – all dogs need and enjoy company. While some will acclimatize to prolonged stays in car and office, it is generally better to avoid having a dog as a pet if the house is empty all day.

(vi) *Family* – not all breeds are suited to sharing their affections with other family members. Generally, a family dog is acquired as a puppy and reared with children. Many believe that the herding dogs (collies etc.) are one-man animals, being for generations bred to obey the commands of one man, and such breeds are often regarded with greater caution for the family situation or for a young couple who may naturally be planning to have children.

(vii) *Longevity* – the average lifespan of the domestic dog is variable, from eight to nine years in larger breeds like Great Danes to fifteen to sixteen years in the smaller breeds such as Chihuahuas and Yorkies. When acquiring a dog, this should be considered carefully, as future plans may preclude keeping a pet several years hence. On the other hand, while one cannot accurately predict the life expectancy, some owners feel resentful and cheated if they lose their companion after comparatively few years.

2   THOROUGHBRED VERSUS MONGREL

There is a great and mistaken belief that mongrels are hardier dogs than pure-bred pedigree animals; in general veterinary practice, this is totally disproved. It is just as easy, for example, for a cross-bred dog to sustain serious road-accident injuries as a pedigree dog, and statistically more likely; equally, there is no evidence that 'hybrid vigour' acts in any way as protection against common infection.

By definition, pure-bred varieties are reasonably predictable as to their ultimate full-grown size, a point worth considering for would-be puppy-purchasers. And, similarly, their feeding capacity, natural tendencies and exercise requirements can be anticipated.

A mongrel is a cross-bred dog; this may be a 'first cross' – for example, the offspring of a mating between a pure-bred Labrador and a pure-bred German Shepherd (Alsatian). Very often, however, the cross is much more complex, dating back many generations, and rough parentage can only be guessed at. Similarly, owners of such pups can only be guided as to full-grown size, appetite etc. by informed surmise. More worrying is the temperamental make-up of such cross-breds, for in the majority of rescued, stray or ex-sanctuary pups, psychological vices are possibly developing, and, as young adults, problems become manifest that may only be seen by the experienced caninist in the puppy (for example, viciousness, destructiveness, car- or sheep-chasing) that may eventually mean drastic action such as re-homing or destruction.

For these reasons, those dedicated to mongrel ownership, especially if acquiring a puppy, should make permanent owning conditional on one or two weeks' trial, during which time they should observe closely and critically for signs of problems, discuss the matter with their vet and, if necessary, consult a trainer or behaviourist before accepting full responsibility 'until death us do part'.

3   DOG VERSUS BITCH

It is *generally* accepted that bitches are more easily trained than male dogs, more placid, less aggressive and less inclined to wander. Furthermore, for those intending to involve themselves in breeding, a bitch is infinitely preferable to a male dog. Stud dogs usually require to have visiting bitches brought to them for mating and the owners are generally required to supervise this, often without help from the bitches' owners; this may sound trivial, but there is no substitute for experience when it comes to mating, especially when a fair percentage of bitches presented are maidens (unbred).

On the other hand, many feel that the inconvenience and mess (albeit slight) of a bitch in season twice yearly for three weeks at a time is unacceptable. Modern-day drugs, however, can be used safely and effectively to control seasons for a bitch intended eventually to have a litter, and surgical neutering will permanently remove the problems of oestrus where no further litters are intended.

Neutering of male dogs is less often undertaken in the United Kingdom than in the United States. Castrated males do tend to alter body shape and appear fat, but surgery or drugs can be used to minimize problems of the male – such as over-sexedness, straying and aggression – in most cases.

4   SIZE

Before buying a car, most wise drivers will research the facts, particularly 'How much will it cost to run?' and 'Will it fit my garage?'. The wise dog-owner would be well advised to do the same. Puppies of the large breeds will eventually grow to fill a three-seater settee or more-than-average hearthrug, and their physical size must preclude them from most caravans, houseboats, one-up one-down country cottages etc. as well as from bijou town flats – for everyone's sake.

The larger breeds also have higher 'running costs' because their food consumption is greater, their kennel-space requirements are greater (boarding kennels and hospitalization) and their drug needs are greater (veterinary fees).

The sheer size also imposes limits. A frail or infirm owner can hardly be expected to control an exuberant young Saint Bernard, nor can even a young, fit owner reasonably expect to carry a collapsed Great Dane a mile back to the car.

Bear these points in mind; it takes an extra-special owner to fulfil all obligations to the large breeds.

5 COATS AND COAT CARE

Some breeds require frequent and regular specialized grooming by a professional or by the owner prepared to learn how. Poodles (all varieties) and Bedlingtons need periodic clipping, the former ideally every six to eight weeks, and this in addition to regular baths and tidying-up, especially for show days or those with the more ornate clip styles.

Most popular terrier breeds (e.g. Scotties, Cairns, West Highland) and spaniel varieties are traditionally hand-stripped at least twice a year for their comfort and to keep coat length manageable. This is a dying art, but is simple for the owner to do with a little practice and the correct instrument.

It is becoming increasingly popular to 'crew-cut' some long-haired breeds once a year, notably the Old English (Bobtail) Sheepdog, for the convenience of owners. This practice is to be deplored; much preferable is to select a breed with less time-consuming coat.

All breeds of dog should be groomed regularly – most once daily. For longer coats, a strong (metal) comb or wire-toothed brush is essential. All should have a daily once-over with a stiff brush. Short-hairs, like the Boxer, are often 'finished' with a satin cloth to give a final sheen. Grooming should include inspection (and cleansing where appropriate) of lips, teeth, nose, ears, eyes, sheath, vulva and anus. A check should be made at the same time on feet, pads and nails. The value of this is early detection or anticipation of skin ailments, wounds etc., for which first-aid or veterinary attention might be necessary.

Bathing should not be done on a regular automatic basis, but is indicated for genuine cleansing reasons, as an adjunct to clipping or pre-showing, or for medical reasons (e.g. flea infestation, veterinary direction).

6 WHERE FROM?

When buying a pedigreed dog, it is advisable to avoid the temptation to acquire it from some sources. Street markets are definitely out, and department stores, pet-shops, dog dealers and homeless dog sanctuaries should be avoided.

There is no doubt that a reliable and reputable breeder or a pet home with an individual litter prove time and time again to be the best sources. Sires are chosen with care, the bitch has full requirements during a well-supervised pregnancy and the pups lack nothing (food, vitamins and minerals, love and attention) during early rearing. Such pups invariably are stronger, healthier and better adjusted mentally.

A safe rule is: 'Don't buy a pup where you can't *meet* its mother (and often father).' Only rarely (where a litter is orphaned) might you encounter pups without mother from a good breeder.

7 HOW MUCH?

We can split down component costs, so you can calculate if you can *afford* a dog.

(i) *Purchase price* – depends on the source of the puppy, the breed and the quality. Good breeders and home-reared sell direct to you – otherwise a middleman's profit must inflate the price. To some extent the asking price depends on the popularity of the breed and on supply and demand. Also, breeds producing large litters are usually cheaper than those with smaller numbers of puppies. Lastly, the quality or potential of the individual animal will govern the price asked. By way of a very rough guide in this very specialized side of the market, be prepared to be asked ten to twenty times the price of an 'average puppy' – but if this is your goal, take great care and plenty of advice from experienced people. You may to some extent be protected in civil (or even criminal) law, but the onus of proof will be on you to show that the 'sure prizewinner' bought at eight weeks is a 'sure loser' at six months!

Realistically, decent pedigree pups will range in price from £50–200 depending on the above factors, and some even less, for sound reasons.

(ii) *Basic essential equipment:*

Solid (buckling) collar	Separate food/drink crockery
Check collar	Separate grooming tools (comb, brush etc.)
Lead	Dog bed
Identification disc	Licence (see below)

(iii) *Feeding* – is the biggest item over the canine lifespan. This can be assessed by talking to the breeder about adult consumption (see 1 (i) above). For the average thirty-pound dog allow, currently, fifty pence per day as a minimum.

(iv) *Vets' fees* – when you get your puppy, it will probably require vaccination against diseases of distemper (hard pad), hepatitis, two leptospirosis forms and canine parvo virus. This sounds long and complicated, but in practice involves two series of injections at an interval of two to four weeks, depending on the age of the puppy at the time of the first jabs. Thereafter, boosters are required, usually at yearly intervals. Such fees vary and can, of course, be checked with the vet's surgery beforehand, but say, currently, initial vaccination costs £20–25 and an annual booster half this amount.

Other costs to be budgeted for, particularly in the case of a bitch, are surgical neutering or medication to control seasons. In the case of a breeding bitch, it is wise to provide for emergencies during whelping or the puppy-nursing period.

Unexpected illness or accident can, in severe cases, result in more substantial fee charges; these can be covered by taking out a pet health insurance. For a modest annual premium, there is protection available from a number of insurance companies. Your vet or insurance broker can provide you with details of policies.

(v) *Kennelling* – annual holidays must be accounted for if there is no reliable friend, neighbour or relation to care for your dog. True, many hotels, camp and caravan sites and self-catering accommodations will allow your dog. Remember, you can't take a dog abroad without suitable documentation or return with it without six months' quarantine (this does not apply to visits to the Channel Islands, the Isle of Man and Ireland).

Provision must, therefore, be made well in advance to have the family pets cared for, in the majority of cases, by a reputable and acceptable boarding establishment for the duration of annual holidays. Also, some owners prefer three weeks of 'solitary' for the in-season bitch, to prevent nuisance and unwanted pregnancy.

Kennel charges vary, but can be expected to range from about £1.50 (for a tiny toy breed) to £6 or more (for large dogs) per day. 'Vet' all kennels to satisfy yourself as to the standards before booking.

(vi) *Dog licences* – are currently 37½p per year for dogs over six months old. Some dogs are exempt (guide dogs, farm Collies). Pressure is being exerted to alter dog licensing, and an annual fee of £5 has been mooted.

(vii) *Grooming* – (see 5 above). With several breeds, professional grooming fees should be taken into account at the outset if the owner is unable to do this. Currently, allow £5–10 per visit, depending on size, complexity of clip and state of the individual dog.

Some terriers and spaniels conventionally are stripped twice yearly – spring and early autumn. Poodles and Bedlingtons are clipped/trimmed every six to eight weeks.

Bathing (all breeds) may be done as required.

8 FIRST STEPS

Puppies are best acquired at about eight to ten weeks of age. By then they will be well weaned, stronger and almost ready for their vaccinations. Before purchase it is wise to visit the public library or to buy a good book on the breed, and to prepare for the pup's arrival fully briefed on what is required of you, the owner, and how to go about training, feeding etc.

Buy the minimum basic equipment necessary; remember that pups grow like children and will outstrip first collars. Good quality beds may be bought once the pup has passed the chewing stage.

Get in some stocks of food and supplements. Most breeders will give sound advice about the type of food the puppies have been reared on, the amount to give and the frequency of feeds. Initially, stick to the diet which the puppies have been fed by the breeder.

It is always advisable for the puppy to have a health check within a week of purchase. The owner should use this opportunity to ask the veterinary surgeon about vaccination, worming and feeding (if in doubt), and can often seek help on house-training and simple obedience-training. Many books and leaflets are available on such subjects – but remember it is normally not thought safe to exercise puppies outside one's garden until vaccinations are complete (twelve weeks or older).

9 YOUR DOG AND THE LAW

Common and statute laws applying to dogs are many and varied. It is (with few exceptions) necessary to buy an annual dog licence (see 7 above). It is necessary for dogs to wear a collar on public highways, giving identification, and indeed on most public roads it is (strictly speaking) necessary to keep a dog leashed. The 'keeper' of the dog has a duty to control it and is held liable for injury or damage done to people or property. Cover against such third-party risks is strongly advisable (and is automatically built in to many household insurance policies). You may be prosecuted for any nuisance caused by your dog – chasing sheep, biting callers and barking, for example. It is illegal to abandon your dog – i.e. to shut it up at home while you take a weekend holiday, or 'dump' it before you go abroad. And, of course, the dog has wide protection under various 'cruelty' laws. Motorists involved in motor accidents with dogs must by law report such incidents to the police.

Veterinarians are protectors against illness and accident for your dog, through vaccination and timely advice. They also remedy disease and trauma, using medical and surgical techniques in which they are trained. They are expert advisers on dietetics, breeding, breed selection, sources of puppies, behavioural problems and many, many other aspects of concern to dog- or puppy-owners, largely through personal experience and expertise.

Your closest vet is often the best to choose; he is convenient and, in cases of emergency, nearest to hand. However, in some cases it may be necessary to travel further afield to avoid a personality clash. Confidence in one's veterinary adviser is essential; this vet/client/patient relationship should be one of mutual confidence.

For first-time owners, lists of veterinary practices appear in Yellow Pages telephone directories and are available from police stations. Even better, contact the local R.S.P.C.A. branch or neighbouring dog owners whose judgement you would trust for the name of a vet with special doggy interests. This may be particularly desirable in rural areas where there may be several veterinarians in a practice, only one of whom concentrates on dogs (as opposed to horses or farm animals).

Costs of veterinary treatments are widely compared. Quite truly, little is to be gained by selecting the cheapest practice; this invariably has lower overheads and these often result from poor staffing or service and less than desirable facilities, and in the long run is probably as costly as the higher-charging next-door practice. In cases of genuine financial hardship, help for the needy dog may be had from the local R.S.P.C.A. or P.D.S.A. (see the addresses of headquarters of these organizations on pp. 13–14).

Veterinary health insurance is worthwhile investigating. There are three or four schemes to choose from. Their particular forte is in cases of protracted illness or major accident. For a yearly premium of from £17.50 (1982) all costs of treatment (excluding the first £5 excess) will be met. Also included is loss of animal by straying or death and third-party cover. Most vets and dog papers have details of these schemes.

11 SHOWS, SHOWING AND BREEDING

Before selecting your dog, think ahead. Might you toy with showing it? Might you toy with breeding?

In obedience-training, most aficionados start by involvement just to instil basic discipline. By the time this is achieved, enthusiasm and the dog's potential often generate a real enthusiasm. Dogs of most breeds – including mongrels –

can be developed and trained for obedience work, though outstanding examples must be collies and German Shepherds.

If you want to show your dog in breed classes, however, much more thought and careful selection is necessary. Advice and inspection of a litter, for example, by an independent and recognized authority (breeder or judge) is to be recommended. 'You can't make a silk purse out of a sow's ear.' Reasonably, a puppy or adult of 'show quality' must be expected to cost more than one of 'pet quality' which may exhibit only the slightest blemish – enough, however, effectively to disqualify it from major competition. In general terms, the value of an animal is enhanced by winning at shows; its progeny (in the case of a bitch) or stud fee (for a dog) will become more valuable assets. This, of course, does not preclude having a litter from a pet (unshown) bitch, or using an unexhibited dog at stud. Both of these require special thought and advice from an experienced breeder or a veterinary surgeon.

Shows, show procedure and show preparation have many books devoted to them; advice is freely available from breed societies and the Kennel Club. If you are not enthusiastic, forget about showing, and the same advice holds true of breeding your dog.

Breeds of Dogs Registrable in the U.K.

Affenpinscher

Land of origin: Europe

Original purpose: Companionship and ratting

Recent popularity ranking by K.C. registration: Rare

HEIGHT: Dogs to 10¼ inches, bitches to 9 inches

WEIGHT: Dogs to 8 pounds, bitches to 7 pounds

COAT: Very important in judging. Hard and wiry and varies from short and dense to shaggy and longer on different parts of body. Longer on face, legs, chest and underparts

COLOUR: Black is considered best, but also black with tan markings, red, grey and other mixtures allowed. Very light colours and white markings are faults

Amount of care coat requires: 1 2 3 4 5 6 7 8 9 10
  ★ ★ ★

Amount of exercise required: 1 2 3 4 5 6 7 8 9 10
  ★ ★ ★

Suitability for urban/flat life: 1 2 3 4 5 6 7 8 9 10
  ★ ★ ★ ★ ★ ★ ★ ★ ★ ★

No one really knows where the Affenpinscher comes from, although it was somewhere in Europe. The breed dates back to at least the 1600s and probably is much, much older than that. The name translates from the German as 'monkey terrier', an appropriate name for this strange, fiery little toy.

It was from the Affenpinscher, some people believe, that the now more popular Bruxellois Griffon was in part derived. The later breed all but eclipsed the older one, but there is some indication that interest in the Affenpinscher is reviving slightly.

Actually, this little dark dog is an ideal flat animal. Although in need of some exercise, he adapts easily to life in a flat. Like a great many of the smaller dogs, the Affenpinscher will wait for an opening and then take over. He needs a firm hand, but he is clever enough to take any training necessary to make him into a suitable canine companion. Heaven help the careless owner; a monkeyish little dog will soon be running the household.

The Affenpinscher is tough, and he seems to take himself seriously. He is devoted and affectionate and usually quiet. He is, though, capable of real temper and will attack anything if seriously challenged. He can be moody and

excitable if not given his own way. Until a real balance has been struck between man and dog, it may be a war of nerves; and it is funny to watch this clever little animal try to work things out to his own advantage.

The Affenpinscher requires little care. The coat is best trimmed slightly about every ten weeks, just often enough to maintain the round, wise facial expression. It is ten minutes' work and little more. An occasional brushing is all that is required beyond that. Although a toy, the Affenpinscher is reasonably hardy, but really bad weather and chills should be avoided.

It isn't easy to find a good Affenpinscher puppy when you want one. Anyone seriously considering this little character had better start the search early and carry on until a good pup becomes available. Those people devoted to the breed say it is worth the hunt and the wait.

Afghan Hound

Land of origin: Sinai peninsula, then Afghanistan

Original purpose: Hunting

Recent popularity ranking by K.C. registration: 30th

HEIGHT: Dogs to 27 inches, bitches to 25 inches

WEIGHT: Dogs to 60 pounds, bitches to 50 pounds

COAT: Thick, silky, very fine in texture. Not clipped or trimmed. Long hair except on back in mature dogs, where saddle is short

COLOUR: All colours are seen, but white markings, especially on the head, are not desirable

Amount of care coat requires: 1 2 3 4 5 6 7 8 9 10
                                  * * * * * * * * *

Amount of exercise required: 1 2 3 4 5 6 7 8 9 10
                                  * * * * * * * * * *

Suitability for urban/flat life:* 1 2 3 4 5 6 7 8 9 10
                                  * * *

* Assuming that the dog will be taken on long walks several times a day and at least occasionally be taken somewhere he will be able to run.

The handsome Afghan Hound is an aristocrat. The breed goes back almost six thousand years, and he was no doubt the companion of kings. He is also a clown, for he loves to play and romp and is almost never mean or petty.

The Afghan Hound is one of the few large active dogs who can be kept in the city. Although this dog requires a great deal of exercise and should be taken on long, fast walks several times a day, he can adapt to flat life. Despite the 'mad' act he puts on and the general prejudice that the coursing, or sight, hounds aren't always the brightest of dogs, the Afghan is a willing dog who is anxious to please. Because of the Afghan's size and his occasional good-natured bumptiousness, it is a good idea for a new owner and his dog to take obedience classes together.

The Afghan is a stunning-looking dog, and the coat should be well brushed to enhance the liquid motion that is so characteristic of this animal of style and beauty. Ropy or matted Afghans are unforgivable and tell one a great deal about the owners who bought a dog they were not prepared to keep properly.

Afghans are fine with children, although there is the problem of small

toddlers being bowled over by a great galumphing hound bounding to the door to see who is there.

This ancient hound does well with other animals and usually will not fight. Of course, two mature males always can be a problem, but perhaps less so with this breed than with a good many others.

There is no doubt that many people like the idea of high style in a dog, and one would have to go far to find a breed better suited to that ego need than this one. And this is not to be condemned. It is just as easy to love a dog who gives an added aesthetic satisfaction as it is to adore one who doesn't. The potential Afghan owner should, however, be certain that it isn't *just* style he wants. This breed is sensitive, constantly in need of affection and a sense of participation; although splendid-looking in a fashion layout, the Afghan is not merely an ornament.

Any dog, once purchased, becomes a long-term commitment. It is no more true of any other breed than it is of this ancient hound. He once shared the tents of sheikhs in the Sinai wilderness and later coursed the rugged mountains of Afghanistan for leopard and gazelle in blistering summer heat and bone-cracking winter cold. Despite his picturesque and seemingly delicate beauty, the Afghan remains a hunting hound – hardy, tough and willing.

Airedale Terrier

Land of origin: England

Original purpose: Hunting small- and medium-sized game; guarding

Recent popularity ranking by K.C. registration: 28th

HEIGHT: Dogs to 23 inches, bitches to 22 inches

WEIGHT: Dogs to 50 pounds, bitches to 45 pounds

COAT: Double. Hard, dense and wiry, lying close to the body. A light, soft undercoat. The outer coat may be slightly wavy

COLOUR: Tan and black or tan and dark grizzle. Some red mixture in black acceptable, as is a small white blaze on the chest

Amount of care coat requires: 1 2 3 4 5 6 7 8 9 10
                               * * *

Amount of exercise required: 1 2 3 4 5 6 7 8 9 10
                              * * * * * * * * * *

Suitability for urban/flat life:* 1 2 3 4 5 6 7 8 9 10
                                  * * *

*With proper exercise.

Once known as the Waterside Terrier, this distinctive animal is today the king of all existing terrier breeds. He is the largest and, in many people's opinion, the most admirable.

The Airedale is descended from a cross between a hunting terrier and the Otter Hound; the latter animal helped improve the nose and performance in the water. The resulting terrier was used on fox, badger, weasel, otter, water rat and other lesser game. It was a breed much beloved and one fostered down to our own time with devotion.

As a terrier, the Airedale is by nature courageous and bold. He is also aggressive, but much calmer than most other terriers and never silly or over-excitable. He will attack anything he is sent against and is one of the best all-time ratters.

With his master and family the Airedale is an affectionate, gentle and loyal animal. He is a first-rate watchdog and thrives on rough and tumble play with children. It is unusual for an Airedale to be mean or nasty. He wants to be a part of everything that goes on in the household, and he expects the right to vet strangers. He just likes to be sure, and in security matters he seems to prefer his own judgement to that of a mere human. He easily softens with non-

threatening strangers, though, and is usually too aloof to take exception to a minor insult from a lesser dog. But be careful of an Airedale who has been egged on, for he is a terror when the fight erupts. Fortunately, he generally elects to give it a miss.

Airedale owners resemble religious converts in the intensity of their affection for this breed; they become missionaries. This apparently has been going on for a long time, since the Airedale remains a popular breed, although less so than in the past.

There is the temptation to suggest that because the Airedale is both a dog of considerable substance and active like all terriers, he is not suited to city life. That is not quite true. While probably very happy with a home in the country, the Airedale will settle down to an urban routine as long as he has his family around him. It remains important, however, that he get a great deal of exercise, and ideally that means several miles every day. Obedience-training is highly desirable, for an ill-mannered Airedale would be more than just a nuisance. Given half a chance, this is one dog who will prove himself under any circumstances to be a gentle, loyal and noble friend. It is more than his size that makes him king of the terrier kind.

Alaskan Malamute

Land of origin: Arctic region, usually given as Alaska

Original purpose: As heavy-duty (freight) sled-dog and camp guard

Recent popularity ranking by K.C. registration: Moderate

HEIGHT: Dogs to 25 inches, bitches to 23 inches

WEIGHT: Dogs to 85 pounds, bitches to 75 pounds

COAT: Thick coarse guard coat, not very long and not soft. Dense undercoat 1 to 2 inches deep, oily and woolly. Guard hairs stick out, neck well maned

COLOUR: Light grey to black with white belly and white markings on feet, legs and face. Only solid-coloured dog allowed is all-white

Amount of care coat requires:* 1 2 3 4 5 6 7 8 9 10
                                   * * * * * *

Amount of exercise required: 1 2 3 4 5 6 7 8 9 10
                                   * * * * * * * * *

Suitability for urban/flat life:† 1 2 3 4 5 6 7 8 9 10
                                  *

---

* Heavy brushing required in spring and early summer due to shedding.
† If enough exercise is given.

No one knows the origin of the breed we call the Alaskan Malamute. The name is derived from the Russian name for the massive northwesternmost portion of North America – Alashak (Vast Country) – and from one of the tribes that were found wandering there centuries ago – the Malemiuts, who had a sled-dog of great stamina and loyalty. The breed is certainly one of the northern spitz dogs, but where it first originated and how it is related to the Siberian Husky, the Samoyed, and the sled-dogs of Greenland and the eastern Canadian Arctic is unknowable.

Some sled-dogs were bred for speed, and are indeed used in races today, but the Malamute is a freight hauler, a heavy-duty animal of great substance and endurance. Because these animals are naturally loyal to their owners, many of the examples kept as pets today are equally good watchdogs. Legend has it that every third or fourth dog generation the Innuit (the group to which the Malemiuts belong) tether their Malamute bitches out on the ice when they come into heat and allow wolves to service them. Whether or not that is true, the Malamute undeniably has wolflike qualities in his appearance.

The Alaskan Malamute is a magnificent animal, a fine pet who is good with children. He is solid and steady and has great endurance. Loyal unto death to his family, he is usually not one-personish. He is good with strangers, although he can be aggressive with strange dogs – not always, but that is a characteristic of some specimens. Of the northern spitz-like dogs, this breed is one of the best for the average household.

The harsh coat of the Malamute is best when not washed often, for washing tends to soften it and alter its desirable character. There is a coat-care consideration, though. That very dense undercoat is shed in spring and summer, and unless it is professionally stripped, it can drive the householder mad, for its shedding is endless.

The Alaskan Malamute is suited for a family with at least some active members, and in general for people who want a large, powerful and wonderfully loyal pet. He is a heavy working dog and needs a great deal of exercise if he is to maintain condition and proper temperament. He will adapt to any living conditions as long as he is close to his human family, but confinement without proper exercise is cruel and foolish.

Great care should be taken in buying a Malamute, and only when two or three generations of a line are known should a final purchase be undertaken. There is a congenital malformation known as 'dwarfism' in this breed, and it can crop up in alternate generations. A puppy should be evaluated carefully before purchase, and only the truly professional Alaskan Malamute breeder should be trusted.

Anatolian (Karabash) Dog

(ANATOLIAN SHEEPDOG)

Land of origin: Turkey and Afghanistan

Original purpose: Guarding flocks

Recent popularity ranking by K.C. registration: Moderate

HEIGHT: Dogs to 32 inches, bitches to 31 inches

WEIGHT: Dogs to 140 pounds, bitches to 130 pounds

COAT: Short, dense, thick undercoat, longer at neck and shoulders

COLOUR: Fawn with black mask. White socks and chest common

Amount of care coat requires: 1 2 3 4 5 6 7 8 9 10

Amount of exercise required: 1 2 3 4 5 6 7 8 9 10

Suitability for urban/flat life: Unsuited

This is a large, fast, hardy breed, unsuited to city dwelling and to all but experienced, dominating, strong-minded owners. The dog's main use is guarding sheep and goat flocks from predators, not herding. The predecessors of the breed have been variously used as hunters of big game (lions, horses) and war-dogs, and their reputation for fearless fierceness is well established. They are reputed to survive without food and water for lengthy periods.

This is not a breed to be selected lightly, for there is no doubt that at least in certain sectors the Karabash has a bad reputation for aggression towards other animals and indeed humans. As with most large breeds the hip-joints can be defective and enthusiasts would be well advised to ensure that stock is bought only from certified 'Hip Dysplasia Free' parent dogs. The breed might have a potential in the U.K. for its flock-guarding ability: when sheep-worrying is an increasing problem there can be no more daunting prospect than an Anatolian to a trespassing dog.

Australian Cattle Dog

(KELPIE)

Land of origin: Australia

Original purpose: Herding and droving

Recent popularity ranking by K.C. registration: Rare

HEIGHT: To 20 inches

WEIGHT: To 35 pounds (Kelpies rather more slight – to 30 pounds)

COAT: Smooth double coat

COLOUR: Blue; red speckle

Amount of care coat requires: 1 2 3 4 5 6 7 8 9 10

Amount of exercise required: 1 2 3 4 5 6 7 8 9 10

Suitability for urban/flat life: 1 2 3 4 5 6 7 8 9 10

These working dogs (Cattle Dogs for driving cattle, the smaller Kelpies for sheep) are thought to have originated from imported Scottish (Rough) Collies to Australia, out-crossed with Bobtails and Dingoes. The Kelpie characteristically will run over the backs of huddled sheep. Reputedly they can thrive and work without water for long periods. Capable of covering vast distances, the breed requires much exercise. However, these dogs have an equable temperament and make good companion animals. Robert Louis Stevenson mentioned 'Water Kelpies' in his novel *Kidnapped*.

In common with virtually all herding dogs, the breed may not be best suited to family life, being inherently a variety used to working for one man. Furthermore, frustration due to insufficient exercise and energy dissipation may result in mischievous trends, especially in young dogs.

Australian Silky Terrier

Land of origin: Australia

Original purpose: Companionship, and to some extent ratting

Recent popularity ranking by K.C. registration: Rare

HEIGHT: Dogs to 10 inches, bitches to 10 inches

WEIGHT: Dogs to 10 pounds, bitches to 9 pounds

COAT: Flat, very fine in texture, glossy; decidedly silky; 5 to 6 inches long on mature dog. Pronounced topknot

COLOUR: Various blues and tan

Amount of care coat requires:	1	2	3	4	5	6	7	8	9	10
Amount of exercise required:	1	2	3	4	5	6	7	8	9	10
Suitability for urban/flat life:	1	2	3	4	5	6	7	8	9	10

The Silky terrier is apparently a cross between the Australian Terrier and the Yorkshire Terrier. Like the latter, he is shown as a toy today, although he is clearly terrier all the way through.

The lovely little eight- to ten-pound Silky is more active than some of the other toy breeds and should get plenty of exercise. He can be an exhausting little creature with his endless demands for attention and action, but most people who have known the breed have felt it was worth the effort.

There are stories of Silky Terriers being used in Australia as ratters and snakers on poultry farms, but knowing something of the character of Australian snakes, I tend to doubt most of those tales. The Silky Terrier is essentially a companion animal, like all toys, and at that task he excels. He is bright to a fault, responsive, demanding and even, at times, aggressive. Apparently no one has bothered to tell the Silky just how small he is. He makes a good little watchdog, for he does tend to be vocal. In fact, when you add up all of the Silky Terrier's qualities, what you have is a perpetual-motion machine. He is seldom still.

A great many people live fairly active lives, even though they are essentially city dwellers. The space available to them may necessitate a small dog, while they may crave an active animal of forceful character. The Silky Terrier is the

answer for those people, for he is really the largest dog in the world pushed
down into a very small body.

The Silky Terrier is one of those breeds with a crowning-glory-type coat, and
it does require care. That lovely silky look will last *only* as long as the dog is
bathed and brushed and combed and his coat kept from getting stringy and
matted looking. It does take all that and some judicious trimming to have a
Silky Terrier look like a Silky Terrier is supposed to look. It is important to
keep that in mind when considering this breed.

There are signs of rising favour for this breed, and it will be wise to be wary
of poorly bred or mass-produced puppies. Some are passed off as Yorkshire
Terriers and vice versa. It is wise to stick with an established specialty breeder
and avoid all risk.

Australian Terrier

Land of origin: Australia

Original purpose: Companionship and hunting small game

Recent popularity ranking by K.C. registration: Moderate

HEIGHT: Dogs to 10 inches, bitches to 10 inches

WEIGHT: Dogs to 14 pounds, bitches to 14 pounds

COAT: Outer coat harsh and straight, about 2½ inches long. Undercoat short and soft. Topknot distinctive feature

COLOUR: Blue black or silver black with rich tan (the deeper the better). Sandy or red markings on head and legs

Amount of care coat requires: 1 2 3 4 5 6 7 8 9 10
                                               * * * *

Amount of exercise required: 1 2 3 4 5 6 7 8 9 10
                                               * * * *

Suitability for urban/flat life: 1 2 3 4 5 6 7 8 9 10
                         * * * * * * * * * *

The Australian Terrier (not to be confused, as so often happens, with the Silky Terrier, a toy dog, also from Australia) is a blend of many other terrier lines. It is quite possible that more different breeds were used to create the perky Australian Terrier than went into any other modern pure-bred dog. At the very least the Scottish, the Cairn, the Dandie Dinmont, the Irish, the Skye and the Yorkshire Terriers all went into its make-up. The original parent stock was what was known as the Broken-haired Terrier, sometimes also known as the Rough-coated. What emerged was a distinctive Australian creation, one of the smallest of the working terriers.

The Australian Terrier is a dog of fire and stamina despite his small size. Barely more than a toy, he can hold his own under any weather and terrain conditions. He has been used on small game in the Australian outback, although the impetus behind his development was undoubtedly the search for a superior companion dog. He was first shown in Melbourne in the middle 1880s and has since attracted attention and devoted followers in a number of countries.

The Australian may be close to the perfect small house and flat dog. Small enough not to intrude, he is a loyal pet with charm and personality. He isn't a

heavy shedder and knows instinctively how to fit in and ingratiate himself. He will hold his own with other animals without being silly and quarrelsome. He makes a good watchdog and will return affection in kind and in depth. Although he is an active little dog by nature, he doesn't need long walks. He is quite satisfied staying indoors but will participate in any outdoor activities offered him. He is fine on a farm, great in the suburbs and almost flawless in a flat.

Although not yet a fad in this country, the Australian Terrier undoubtedly will grow in popularity over the years, and care should be taken to obtain specimens only from the most reliable sources. This is not a breed to be mass-produced, for it would not hold its present fine style. This terrier was evolved so recently and from such a variety of lines that only careful breeding will enable it to consolidate all it has gained from the care taken so far.

Basenji

Land of origin: Central Africa

Original purpose: Hunting

Recent popularity ranking by K.C. registration: Moderate

HEIGHT: Dogs to 17 inches. bitches to 16 inches

WEIGHT: Dogs to 24 pounds, bitches to 22 pounds

COAT: Short and silky. Coat very pliant

COLOUR: Chestnut red, pure black, black and tan – always with white feet, chest and tail tip. White legs, blaze and collar allowed as optional

Amount of care coat requires: 1 2 3 4 5 6 7 8 9 10
                           *

Amount of exercise required: 1 2 3 4 5 6 7 8 9 10
             * * * * * *

Suitability for urban/flat life: 1 2 3 4 5 6 7 8 9 10
     * * * * * * * * *

There aren't many animals from Africa on the European scene, and for that reason alone the Basenji began catching on almost as soon as he was first seen. He was a curiosity with a fascinating history. This dog was brought to Egypt for the pleasure of the pharaohs thousands of years ago. With the fall of that ancient civilization, the breed was able to continue in its native central Africa, where it was used for hunting.

The Basenji is a swift, silent dog with a remarkable nose and great determination. He is an active animal and should be given a great deal of exercise every day. He has a lovely, high-stepping gait and is great fun to watch. When happy, he bounds and leaps and is like a little deer with a glistening coat.

It is not true that the Basenji is mute. He does not bark like other dogs, but he does make a giggling, yodelling sound that is impossible to describe or imitate. It is a happy sound, generally reserved for close friends.

The Basenji is one of the cleanest dogs. His coat needs almost no care, and he rarely if ever needs bathing – certainly not more than a couple of times a year. Almost unique in the dog world is his habit of washing himself all over, just like a cat. The result is a perfect pleasure of a dog for the fastidious home-owner.

Naturally well-behaved and intelligent, the Basenji will take training easily, especially if he is included within the family circle. He is a calm dog, surprisingly so for one so active. He seems to have everything under control, however, and to know instinctively how to please.

Basenjis can be good with children – in almost any family situation – but they do insist on being a part of the action and are often suspicious of strangers. A Basenji who is left out, even inadvertently, is an unhappy dog.

In play and pleasure, in the show-ring and on the street, the handsome, sprightly little fox-terrier-sized hound called the Basenji never fails to attract attention.

Basset Hound

Land of origin: France

Original purpose: All-purpose hunting

Recent popularity ranking by K.C. registration: Moderate

HEIGHT: Dogs to 15 inches, bitches to 14 inches

WEIGHT: Dogs to 45 pounds, bitches to 35 pounds

COAT: Hard, smooth, short and quite dense. Skin loose and elastic

COLOUR: Any recognized hound colour. Distribution of markings of no importance in judging

Amount of care coat requires:	1 2 3 4 5 6 7 8 9 10
Amount of exercise required:	1 2 3 4 5 6 7 8 9 10
Suitability for urban/flat life:*	1 2 3 4 5 6 7 8 9 10

* But plenty of exercise *is* required – preferably three or four long walks a day.

The Basset Hound is an old breed developed in France and Belgium mostly from the Bloodhound, whose saintlike disposition it shares.

The Basset has been popular in Europe for centuries and has always been highly regarded for his many fine qualities. He is a slow, trailing dog but one with tremendous stamina and deliberateness. He is said to have a nose second only to that of the Bloodhound, that grandfather of all scent hounds. The ears of the Basset, designed to swirl up stale scent particles into the ever-receptive nose, also point to the undoubted Bloodhound ancestry of the breed. Because of a naturally oily skin, he does have a pleasant, somewhat musky, 'doggy' odour.

The Basset is one of the most pleasant and adaptable of dogs. Almost never snappy or aggressive, he gets along well with his master (whom he adores), family and friends (whether two- or four-legged) and he should always be included in family activities. He is peaceful, sensible, affectionate and simply marvellous with children. As a puppy he is as engaging as an animal can be, and his cheery outlook remains with him all his life. He can be serious, of course, and when charged with a job the Basset goes about it with almost comic intensity.

More agile than he appears, the Basset requires a great deal of exercise. It would be unfair to keep a Basset Hound shut in week in and week out. This is an active field animal, and he has been bred for that purpose for hundreds of canine generations. He should not be penalized just because he also happens to be almost unbelievably pleasant. The Basset Hound should be walked several times a day – long, well-paced walks – and taken to the country for an open-air run as often as possible. Because family is far more important to a Basset than anything else, he will adapt to flat life and is quiet and reasonable when inside.

Bassets are fairly long-lived, are generally strong and healthy, and can be good watchdogs. They have very loud voices. Naturally obedient and easy to train, they are good natured about taking orders. A large, fine hound of many exceptional qualities, the Basset deserves all the favour he is experiencing. Very few hounds outrank him in popularity.

Beagle

Land of origin: probably Wales and England

Original purpose: Hunting rabbits

Recent popularity ranking by K.C. registration: 34th

HEIGHT: Dogs 13 to 15 inches, bitches 13 to 15 inches

WEIGHT: To 20 pounds

COAT: Close, hard, typical hound; medium length

COLOUR: Any true hound colour – white, tan, black in different combinations and markings

Amount of care coat requires: 1 2 3 4 5 6 7 8 9 10
     *

Amount of exercise required: 1 2 3 4 5 6 7 8 9 10
     * * * * * * * *

Suitability for urban/flat life:*   1 2 3 4 5 6 7 8 9 10
     * * * *

* But only if properly exercised.

The Beagle is one of the oldest of the scent hounds, probably dating back to pre-Roman times. It is believed that the breed formed in England and possibly in Wales, although we can never know for sure. Beagles have been evident all through recorded history in that part of the British Isles.

The Beagle is a hunting hound who works well alone or in small groups or large packs. He has been used on rabbit and hare and other game as well. The ancestry of some packs in England is very old, and their blood-lines are jealously guarded. The breed is by nature loyal, very easily trained and courageous. For his size this tough little dog will take almost anything that any other dog can handle. No weather bothers him, no terrain – no matter how rough and broken – is too hard, and no amount of running will wear him down. For endurance and courage this dog is not to be beaten.

All of that, though, has to do with the dog in the field. Many Beagles today are house pets, and they excel at that assignment as well. Beagles and children are a natural mix, and the dog gets along splendidly with other animals. Beagles are often good little watchdogs, although they are fine with strangers once they have been introduced. They are affectionate and outgoing, and they have a lovely hound voice. In the city young beagles need to be trained not to

overdo the vocalizing. A Beagle loves a good howling session and may tend to do a solo when left alone. That can be a bit tiresome for the neighbours.

Beagles are splendid country dogs, fine in the suburban home and in a flat as well – as long as they get exercise. They are not silly or ever unpleasant; they are calm, gentle and loving. They are also clean and quite easy to train.

Great care must be taken to obtain a really good example of the breed. It is wise to by-pass the mass-producers and seek out the specialist. There are two distinct sizes of Beagle. The smaller (less than 13 inches) is often referred to as the 'American' or 'Pocket' Beagle. These cannot be registered at the Kennel Club.

Bearded Collie

Land of origin: Scotland and England

Original purpose: Drover

Recent popularity ranking by K.C. registration: 31st

HEIGHT: Dogs to 22 inches, bitches to 21 inches

WEIGHT: Dogs to 55 pounds, bitches to 45 pounds

COAT: Double – undercoat soft, furry and close; outer coat harsh, strong, flat, *not* woolly, *not* curly

COLOUR: Slate grey, reddish fawn, black, all shades of grey, brown and sandy. May or may not have typical white Collie markings on head, chest, neck, legs, feet and tail tip

Amount of care coat requires:* 1 2 3 4 5 6 7 8 9 10

Amount of exercise required: 1 2 3 4 5 6 7 8 9 10

Suitability for urban/flat life:† 1 2 3 4 5 6 7 8 9 10

* Slightly more during first two years
† If properly exercised *every* day.

This breed of British sheepdog may be the oldest of English droving dogs. Certainly it is much older than the Old English Sheepdog.

The 'Beardie', as his fanciers refer to him, is a working dog first, a pet second. He is a natural herder and drover. Children, especially small tots, must expect to be directed, guided and nudged to where the family Beardie thinks they should be. He is generally excellent with children and ultimately friendly with strangers the family accepts.

The Bearded Collie makes a perfectly awful guard-dog. That is not part of his make-up, although he is a satisfactory watchdog. He will bark at a strange sound in the night, but don't expect a Beardie to go for a stranger's throat, even an unwelcome stranger. Tail wagging is more likely.

The breed is slow to mature, and a Beardie's coat for the first two years requires about forty-five minutes of vigorous brushing a week. After two

years, about twenty minutes a week will do. In the breed's favour is the fact that Beardies shed very little.

This dog is active; he has a long, lean body and he does not normally run to fat. He has an easy, free movement and does require exercise. Any Beardie kept in the suburbs or city should get an absolute minimum of a half an hour to an hour of real exercise every day. That double coat means the Beardie can take any weather, certainly more than his owner is likely to appreciate. A run in an open field is really what a Bearded Collie needs and wants, and for that reason I prefer to see this breed in the country. Still, the dog is not so large that he is a handicap in a flat, and he is flexible enough to manage the situation as long as he is loved and is walked – a lot. Running is better than walking, when possible.

One hopes that popularity will not harm this fine, old working dog.

Beauceron

(FRENCH SHORT-HAIRED SHEPHERD)

Land of origin: France

Original purpose: Herding and possibly hunting

Recent popularity ranking by K.C. registration: Rare

HEIGHT: Dogs to 28 inches, bitches to 27 inches

WEIGHT: N.S.G.

COAT: Moderately short, dense coat

COLOUR: Predominantly black; brown points legs, feet and muzzle

Amount of care coat requires: 1 2 3 4 5 6 7 8 9 10
                               * * *

Amount of exercise required: 1 2 3 4 5 6 7 8 9 10
                               * * * * * * * * * *

Suitability for urban/flat life: 1 2 3 4 5 6 7 8 9 10
                                 *

This breed resembles a cross between a Doberman and a German Shepherd. It is used predominantly for herding, and is a large resilient breed, also well capable of guarding. By reputation, Beauceron temperament is variable and dubious. Because of this and its almost limitless exercise capability, it is generally not suited to house life.

As with many of the more exotic working breeds great caution is to be advised before selecting such an 'unknown quantity' as a potential house-dog. Many animals will adapt reasonably well, providing they have enough exercise and activity to keep themselves interested. Inactivity and boredom are great enemies of breeds barely removed from their working roles, and destructiveness and ill-temper are likely sequels.

Bedlington Terrier

Land of origin: England

Original purpose: For use on vermin

Recent popularity ranking by K.C. registration: Moderate

HEIGHT: Dogs to 16 inches, bitches to 15 inches

WEIGHT: Dogs to 23 pounds, bitches to 22 pounds

COAT: Crisp but not wiry – stands out from skin. Not to exceed 1 inch when shown. Has tendency to curl

COLOUR: Blue, sandy, liver, blue and tan, sandy and tan, liver and tan

Amount of care coat requires:	1	2	3	4	5	6	7	8	9	10
	*	*	*	*	*	*	*	*		

Amount of exercise required:	1	2	3	4	5	6	7	8	9	10
	*	*	*	*	*	*				

Suitability for urban/flat life:	1	2	3	4	5	6	7	8	9	10
	*	*	*	*	*	*	*	*	*	*

This spunky little terrier has had a number of names down through the years. He evolved in the north of England from stock that has never really been identified. Known as the Rothbury terrier and the Northumberland Fox Terrier, he was admired both in England and Wales for his great pluck. He would fight any other dog or any vermin, and was used in pits and demonstrations against his own kind as well as against badgers, rats, foxes and anything else that would put up a fight.

The fire behind that behaviour still burns in the Bedlington Terrier, and he generally does better in a one-animal household. He will fight anything that intrudes on his proprietorship. A good pet when properly raised, he will be fine with children and is not bad with strangers, if a little cautious. But he doesn't want any other animals around to steal his thunder. In owning a Bedlington, that should be kept in mind. He should not wander where he is likely to encounter other dogs and cats. Away from other animals, he can be quite placid.

The Bedlington can make an ideal pet for a couple whose children have grown up and who want to share their home with a devoted friend. Because he is a highly spirited terrier, he should be exercised regularly. He needs those long, steady walks on a lead, and he needs a good romp in the country

whenever there is an opportunity. He should not be let free near traffic, however, because if he sees another animal, he might take off in pursuit, letting his spirit rather than his good sense guide him.

The Bedlington's coat must be seen to if he is to have that appealing if deceptive 'little-lamb' look. That does require some instruction to be done well. Many owners prefer to let a professional groomer see to the job. Unique in appearance and full of fire, will and devotion, the Bedlington Terrier is an interesting pet for the right household.

Belgian Shepherd Dog

(GROENENDAEL)

Land of origin: Belgium

Original purpose: Shepherding

Recent popularity ranking by K.C. registration: Moderate

HEIGHT: Dogs to 26 inches, bitches to 24 inches

WEIGHT: N.S.G.

COAT: Guard hairs long, straight and very abundant, particularly around neck, back of front legs; long trimming on hindquarters and on tail. Dense undercoat very protective

COLOUR: All black, or black with restricted amounts of white: moderate strip or patch on chest, between pads of feet, on tips of rear toes only, and grey or white on chin and muzzle. White on tips of front toes a fault

Amount of care coat requires: 1 2 3 4 5 6 7 8 9 10

Amount of exercise required: 1 2 3 4 5 6 7 8 9 10

Suitability for urban/flat life: 1 2 3 4 5 6 7 8 9 10

These intelligent dogs have been used extensively for police work in Europe and other parts of the world, including the United States, and indeed may have been the first breed in Europe to be trained for such work. They are loyal and willing animals who want to please their masters; they are affectionate with people they know but are suspicious of strangers. They were used as patrol- and courier-dogs in World War I, and hundreds gave their lives in battle. They are without fear and will attack anything they feel threatens their family and their property. They are possessive and territorial, as goes with being an outstanding guardian of home and flock. The Belgian Shepherd Dog is not at all casual about his responsibilities.

When one considers that the German Shepherd ranks high in this country in popularity and the Belgian Shepherd Dog much lower, one realizes how unspoiled and still true to purpose and form this dog probably is. Anyone who finds that distinction appealing and who wants to work towards maintaining such early and original perfection might well consider this intelligent breed.

The Belgian Shepherd Dog requires a lot of exercise. He is a rough, tough outdoor animal designed to handle any weather and any assignment. To coop him up and deny him an opportunity to move, to protect, and to participate in an active, outdoor life is to start the breed on the road to disintegration. Training of the Belgian Shepherd Dog should start early and continue long, and his distrust of strangers should be carefully supervised. He is far too intelligent an animal to be allowed to get the upper hand. Once you surrender it, you might never be able to get it back.

Belgian Shepherd Dog
(LAEKENOIS)

Land of origin: Belgium

Original purpose: Hunting and herding

Recent popularity ranking by K.C. registration: Moderate

HEIGHT: Dogs to 26 inches, bitches to 24 inches

WEIGHT: N.S.G.

COAT: Rough, dry, untidy-looking without curls or fluffiness. No plumes on tail

COLOUR: Reddish-fawn with black shading muzzle and tail

Amount of care coat requires: 1 2 3 4 5 6 7 8 9 10
                               * * * * *

Amount of exercise required: 1 2 3 4 5 6 7 8 9 10
                             * * * * * * * *

Suitability for urban/flat life: 1 2 3 4 5 6 7 8 9 10
                                 * * *

This is one of the four Belgian Shepherd Dogs – the one with the wiry coat. It is not an admissible breed in the U.S.A. and is the rarest of the Belgian Shepherd Dogs. Although originally herding and hunting dogs, they make good guards, and have been used as wardogs. They need lots of exercise, sound training and firm handling. The Laekenois is an ideal out-of-doors dog with an excellent thick coat. It is, from several aspects, not the best choice of dog for urban dwellers.

The coat requires daily grooming but this may be less arduous than with a long-coated variety unless bathing is indicated, when the washing and drying of a large dog may prove a daunting prospect. In common with the other Belgian sheepdogs most first-time owners find them over-exuberant, certainly until they attain the age of about three years. This can be minimized by lengthy exercise periods to tire out the young Laekenois, but few people can afford the time to devote several hours a day purely to this. As with most animals, sobriety develops with ageing, but the puppy and young dog may, unless given the required exercise, resort to destructiveness, excessive barking and even aggression.

Belgian Shepherd Dog

(MALINOIS)

Land of origin: Belgium

Original purpose: Shepherding

Recent popularity ranking by K.C. registration: Moderate

HEIGHT: Dogs to 26 inches, bitches to 24 inches

WEIGHT: N.S.G.

COAT: Short and straight with a dense, protective undercoat. Somewhat longer around the neck and on tail and back of thighs

COLOUR: Fawn to mahogany with black overlay; black muzzle and ears. Lighter underneath but not washed out. White on toe tips and *small* white spot on chest permitted

Amount of care coat requires: 1 2 3 4 5 6 7 8 9 10

Amount of exercise required: 1 2 3 4 5 6 7 8 9 10

Suitability for urban/flat life: 1 2 3 4 5 6 7 8 9 10

The Belgian Malinois is one of four virtually identical Belgian shepherding dogs that differ only in colour and to some degree in coat (see also the other Belgian Shepherd Dogs). All four breeds evolved from the basic shepherd stock of Holland, Belgium and France that was known as Chien de Berger, an animal bred for loyalty, endurance and intelligence. The livelihood and therefore the lives of the shepherding people depended in no small part upon the quality of their dogs. Dog-owning was not a luxury. You fed an animal who earned its keep, and the herding dogs of Europe, in the Middle Ages, earned their keep and more. Bandits, stock thieves and wolves prowled the countryside, and it took no small amount of canine courage to protect flocks and families against intrusion and ruin.

The Belgian Malinois, like the other three breeds, is obviously related at some point to the German Shepherd. The earlier shepherd dogs of western Europe were not bred for colour and style but for performance, and it is only in relatively modern times that an effort has been made to standardize them. The Malinois is a short-haired mahogany dog, the Belgian Groenendael a black

breed and the Belgian Tervueren a longer-haired, mahogany-russet breed.

The overall impression the Belgian Malinois gives is of a square and well-balanced dog. The male is masculine looking, and the bitch unmistakably feminine. The expression is alert, sure and inquiring. The Belgian Malinois wants to know what you want, whether you are a friend or a stranger. If you are a stranger, the dog certainly wants to know that you are not a threat to the household he was born to protect.

Because they are natural watchdogs and at times openly suspicious of people they do not know, these dogs should be trained early and well. They were used to drive wolves and feral dogs away from flocks, so they had fear bred out of them. They can be quick to fight, and when they do, there is no stopping them. They will fight to the death.

The Belgian Malinois is a fine, intelligent and affectionate dog. Anyone looking for a breed that has not been watered down by mass-production might well turn to this fine working dog. As a working dog, however, it is a breed more suited for open country than for city life, and it should be given a great deal of exercise every day.

Belgian Shepherd Dog

(TERVUEREN)

Land of origin: Belgium

Original purpose: Shepherding

Recent popularity ranking by K.C. registration: Moderate

HEIGHT: Dogs to 26 inches, bitches to 24 inches

WEIGHT: N.S.G.

COAT: Guard hairs long, straight and very abundant, particularly around neck, back of front legs; long trimming on hindquarters and on tail. Dense undercoat very protective

COLOUR: Attained at eighteen months: rich fawn to russet mahogany with black overlay. Hairs two-coloured (black-tipped). In males, pronounced on shoulders, back and rib section. Chest mixture of black and grey. Mask and ears largely black. Tail with darker tip. Lighter underbody but not washed out

Amount of care coat requires: 1 2 3 4 5 6 7 8 9 10
                                      * * *

Amount of exercise required: 1 2 3 4 5 6 7 8 9 10
                                      * * * * * * * * *

Suitability for urban/flat life: 1 2 3 4 5 6 7 8 9 10
                                      * *

This is the breed known in France and Belgium as the Chien de Berger Belge. It is a stunningly handsome version of the black Belgian Groenendael, different only in colour. Before the 1880s, when dog-shows became popular and tended to direct attention to a dog's appearance, European shepherds were not concerned with conformation. They were looking for dependability and durability, and they had that in their Chiens de Berger no matter what they looked like. But by the 1880s fencing and corralling were commonplace, and the wolves were gone. It was time to start dressing up the working breeds in dependable finery.

The Belgian Tervueren, like his very close cousins, the Belgian Malinois and the Belgian Groenendael, is an elegant-looking animal with a lively and graceful gait. His whole attitude is one of willingness, even eagerness to work, to please, to belong. He is obedient when trained well and early and has a long memory for friends and foes. He can be a fighter, because he was made to drive off or kill the feral dogs that ranged across Europe spreading rabies and

terror, but his possessiveness and fearlessness must be held in check. Although they are fine qualities, they are not needed the way they once were.

Once again, we find in the Belgian Tervueren an animal still close to some original ideal pragmatically arrived at a long time ago in a very rough world, but a breed little known in this country. Only the fine points of appearance have been modified or clarified in modern times – in the last century – and the rest is still probably pretty close to original design. This has great appeal for many people, and so does the fact that the spoilers have not yet chosen this breed for their quick-money machinations.

The Belgian Tervueren, like his first cousins, needs a great deal of exercise and is of limited appeal in the city. By nature a watchdog, he is best in the suburbs or country, where he still should be controlled and not allowed to fight with other dogs, as some specimens are likely to do. Early and careful obedience-training are in order for this working dog of western Europe.

Bernese Mountain Dog

(BERNESE SENNENHUND)

Land of origin: Switzerland

Original purpose: As draught animal and herder

Recent popularity ranking by K.C. registration: Moderate

HEIGHT: Dogs to 27½ inches, bitches to 26 inches

WEIGHT: N.S.G.

COAT: Soft and silky with bright, natural sheen. Slightly wavy but never with actual curl

COLOUR: Jet black with russet brown to deep tan markings on all four legs, a spot just above forelegs, each side of white chest markings, and spots over eyes. Over-eye spots are expected and required. Brown on forelegs must separate black from white

Amount of care coat requires: 1 2 3 4 5 6 7 8 9 10
                                 * * * *

Amount of exercise required: 1 2 3 4 5 6 7 8 9 10
                                   * * * * * * * * *

Suitability for urban/flat life: 1 2 3 4 5 6 7 8 9 10
                                 *

The Bernese is a Swiss dog descended from dogs of ancient Rome. Two thousand years ago Roman legions crossed Switzerland into northern Europe accompanied by large and probably ferocious war- and guard-dogs. Inevitably some of these animals fell by the way, and some of them survived. From the latter it is believed that at least four large breeds evolved in the Alpine country alone. Three of them were used to herd sheep, but one was a draught animal, and that was the dog we today call the Bernese Mountain Dog. The name comes from the canton of Berne, where the weavers kept the dogs to draw their carts to market right up until quite modern times.

The Bernese – seventy pounds and more, and almost twenty-eight inches tall – is a large animal. With his heavy coat and rugged constitution, he is an outside dog primarily and will do well in a kennel as long as he is shielded from sleet and freezing rain. He is hardy, healthy and quite aristocratic. Adorable as a puppy, the Bernese matures into a steady, stable animal fearlessly loyal to his master. One-personish by nature, the Bernese will adjust to a family situation

and accept family members and often-seen friends. Strangers, however, will be ignored, and are themselves better off if they ignore the dog until he is ready to attempt first overtures. The Bernese belongs to a few people and doesn't like to have his situation altered or expanded. He can be a good watchdog but should never be used for attack or other aggressive behaviour.

The Bernese needs a lot of exercise and is happier in colder climates than in warm ones. He is not a satisfactory flat pet. The big city with its restrictive environment is not Bernese Mountain Dog country.

The Bernese should be obedience-trained, and that training should start early and continue long. It is best if the owner takes the training sessions with the dog. In the Bernese Mountain Dog we have once again an animal too large to be tolerated as a brat. That kind of behaviour may be attractive and even acceptable (to a degree!) in a toy, but in a large, powerful animal like a Bernese it is quite intolerable. When it occurs, and certainly when it persists, the owner, not the dog, and certainly not the breed, is to blame.

Bichon Frise

Land of origin: France

Original purpose: Companionship

Recent popularity ranking by K.C. registration: Moderate

HEIGHT: Dogs to 12 inches, bitches to 12 inches

WEIGHT: N.S.G.

COAT: Double – outer coat is profuse, silky, loosely curled; 2 inches or longer

COLOUR: Pure white; sometimes with cream, apricot or grey on ears

Amount of care coat requires: 1 2 3 4 5 6 7 8 9 10
           * * * * * * * * * *

Amount of exercise required: 1 2 3 4 5 6 7 8 9 10
           * *

Suitability for urban/flat life: 1 2 3 4 5 6 7 8 9 10
           * * * * * * * * * *

The Bichon Frise is a small French toy-like companion dog whose derivation is cloaked in mystery. The breed has been known by many names, we think, and among them may be Tenerife Dog, Curly-coated Poodle, and Bichon à Poil Frise. In all likelihood any number of old French toy breeds went into the make-up of this little white bundle of charm.

The Bichon Frise was bred to be a companion animal. If he fails at that, he fails at everything. He should be gay, playful, affectionate and lively. The whole attitude should be one of involvement, participation and willingness. Shy, snappy or overly moody specimens were probably poorly bred or badly raised. The Bichon Frise should give the impression that he is smiling. When he is serious, he is even more endearing. He is an ideal flat dog and requires little exercise, although a chase around the coffee table after a rubber toy will be appreciated, perhaps more for the pleasure of interacting with a human being than for the exercise obtained.

Anyone contemplating this breed should keep that coat in mind. It does require care, and the dog you so admire in the show-ring or in photographs will not be the dog you have at home unless you are prepared to give it some time each day. A Bichon Frise can be a matted, ropy mess or a picture-book white muff of a dog. The difference is the time spent allowing the one or achieving the other.

The Bichon Frise is attracting a great deal of attention because of the continual demand for ideal urban pets. Its small size and predictable popularity are going to bring a great many unscrupulous backyard breeders into the field. Bichons Frises should be purchased with care. They are enough like other European toy and non-sporting dogs to tempt less-than-honest breeders to use what they can find – the Maltese and other breeds as well. Stick with the professional breeder who is devoted to perfecting and perpetuating this delightful breed. Any would-be owner of this newish breed may well be in the vanguard with what could be one of the most popular dogs in the country ten to fifteen years from now.

Bloodhound

Land of origin: Probably ancient Greece or Rome

Original purpose: Hunting, then man-trailing

Recent popularity ranking by K.C. registration: Moderate

HEIGHT: Dogs to 27 inches, bitches to 25 inches

WEIGHT: Dogs to 90 pounds, bitches to 80 pounds

COAT: Short, dense and able to withstand rough country

COLOUR: Coal black with rich tan above eyes, on sides of muzzle, chest, legs and breeching. Black pencilling on toes

Amount of care coat requires: 1 2 3 4 5 6 7 8 9 10
                                 *

Amount of exercise required: 1 2 3 4 5 6 7 8 9 10
                                * * * * * * * * *

Suitability for urban/flat life: Unsuited

The Bloodhound often is referred to as the grandfather of all scent hounds. His origins go back to ancient times, and he probably has been known in something like his present form for two thousand years. The modern scent hounds (as distinct from sight hounds such as the Greyhound and Borzoi) – the Beagles, Bassets and Foxhounds, for example – all carry the blood of the Bloodhound.

Interestingly, Bloodhounds probably got their name from the fact that in the Middle Ages in England it was only people of blue blood – aristocrats, that is – who owned this animal. To suggest that the name Bloodhound comes from any sanguinary propensity is just plain silly. Bloodhounds do not *hunt* men; they follow trails, and that is their game. The Bloodhound's almost unimaginably keen nose enables him to follow trails no other dog could detect. When he gets to his quarry, be it a child or an escaped convict, he does not attack but wags his tail and often tries to kiss.

Apart from the nonsense myth of the attacking, bloodthirsty hound, there are other nonsense tales. Bloodhounds normally are used alone, not in packs. Occasionally a brace (pair) may be used, but no more than that. They do not follow a trail yowling – almost all Bloodhounds trail silently. A Bloodhound is not allowed off a lead for two reasons: he would soon leave his trainer behind, and since he has absolutely no road sense, he would be liable to be hit on the first road he had to cross.

70

The Bloodhound is a loving, gentle pet who should never be quarrelsome with people or other animals. He does not do especially well in the obedience department because his whole nature is to tell you where to go, not take directions *from* you.

The Bloodhound is not a casual dog-owner's dog but rather a special breed for dedicated people. Good examples do not come cheaply, and Bloodhounds are suited to country living. They like to be in the company of other animals and people. Their voices are glorious, and they are more apt to 'sing' in greeting to someone they love than when on a trail. Bloodhound owners should consider training their dogs to trail and registering them with the police. Many children and confused old people have been saved by hounds owned by hobbyists. The Bloodhound does require a great deal of exercise, and his feeding must be scheduled and precise, since he is particularly subject to bloat. This gastric disorder of uncertain origin can kill an otherwise healthy dog within an hour.

Border Collie

Land of origin: Scotland and England

Original purpose: Shepherding

Recent popularity ranking by K.C. registration: Moderate

HEIGHT: To 21 inches

WEIGHT: N.S.G.

COAT: Undercoat short and dense; topcoat may be smooth or long (latter forming mane, brush and leg feather)

COLOUR: Black, black and white, tricolour – white never to predominate

Amount of care coat requires:

	1	2	3	4	5	6	7	8	9	10
Long:	*	*	*	*						
Smooth:	*									

Amount of exercise required:

1	2	3	4	5	6	7	8	9	10
*	*	*	*	*	*	*	*		

Suitability for urban/flat life:

1	2	3	4	5	6	7	8	9	10
*	*	*	*	*	*				

Most frequently seen working on farms or in the obedience ring, this breed became registrable as recently as 1976. These dogs will automatically 'herd' children (and adults) as well as animals other than sheep, so strongly inbuilt is this characteristic. They are highly intelligent and easily trained, but are used to working for one master. Despite this, they are considered generally to be good family dogs, given plenty of exercise, a firm upbringing and handling.

Though sometimes wrongly referred to as the Welsh Collie, the standard working collie is still jealously bred by shepherds and farmers who pay particular attention to working ability when selecting a suitable mate for their dogs. Frequently one puppy only is kept from a litter and it is trained invariably with an older working dog to the handler's spoken commands, whistles and arm gestures. The working collie perhaps surprisingly made its mark with the television series *One Man and His Dog* which took British viewers by storm and promoted sheepdog trials to prime-viewing ratings.

Border Terrier

Land of origin: England and Scotland

Original purpose: Killing foxes and vermin

Recent popularity ranking by K.C. registration: 33rd

HEIGHT: N.S.G.

WEIGHT: Dogs to 15½ pounds, bitches to 14 pounds

COAT: Short, dense undercoat with very wiry outer coat that is close lying. No curl or wave. Thick, loose hide

COLOUR: Red, grizzle and tan, blue and tan, or wheaten. A small amount of white allowed on chest but not on feet

Amount of care coat requires: 1 2 3 4 5 6 7 8 9 10
                                       * *

Amount of exercise required: 1 2 3 4 5 6 7 8 9 10
                                    * * * * * * * * *

Suitability for urban/flat life: 1 2 3 4 5 6 7 8 9 10
                                      * * * * * * * * *

This is a hardy, tough little action terrier from the border country. For several hundred years this wiry dynamo has been used to drive away and kill foxes and other animals that might attack the lambs. Extremely alert and active, this dog can tolerate any weather, any terrain, and will run behind a horse for hours. When a fox is spotted, he will chase it to ground and kill it from above or below, wherever he can catch the quarry. He can burst through any tangle of wire or brush because his loose skin keeps him from getting trapped. He will climb any wall or overcome any obstacle to get at his enemy.

The tough little Border Terrier is a hard-working field animal and cannot always be expected to behave as a pet as well. He is, though, loyal to his master and anxious to please. If raised in a home, he will respond because he is intelligent and eminently trainable.

It must always be remembered that the Border Terrier has been bred to kill other animals. That is his original calling, and that can lead to trouble unless the dog is held in some kind of check. Border Terriers need early training and a strong-willed master to see to it that deportment is given high priority. The dog is so active and so assertive that if ill-mannered, he could become the neighbourhood pest or even menace. That need not be, however, since the

breed is so bright and anxious to please. A good trainer can do wonders with this dog, the largest single problem being his penchant to go after other animals, cats included.

This breed is attractive and spunky and could enjoy greater popularity in this country at some future time. Anyone now contemplating the purchase of one should see to it that plenty of exercise is provided. The breed is active enough, and having one become hyperactive for lack of proper exercise is quite unnecessary.

Borzoi

Land of origin: Russia

Original purpose: Coursing wolves and game animals

Recent popularity ranking by K.C. registration: Moderate

HEIGHT: Dogs to 29 inches, bitches to 27 inches

WEIGHT: N.S.G.

COAT: Long and silky but not at all woolly. May be flat or wavy or even somewhat curly. Neck well frilled, profuse and curly. Feathering on hindquarters and tail, less on chest

COLOUR: Any colour or combination of colours is acceptable

Amount of care coat requires:	1 2 3 4 5 6 7 8 9 10
Amount of exercise required:	1 2 3 4 5 6 7 8 9 10
Suitability for urban/flat life:	1 2 3 4 5 6 7 8 9 10

The Borzoi, originally known in the United States as the Russian Wolfhound, is one of the most aristocratic of all dogs in style, bearing and ancestry. Arabian Greyhounds, gazelle-coursing animals of great speed, were imported into Russia by members of the royal circle. When they failed to survive the Russian weather, others were imported and crossed with a native working dog. The result, after considerable effort, was what we know as the Borzoi.

Few dogs are as beautiful to behold as this magnificent hound, who is even more spectacular when seen in pairs. If a standing Borzoi is lyrical, the hound in motion is an epic poem. He floats when he gets into full stride. He is a powerful, aggressive, purposeful animal with deadly accuracy once he is set loose. He will run a wolf to the ground and kill it, whatever its size. This should be kept in mind when other dogs are around – a Borzoi in a fight is big trouble, not only because of size and power, but also because of the breed's extraordinary speed.

Any prospective owner should weigh carefully the exercise this animal must have. Since few city dwellers can provide an opportunity for the Borzoi to course, very long walks and, if there is a place where conditions are right, a chance to run are the minimal requirements. It must be remembered, though,

that before a Borzoi is allowed to run, he must be thoroughly trained. He will be out of sight in seconds and well beyond a casual whistle of recall. The dogs certainly should not be allowed to molest native wildlife or other people's pets.

The Borzoi makes a good pet. He is generally a calm animal, considering his purpose and design, and is affectionate with youngsters and adults. Because of the animal's lightning-like reflexes, incredible speed, agility and great size, any sign of aggressiveness towards people must be discouraged. A puppy should be trained early, and that training should be maintained throughout the dog's life.

The Borzoi is not always superb, however. There are an unfortunate number of poor examples around, animals who are too long for their height, with a disproportionate head, too short a tail, or who lack the liquid motion that so enhances the beauty of this breed; such specimens are to be avoided by knowing the parents of the animal and by not buying a puppy too young to be properly evaluated. Care in purchase is required, for relatively poor examples are found even in the show-ring. In the pet trade they can be horrendous. Beware of an inexpensive Borzoi.

Boston Terrier

Land of origin: United States

Original purpose: Companionship

Recent popularity ranking by K.C. registration: Moderate

HEIGHT: N.S.G.

WEIGHT: To 25 pounds

COAT: Short, smooth, bright and fine. Must be shiny and alive

COLOUR: Brindle and white or black and white. Brindle and white with nicely balanced distribution considered best

Amount of care coat requires: 1 2 3 4 5 6 7 8 9 10
                                                 *

Amount of exercise required: 1 2 3 4 5 6 7 8 9 10
                 * * * *

Suitability for urban/flat life: 1 2 3 4 5 6 7 8 9 10
               * * * * * * * * * *

The Boston Terrier, the descendant of the crossing of an English Bulldog and a white English terrier, is an American breed, one of the few. He is also one of the most delightful of canine companions. Naturally bright and high-spirited, this is a consummate pet dog for any setting; farm, suburban home and city flat are all equally his natural turf.

The Boston has only one use: love. He is certainly not a hunting dog and not a working or herding animal, and although he will bark when strangers approach, he isn't much of a guard-dog either. He was bred for loving, and that is what he does best, first and always.

There is great need for city dogs, dogs that, although they like exercise and should get their share, are not demanding and do not require long walks in foul weather. The Boston Terrier may fit the bill of the perfect city dog. Any Boston will be grateful for the chance to chase a ball (the breed seems addicted to this sport), but he is content to sit and be quiet or play with a rubber toy on the kitchen floor. He wants to be in on everything in the family, but he gives as good as he gets. This is one of the most affectionate of all breeds. The Boston is also intelligent and takes to training with enthusiasm. To a Boston it is all part of the lovely game of living. Fortunately, he tends to be very long-lived, often continuing into the upper teens.

Bostons hardly shed at all, and they do not have a 'doggy' odour. They seldom need bathing, and a minute or two a week with a brush does it all. They are shiny, clean little animals.

Like the other short-nosed dogs, Bostons snort and gulp enough air to make them gassy. They may vomit when upset, but none of these things are bad enough to be a problem. Counter them with the fact that you can house-train a Boston Terrier in a matter of hours or days.

Be careful when you buy a Boston; if you buy from the wrong line, you may not get a superb companion but an idiotic, neurotic, snappy monster. Buy *only* from a recognized specialty breeder and when you have a chance to meet your puppy's parents and see what manner of dogs they are. When you set out to buy this super little dog, you have every right to expect the best in performance and character.

Bouvier des Flandres

Land of origin: Belgium

Original purpose: All-purpose (draught, shooting, herding)

Recent popularity ranking by K.C. registration: Moderate

HEIGHT: Dogs to 27 inches, bitches to 25½ inches

WEIGHT: Dogs to 88 pounds, bitches to 77 pounds

COAT: Rough and tousled. Able to tolerate any weather. Outer coat harsh, rough and wiry; very, very thick. Undercoat fine and soft

COLOUR: Fawn to black, salt and pepper, grey and brindle. White star on chest permitted. Chocolate brown with white spotting not desired

Amount of care coat requires: 1 2 3 4 5 6 7 8 9 10
                                              * * * *

Amount of exercise required: 1 2 3 4 5 6 7 8 9 10
                                            * * * * * * * * *

Suitability for urban/flat life: 1 2 3 4 5 6 7 8 9 10
                                            *

The cattle-herding people of the northern French hill country and south-western Flanders needed a really tough dog to guard, herd and drive their animals. The Bouvier des Flandres emerged as that animal. He is a rough and intelligent dog who was of help to the small farmer and the butcher alike. The itinerant strangers and packs of feral dogs who wandered those hills all needed to be watched, and occasionally attacked, and the Bouvier was the right dog for the job. Afraid of nothing, undeterred by any kind of weather or terrain, and boundless in his devotion to his master, the Bouvier set about his task with particular skill and energy.

The seventy-pound Bouvier des Flandres served faithfully in World War I as well. He was an ambulance dog and a messenger. That war, however, nearly did the breed in. The areas where he was best loved and where most of the significant breeding was going on were devastated by the battles that raged back and forth. Most of the stock was lost, and many examples were carried off to Germany. A few good specimens survived, though.

The Bouvier can be a family dog and is usually good with children. He is loyal and obedient when trained and is a watchdog. But he is also rough-and-tumble and hard to maintain in close quarters. He really is a dog for the

countryside, although a suburban neighbourhood will do as long as the dog is well trained and well controlled. It must be remembered that the Bouvier des Flandres was used to drive away whole packs of stray dogs, and he is not likely to back down from a fight. Like many herding and driving breeds, the Bouvier des Flandres is protective and territorial, and that can lead to fights, even though the strange dog's intentions are inoffensive. This must be watched, for the Bouvier is far too powerful to be allowed to perform his ancient responsibilities unchecked.

A good household pet if there is an opportunity for plenty of exercise, the Bouvier is an interesting large dog with a long and noble tradition of service to man.

Boxer

Land of origin: Germany

Original purpose: Probably for bull-baiting and other blood-sports; later guard and companion

Recent popularity ranking by K.C. registration: 11th

HEIGHT: Dogs to 24 inches, bitches to 23 inches

WEIGHT: Dogs to 70 pounds, bitches to 65 pounds

COAT: Short, shiny and smooth. It should lie tight to the body and never be curly, wavy or woolly

COLOUR: Shades of fawn ranging from light tan to dark red and mahogany. Darker colours preferred generally. May also be brindled, with black standing out from fawn background. White markings often handsome, but generally not on back of torso. White face marking may replace dark mask

Amount of care coat requires: 1 2 3 4 5 6 7 8 9 10

Amount of exercise required: 1 2 3 4 5 6 7 8 9 10

Suitability for urban/flat life: 1 2 3 4 5 6 7 8 9 10

The Boxer was derived in Germany from a number of strains common to Europe in the Middle Ages. Great Dane and English Bulldog may be included, and some of the mastiff line from Tibet is also likely. They all go back to what is called the Molossian strain, which undoubtedly came out of the Asian mountains to spread westward thousands of years ago.

This is a breed of enormous courage and stamina. Boxers were probably first bred for blood sports – baiting bulls and hunting boar and possibly dog-fighting as well. They were bred for ferociousness, but that is gone now, and except for an occasional penchant for a good scrap, the Boxer is a gentleman.

Alert, willing and anxious both to participate and to please, the Boxer is an ideal family dog. He is affectionate, a fine watchdog and good with children. He can be fine with other animals he knows and can be raised in a multi-animal household. When he does fight, however, he is deadly serious.

A Boxer is by nature careful with strangers, although not snappy or silly. He

checks things thoroughly, and if he decides a stranger is all right, he is open and friendly. He is not complicated and sneaky. A Boxer lets you know what he has on his mind. The agility, fearlessness and intelligence of this breed led to it being chosen as one of the first in Germany to work with the police. Boxers also have been used to lead the blind and for guard work. There is little this dog cannot learn to do.

Because they are so popular in this country, Boxers have been mass-produced, and that has been destructive to many lines. There are still many fine examples of the breed being shown and sold as companion animals. Since a poorly bred Boxer may be ugly in disposition as well as in conformation, the prospective buyer should be willing to go far to buy from only the finest breeders. You must see the parents of a puppy and know something about them before you can properly judge the puppy itself. All Boxer puppies are adorable, but not all grow up to fulfil the breed's promise.

Briard

Land of origin: France

Original purpose: Shepherding

Recent popularity ranking by K.C. registration: Moderate

HEIGHT: Dogs to 27 inches, bitches to 25½ inches

WEIGHT: N.S.G.

COAT: Long, stiff and slightly wavy

COLOUR: All solid colours allowed with the exception of white. Dark preferred – black, black with some white hairs, dark and light grey shades, tawny. Or two of these in combination but with no spots – transition between colours to be gradual and symmetrical

Amount of care coat requires:	1 2 3 4 5 6 7 8 9 10
Amount of exercise required:	1 2 3 4 5 6 7 8 9 10
Suitability for urban/flat life:	Unsuited

The Briard is probably the oldest of the true French shepherding dogs. These animals originally were used to protect flocks against thieves and feral dog packs. They have exceptional hearing, are extremely agile and are loyal. They are still the top-rated sheepdog in France and are in use all over the country. Although often known as Chiens Berger de Brie, they are popular well beyond Brie. They have had their place of eminence for over seven hundred years, which speaks well for their qualities.

The Briard does not learn as quickly as some of the other herding dogs, but once he has been trained, he is trained for life. Further, nothing will deter him. He can stand any terrain and any weather, and he has enormous endurance. He is so willing a worker that his short career as a cart-dog proved undistinguished, as he tended to overdo and hurt himself. The Briard served well in World War I, carrying supplies and munitions to the front.

The Briard is a quick mover – he turns fast, as suits a shepherder. These dogs are definitely not keen on strangers and tend to remain suspicious even after

some time has passed. They are not yappy and silly about newcomers, but they will watch quietly for some sign that they are needed. As natural watchdogs, they can be quite protective.

Because they have been bred through so many centuries as active field-dogs, they do need exercise to remain happy and in good shape. They cannot be kept easily in a flat. In any circumstances there must be active members of the family to take them on long walks and runs, and more than once a day. In general the Briard is a well-mannered dog, stoic and reserved. He is a good breed with children that he knows. He does not tend to stray, preferring to stay near the property of his master so that he can protect it.

The Briard is not the most elegant of breeds, but he does have a nice square, solid appearance. He looks as purposeful as he is, and in the right setting he makes a good family pet and household guardian. Training has to start early and last long. Once you have brought your Briard to the right point of training, though, you have an exceptionally well-mannered canine friend.

Brittany Spaniel

Land of origin: France, from ancient Spanish stock

Original purpose: Hunting

Recent popularity ranking by K.C. registration: Moderate

HEIGHT: Dogs to 20½ inches, bitches to 19½ inches

WEIGHT: N.S.G.

COAT: Dense and flat, wavy but not curly. Skin loose but not so loose as to form pouches

COLOUR: Dark, rich orange and white or liver and white. Never to be tri-coloured or to show any black at all. Colours should be strong and not faded.

Amount of care coat requires: 1 2 3 4 5 6 7 8 9 10
                                 * * *

Amount of exercise required: 1 2 3 4 5 6 7 8 9 10
                                 * * * * * * * * *

Suitability for urban/flat life: 1 2 3 4 5 6 7 8 9 10
                                 * * *

The Brittany is actually too leggy to be called a spaniel, or at least he is one of the least spaniel-like of all spaniels. He is as high in the withers as he is long. He comes from ancient Spanish stock carried across Europe so long ago we can't pinpoint the period. While most spaniels developed in the British Isles, this breed was developed in France and has been known to European sportsmen for centuries. He shares common ancestry with all the other spaniels, the setters and the pointers. In size and appearance he may be close to those ancestral dogs from which all three groups arose.

The Brittany is never shown with a tail substantially longer than four inches. The tail is sometimes docked, but many Brittanies are born with mere stubs, and some are born without tails at all. The first tailless specimens we know of appeared about a century ago in the Douron Valley in France.

The Brittany is an excellent field-dog, and as such his true qualities show best. The breed is by nature aggressive and loyal. Since Brittanies are not keen on strangers, they are natural watchdogs and are quite fearless. They should, though, be watched around strangers, for they can become a little too tough and may be quite intimidating. They tend to be one-personish but will live with a family most amicably. They can be raised with other animals.

The Brittany is not as elegant as some of the other spaniels, although he has a certain keenness about him that is attractive. His coat can be handsome although it is not as fine as those of other spaniels. Brittanies are sturdy, well boned, strong and driving. Never clumsy or awkward, they move fast, their long legs serving them well. They have minimum feathering and their ears are not long, so coat care is less than for the other spaniels.

The Brittany needs a great deal of exercise, and if one is brought into a confined suburban home or a city dwelling, that should be kept in mind. All the wonderful drive and energy that make this breed so desirable in the field *can* degenerate into plain silliness and hyperactivity. The splendid field-dog improperly cared for can become a pest. If you keep a Brittany, long walks on a regular basis are a must.

Beware of poor breeders and mass-producers. You should know the original source well, and buy only after careful consideration. The range in looks, and especially in behaviour, is great.

Bulldog

Land of origin: England

Original purpose: Bull-baiting

Recent popularity ranking by K.C. registration: Moderate

HEIGHT: N.S.G.

WEIGHT: Dogs to 55 pounds, bitches to 50 pounds

COAT: Straight, short, flat, close lying, fine, smooth and glossy

COLOUR: Brindle or red brindle, solid white, solid red or fawn, piebald; colours should be bright and clearly defined

Amount of care coat requires: 1 2 3 4 5 6 7 8 9 10
                                *

Amount of exercise required: 1 2 3 4 5 6 7 8 9 10
                              * * *

Suitability for urban/flat life: 1 2 3 4 5 6 7 8 9 10
                                  * * * * * * * * *

The Bulldog was designed to fight bulls, and that, simply, is how he got his name. He probably also was used to fight bears and other pit animals in a much more cruel era of England's history. Despite all that nasty background, the English Bulldog of today is a gentle, companionable animal.

The Bulldog is adoring and wants to be adored back. He can do well with other animals as long as they will recognize who is at the top of the order. Bulldogs do not like being challenged or insulted. When a fight does start, all hell breaks loose, and the other dog may be dead before anything effective can be done. Bulldogs should definitely be on leashes when they are apt to encounter strange dogs.

Curiously, bulldogs and cats get along very well together as long as the cats understand the position Bulldogs take over a food dish – total possessiveness. There can be unfortunate accidents involving otherwise extremely sweet Bulldogs if this fact is overlooked. If the household contains other animals, Bulldogs are best fed by themselves, and food dishes should not be left around.

With children Bulldogs are another story. They seem to have a built-in sense of manners, and even the smallest child is unlikely to be knocked over. Bulldogs approach babies as if they really did understand their own weight and

power. They are flawless pets, giving and getting love endlessly and never tiring of the opportunity to interact with human beings.

There has to be a debit side, and in that column can go snoring. Bulldogs seem to sleep more contentedly than almost any other breed, and they certainly let you know it. The variety of snorts, wheezes, grunts, huffs and snores that can come from a sleeping Bulldog is nothing less than astounding.

Bulldogs are immensely appealing with their marvellous shoulders-out attitude, and they tend to enslave their owners. They are like super-powered tanks when faced with a challenge, charging forward even when in doubt because of their poor eyesight. Much of that is bluff, however, and a harsh word will turn most Bulldogs off.

Bulldogs like a walk and can be downright frisky pups, but as they mature, they need little strenuous activity. They are fine on the farm, in the suburbs or in a flat. They are not long-lived dogs, and ten years would be an old and perhaps even unusual Bulldog. They should *never* be locked in a car, for they feel heat terribly. More than one Bulldog standing in the sun at a dog-show has ended up with an oxygen mask over his face. Their health generally requires careful watching under all circumstances.

Bullmastiff

Land of origin: England

Original purpose: Night patrol against game poachers on private estates

Recent popularity ranking by K.C. registration: Moderate

HEIGHT: Dogs to 27 inches, bitches to 26 inches

WEIGHT: Dogs to 130 pounds, bitches to 110 pounds

COAT: Short and dense, offering good protection against harsh weather

COLOUR: Red, brindle or fawn, the latter usually with a dark face and ears. A small white spot on the chest is allowed but no other white markings. Originally darker dogs were favoured because they were more difficult to see at night. Now lighter-coloured animals are as highly regarded

Amount of care coat requires: 1 2 3 4 5 6 7 8 9 10

Amount of exercise required: 1 2 3 4 5 6 7 8 9 10

Suitability for urban/flat life: Unsuited

The Bullmastiff is not to be confused with the Mastiff. He is only 60 per cent Mastiff; the rest is Bulldog.

This breed is one of the few animals actually bred to attack man. Once known as the 'gamekeeper's night-dog', he was used to track and knock down poachers on private estates. He was sometimes muzzled and was not meant to maul his victims, just keep them on the ground until the gamekeeper arrived. The Mastiff was tried for this task, but he was neither fast enough nor sufficiently aggressive. That is why the old Bulldog – a bigger, rougher animal than the breed we know today – was blended in.

All that is history. Today's Bullmastiff, while not exactly a dog to challenge in open combat, is usually a gentleman. He is not a fearsome beast, as he once may have been from the poacher's point of view. He is fine with his owner's family and generally open and willing with strangers. It might be quite another thing, though, if a Bullmastiff's family seemed threatened, for this is an alert animal. He also happens to be without fear. It is doubtful that another dog could make a Bullmastiff back down once his hackles were up. For this reason he must be trained to live with other animals. Like the Bulldog, which constitutes nearly half his blood-line, he doesn't like other animals to challenge him.

There is no doubt that the sight of a Bullmastiff on the premises would be a deterrent to almost anyone, but in reality a dog is no harder than a man to disable, for instance with teargas. No one should think that a Bullmastiff or any other breed will make their property crime-proof, and for this reason the animal should never be attack-trained, nor should any aggressiveness toward people be tolerated. With giant breeds and super-dogs like Bullmastiffs, this is asking for trouble. Let the sight of him alone be the prime deterrent. A professional criminal will not deliberately put himself in a position to get hurt, so it is the innocent or minor-nuisance trespasser who is likely to be seriously hurt or killed by an attack-trained dog.

The Bullmastiff is a family dog, but he is hardly suited to flat living. He is an estate dog, a dog-person's dog and a magnificent pet in the right setting. The fact that he will scare off lesser intruders is secondary. What is important is that the breed is a splendid one, represented by regal, powerful animals who are by nature devoted to their masters and without meanness or pettiness in their make-up.

Bull Terrier and Bull Terrier (Miniature)

Land of origin: England

Original purpose: Fighting

Recent popularity ranking by K.C. registration: 26th

HEIGHT: N.S.G.

WEIGHT: N.S.G.

COAT: Short, hard, flat and glossy

COLOUR: Two varieties. White – all white or white with some markings on head. No other markings allowed. Coloured – any colour other than white or any colour with white markings as long as white does not predominate. Brindle is the preferred colour

Amount of care coat requires: 1 2 3 4 5 6 7 8 9 10
            *

Amount of exercise required: 1 2 3 4 5 6 7 8 9 10
            * * * * * * * * *

Suitability for urban/flat life: 1 2 3 4 5 6 7 8 9 10
            * * * *

The Bull Terrier is a much maligned dog. It is true that he was originally bred for blood-sports, but those were rougher times. There is a kind of nobility to the breed, and he is not generally a nasty creature. But neither is he a wise choice for an inexperienced owner. He should not be one's first dog.

The Bull Terrier, a cross between the Bulldog and an extinct variety of white terrier with some Pointer blood thrown in, is a powerful and assertive animal who will answer the ancient call of his kind if challenged. When that happens, he can kill almost any dog alive. Bull Terriers, because there is always the danger that they will be provoked into a fight, must at all times be kept under control and never allowed to wander. They don't necessarily look for trouble, but trouble has a way of presenting itself. Unfortunately, Bull Terriers don't just get into fights, they finish them.

With people Bull Terriers can be affectionate, playful and loyal. They make excellent watchdogs. There is something about them that frightens unwelcome people away.

The Bull Terrier eats a great deal and must be walked often and long. They are not a good breed for inactive people. They require an active, lively family

who wants to romp, run and tussle. Activity is the keynote of this dog's existence.

As for appearance, there are people who detest it and people who love it. That seems to be true of the breed in general – no one *likes* a Bull Terrier, they either hate or adore him.

Some people insist that there is a greater difference between the disposition of dog and bitch in this breed than in any other. However that may be, the bitch is certainly a softer dog, milder and perhaps easier to train and manage.

The Miniature Bull Terrier is in all respects identical to the Bull Terrier with the exception of size.

The Miniature Bull Terrier should have a maximum height of 14 inches and a maximum weight of 20 pounds.

Cairn Terrier

Land of origin: Isle of Skye, Scotland

Original purpose: Killing vermin

Recent popularity ranking by K.C. registration: 18th

HEIGHT: N.S.G.

WEIGHT: To 14 pounds

COAT: Hard and weather resistant. Double – outer coat profuse and harsh, undercoat short, soft and close

COLOUR: Any colour except white. Dark ears, muzzle and tail tip are desirable. Often seen wheaten, grizzle and tan

Amount of care coat requires: 1 2 3 4 5 6 7 8 9 10
                                   * * *

Amount of exercise required: 1 2 3 4 5 6 7 8 9 10
                              * * * * *

Suitability for urban/flat life: 1 2 3 4 5 6 7 8 9 10
                          * * * * * * * * *

The Cairn is one of Scotland's super little working terriers, and for hundreds of years he has been used to pursue vermin. He has a game, hunting spirit and is bold and fearless, but he is also a little hardheaded. Some writers insist that the Cairn is the ancestral breed for the Scottie, the West Highland White and the Skye. He certainly has contributed to all those breeds and to others that we don't even know in this country.

The Cairn Terrier has managed to survive fads and quirks and remains, thanks to the determination of his fanciers, much the dog he was hundreds of years ago on the Isle of Skye. He has a broader head than most terriers and a relatively short, pointed muzzle. He is built close to the ground, but he is not heavy. At least he should not give that impression. The whole feeling should be of an alert, intelligent, active and assertive dog. And all those things are true.

Cairns are perfect house pets and are fine in flats. They require only a reasonable amount of exercise, although any time a good romp is available, it should be encouraged. They shed, but not very much, and they are devoted to their master. They can be a little one-personish, but certainly not to the point of being a nuisance or menace. They are generally cheerful, they are always busybodies, and they want to be in on everything going on in their household.

Let there be no mistaking the point: the house where a Cairn lives is *his* property. Cairns make good little watchdogs.

The Cairn coat is very important to the animal's appearance, but no real clipping is involved. The coat is tidied and brushed; for top show form a little trimming is required. The hair on that broad head is all-important. Although the coat can have a slight wave, any tendency to silkiness or to curl would be a severe fault.

The Cairn is hardy and ready to go at all times. Weather doesn't bother him, and he is a very responsible animal, sensing almost magically the moods of his owner. He watches and waits and takes his cues automatically. He is an ideal dog for a single person or a couple without children who want to add a spot of constant cheerfulness to their life.

Canaan Dog

Land of origin: Israel

Original purpose: Guard, flock protector, war-dog

Recent popularity ranking by K.C. registration: Rare

HEIGHT: To 23½ inches

WEIGHT: To 55 pounds

COAT: Short coat, slight tail feather

COLOUR: N.S.G.

Amount of care coat requires: 1 2 3 4 5 6 7 8 9 10
                                             * *

Amount of exercise required: 1 2 3 4 5 6 7 8 9 10
                                             * * * * *

Suitability for urban/flat life: 1 2 3 4 5 6 7 8 9 10
                                             * *

This is a sturdy guard-dog – fearless and easy to train. It has an inbuilt distrust of strangers and an inherent aggression. It is very much a specialist's breed and not to be recommended for the average household – especially in urban areas. Indeed the natural characteristics of the dog may be well suited only to conditions in the Near East.

At the time of writing, no examples of this breed are in the country, but their potential as flock protectors could possibly result in their importation to defend farm stock against worrying dogs and other predators, and possibly even to discourage human rustlers. As a general rule, anyone contemplating selection of a rare breed such as this would be well advised to spend some time observing the dogs in their original habitat and speaking at length with their owners before committing themselves to the expensive and hazardous exercise of purchase, transportation and quarantine, only to find the animal is unsuited to the life-style in Britain.

Cavalier King Charles Spaniel

Land of origin: Britain

Original purpose: Companion dog

Recent popularity ranking by K.C. registration: 5th

HEIGHT: N.S.G.

WEIGHT: To 18 pounds

COAT: Long, silky and free from curl, though a slight wave is permissible. There should be adequate feather

COLOUR: There are four accepted colours – tri-colour (black, red and white), ruby (self-coloured red), black and tan and Blenheim (rich chestnut on white ground)

Amount of care coat requires: 1 2 3 4 5 6 7 8 9 10
                                                 * * * * *

Amount of exercise required: 1 2 3 4 5 6 7 8 9 10
                                                 * * *

Suitability for urban/flat life: 1 2 3 4 5 6 7 8 9 10
                                                 * * * * * * * * * *

The Cavalier is among the top popular small breeds. These dogs are generally of excellent temperament, though some strains may be nervous or apprehensive. They originated from the same stock as King Charles Spaniels, but are a larger, stronger breed with a much less snub nose.

The Cavalier was very highly thought of by King Charles II and has been widely reported by Pepys and his contemporaries. They are a hardy breed, extremely adaptable and generally happy to get on with other household pets, children etc., and have very few disadvantages. In addition to daily grooming, many Cavaliers, especially those with large areas of white coat, require regular bathing – say once a month – to keep them really presentable.

Although they are thought of as small companion dogs, they are extremely hardy and game for anything, and country-dwelling Cavaliers are often seen to hunt smaller rodents when they go burrowing.

Chihuahua
(LONG COAT AND SHORT COAT)

Land of origin: Mexico

Original purpose: Probably status and companionship

Recent popularity ranking by K.C. registration: Long Coat: 20th
Short Coat: 35th

HEIGHT: N.S.G.

WEIGHT: To 6 pounds, show-weight: up to 4 pounds

COAT:
Long Coat – soft, flat or slightly curly, with undercoat desirable. Ears fringed;
feathering on feet and legs. Large ruff on neck desired. Tail as plume
Short Coat – soft, close and glossy, should be smooth and well placed over body.
Undercoat permissible

COLOUR: Any colour; may be solid, marked or splashed. No preferences

Amount of care coat requires:

Long Coat:	1*	2*	3*	4	5	6	7	8	9	10
Short Coat:	1*	2	3	4	5	6	7	8	9	10
Amount of exercise required:	1*	2	3	4	5	6	7	8	9	10
Suitability for urban/flat life:	1*	2*	3*	4*	5*	6*	7*	8*	9*	10*

The true origin of this smallest of all dogs (he may weigh as little as one pound)
is unknown. Apparently the Toltecs had them in Mexico before they were
conquered by the Aztecs, who took over the breed. This dog was apparently a
status symbol among the ruling class, but there is reason to believe that the
common people ate them. There is some tradition to suggest that a hairless or
nearly hairless dog reached Mexico from China or some other Asian land in
ancient times and that this animal appeared in the ancestry of the dog we call
the Chihuahua today. The original Toltec dog may have been the Techichi.
The name Chihuahua comes from the Mexican state of that name, but the dog
is no more common there than in any other part of Mexico. Actually, the breed
as we know it is more an American creation, its popularity there being great
and consistent year after year.

Short Coat Chihuahua   Long Coat Chihuahua

The Chihuahua, in the long coat or short coat variety (the latter is much better known), is the ultimate toy. This is a dog which need never go out, should not be exposed to weather extremes, and who really must be spoiled to be appreciated. He is companionable but highly temperamental, and he despairs if left out of anything that is going on. He does not like other breeds of dogs, and this is often referred to as clannishness. An important factor probably is that all other dogs are bigger than the Chihuahua and may seem challenging and dangerous.

The Chihuahua is an ideal dog for middle-aged and elderly people who want to fuss over and be fussed at by a tyrant of a toy. Chihuahuas are no trouble to keep, since they are neat and don't have to be walked. Although small eaters, as might be expected, they are fussy, and that generally pleases the people most interested in the companionship of the world's smallest dog. A bit of white-meat chicken will please the Chihuahua to get and the owner to give. That really is what the Chihuahua is all about. He has a job to do and a niche to fill. He accomplishes his mission with commendable skill.

The Chihuahua has long been popular and is variable in quality. Care should be taken in buying one of these fine little characters. The really serious fanciers and breeders are slow to part with a puppy. They want to know the kind of home he is going to get. You must be very reassuring if you want to own a really fine Chihuahua.

Chinese Crested Dog

Land of origin: China

Original purpose: Companion dog

Recent popularity ranking by K.C. registration: Rare

HEIGHT: N.S.G. (varies considerably)

WEIGHT: Also variable, maximum 12 pounds

COAT: As the name suggests, the dog is hairless with the exception of tufts on the crown of the head, tip of the tail and feet

COLOUR: N.S.G.

Amount of care coat requires: 1 2 3 4 5 6 7 8 9 10

Amount of exercise required: 1 2 3 4 5 6 7 8 9 10

Suitability for urban/flat life: 1 2 3 4 5 6 7 8 9 10

The Chinese Crested Dog must be one of nature's curiosities. These dogs are only recently being seen in Great Britain. Because of their lack of general coat hair, they have one obvious advantage in that they do not cast, and this may be a boon to owners or families that have an allergic problem to dog hair.

They tend to lack the 'doggy' smell, and their skin feels hot to the touch. Because of heat loss and lack of insulation, the crested dog's body temperature is slightly higher than that of other breeds. Despite the genetic disposition to hairlessness, occasionally in a thoroughbred litter fully haired pups are born, referred to as 'powder puffs'.

Because of the curious skin, the Chinese Crested Dog needs frequent bathing, say weekly, and oiling of the hairless parts is recommended, using a baby oil. Care should also be taken with such dogs in very sunny weather, due to the risk of sunburn and heat stroke.

Chow Chow

Land of origin: China

Original purpose: Probably hunting; also bred for meat and fur

Recent popularity ranking by K.C. registration: 32nd

HEIGHT: From 18 inches

WEIGHT: N.S.G.

COAT: Dense, abundant, straight and off-standing. It is rather coarse in texture, and there is a woolly, much softer undercoat

COLOUR: Any clear colour, solid throughout. There are generally lighter shadings on ruff, tail and breechings

Amount of care coat requires:	1	2	3	4	5	6	7	8	9	10
	★	★	★	★	★	★	★	★		

Amount of exercise required:	1	2	3	4	5	6	7	8	9	10
	★	★	★	★	★	★	★			

Suitability for urban/flat life:	1	2	3	4	5	6	7	8	9	10
	★	★	★	★	★					

This dog of China is at least two thousand years old. There are endless suggestions as to what animals were ancestor to this breed and to which breeds it in turn gave rise. No one knows, and the mystery is compounded by the fact that the Chow Chow is the only breed of dog left on earth with a black tongue. Because the polar bear also has a black mouth, there are absurd stories about a direct line of descent from the great white bear of the North. It may in fact be the ancestral breed to many of the sled-dogs and Spitz-type dogs we know today – for example, the Japanese Akita. It is generally agreed that it did not come from any familiar Western breeds.

The Chow Chow (very often just referred to simply as the Chow) is an aloof and dignified dog. He was used extensively for hunting in China and also, apparently, for guard work. He is not at all demonstrative and can be very hardheaded. He is a massive-looking animal, handsome and powerful, and to some people he appears to be ferocious. The heavy head and ruff and the thick muzzle may give that impression. In fact this dog is not ferocious; he is just very self-contained. He should not be expected to act like a romping hound or a terrier looking for a game; that is not his style. He is loyal, may be affectionate towards his owner, and can be an excellent watchdog. Because he can be a little

on the tough side, he should be watched around other animals. This is not always the best breed for a household with children. The Chow Chow may be fine with an owner's children, but friends of the children are another matter.

That magnificent Chow Chow coat does require a lot of care. Bathing tends to soften it, so it is not recommended any more often than necessary. Constant brushing is essential if matting is to be avoided. There is considerable shedding in the summertime.

People looking for a cuddly pet should not look to a Chow Chow. This is an animal of high style; he is both decorative to the discerning and formidable to the uninvited. He is a stunning dog in the show-ring and should be obedience-trained simply because he is powerful and is a bit on the stubborn side. Strangers should not expect much in the way of a greeting. In fact, they should expect to be ignored as long as they do not appear to be threatening towards the household.

Collie

(ROUGH AND SMOOTH)

Land of origin: Scotland

Original purpose: Herding, farm work

Recent popularity ranking by K.C. registration: 8th

HEIGHT: Dogs to 24 inches, bitches to 22 inches

WEIGHT: Dogs to 65 pounds, bitches to 55 pounds

COAT: Well-fitting, straight and harsh outer coat with very dense soft, furry undercoat. Very abundant and the dog's 'crowning glory' in the rough-coated variety. The smooth variety has a hard, dense and smooth coat

COLOUR: Four varieties: sable and white (sable running from light gold to dark mahogany), tricolour (predominantly black with white and tan markings), blue merle and white. The latter is really predominantly white with sable or tri-colour markings. Colours are the same for both coat styles

Amount of care coat requires:

	1	2	3	4	5	6	7	8	9	10
Rough:	★	★	★	★	★	★	★	★	★	
Smooth:	★									

Amount of exercise required:

	1	2	3	4	5	6	7	8	9	10
	★	★	★	★	★	★	★	★	★	

Suitability for urban/flat life:

	1	2	3	4	5	6	7	8	9	10
	★	★	★							

The Collie dates back several hundred years to the Scottish Highlands, and given the antiquity of shepherding, the breed undoubtedly had much earlier origins on the Continent. No one will ever sort out the early history of the Collie, for no records were kept by breeders of working dogs. These animals were essential to their masters' livelihood rather than to their sense of aesthetics.

There are two varieties of Collie, the rough and the smooth, with the former being the more popular. Records indicate that as late as the end of the last century the two varieties might appear in the same litter, but some authorities believe that the two had different origins. Today, though, they are considered varieties of the same breed, and all the rest must remain conjecture.

The standards for the two forms are the same except for the coat, and therein lies a world of difference. The Rough Collie requires a great deal of care if he

Smooth Collie

Rough Collie

is to look as he should. His coat is long and dense and soon will become a hopeless tangle unless brushed out regularly. The smooth-coated variety requires virtually no care, but he is not at all popular with American fanciers of the breed.

The Collie is a working dog designed for living in the open. He requires a lot of exercise on a regular basis, for working dogs are creatures of habit. No one should think of owning a Collie unless he plans to exercise him and care for him properly.

By nature the Collie is careful with strangers – not hostile, just cautious. He is very affectionate with family and with people he knows well. He is loyal, a good watchdog and sensible in all things. Like many other breeds, the Collie has suffered from extreme popularity. As a result of books, films and television series starring Collies, the breed consistently has been one of the most popular. Many breeders far more interested in profit than in the welfare of their breed have capitalized on the demand, and there are many sub-standard specimens around. They can be unreliable and nervous, the last things one should expect of a fine Collie.

Perhaps as much as with any breed today, great care should be taken when buying a Collie. Only the most responsible breeders should be considered, and only after the adult dogs in their line have been seen. There is no finer dog than a fine Collie, and no greater disappointment than a bad one.

Dachsbracke

Land of origin: Sweden, then Germany

Original purpose: Game-dog

Recent popularity ranking by K.C. registration: Rare

HEIGHT: To 16½ inches

WEIGHT: N.S.G.

COAT: Short, dense coat

COLOUR: N.S.G.

Amount of care coat requires:	1 2 3 4 5 6 7 8 9 10
	* *
Amount of exercise required:	1 2 3 4 5 6 7 8 9 10
	* * * * * * *
Suitability for urban/flat life:	1 2 3 4 5 6 7 8 9 10
	* * * * *

Thought very similar to the Drever (one of Sweden's most popular game-dogs), there is a resemblance to the Dachshund. There are three regional varieties of Dachsbracke, one of which is nearly extinct. Like the Drever, this breed was formerly a scenting and driving dog for small-game shooting. Nowadays it has become more accepted as a house dog.

At the time of writing, this breed is rare on the Continent and non-existent in Britain. Specific comment on the variety is therefore not possible, and would-be importers would be well counselled to make detailed inquiries in the dog's native Germany before choosing the breed. In general terms one should be very cautious before deciding on a hound variety (or near relation) as a domestic family pet, for their reaction to full domestication can be very variable and sometimes totally unsatisfactory.

Dachshund

(LONG-HAIRED, SMOOTH-HAIRED, WIRE-HAIRED; MINIATURE
LONG-HAIRED, MINIATURE SMOOTH-HAIRED, MINIATURE WIRE-
HAIRED)

Land of origin: Germany

Original purpose: Hunting, especially of badger

Recent popularity ranking by K.C. registration: Miniature Long-haired: 21st
Miniature Short-haired: 37th

HEIGHT: N.S.G.

WEIGHT:
Standard Long-haired: Dogs to 18 pounds, bitches to 17 pounds
Standard Smooth-haired: Dogs to 25 pounds, bitches to 23 pounds
Standard Wire-haired: Dogs to 22 pounds, bitches to 20 pounds
Miniature: Ideally to 10 pounds (not to exceed 11 pounds)

COAT: (Standard and Miniature):
Long-haired variety – soft, sleek, glistening, slightly wavy, feathered
Smooth-haired variety – short, thick, smooth, shiny. Not coarse or too thick
Wire-haired variety – uniform, tight, short, thick, rough and hard. Good undercoat.
Beard on chin. Eyebrows bushy

COLOUR: Red or tan, red-yellow, brindle; deep black, chocolate, grey, or blue and
white. Dappled. Foregoing for smooth variety. All colours permissible in wire-haired
variety. Long-haired has same range as smooth except red and black is allowed and
classed as red

Amount of care coat requires:

Long-haired:	1*	2*	3*	4*	5*	6*	7	8	9	10
Smooth-haired:	1*	2	3	4	5	6	7	8	9	10
Wire-haired:	1*	2*	3*	4	5	6	7	8	9	10
Amount of exercise required:	1*	2*	3	4	5	6	7	8	9	10
Suitability for urban/flat life:	1*	2*	3*	4*	5*	6*	7*	8*	9*	10*

Today's Dachshund is the descendant of a fiery German hunting dog of perhaps
thirty-five pounds or more. He was used initially on badger, or so tradition
goes ('Dachs' is the German word for badger), but also on a wide variety of

Smooth-haired Dachshund

Long-haired Dachshund

Wire-haired Dachshund

other wildlife. He should exhibit the character and assertiveness this background suggests.

The Dachshund is a wonderfully responsive and loyal dog, seemingly a hound but with many terrier-like characteristics. He is intelligent, willing to learn and a true participant. He loves play, and he travels well. He is a perfect flat dog.

The three coat styles require different degrees of care, of course, but it is never oppressive, for the naturally clean little Dachshund is never very large. The Miniature variety sports all three coats. He is a true lapdog and can be carried anywhere.

Dachshunds get along well with children and with other animals, although when young they are very playful and can drive other animals up the wall. They soon learn their manners, though, and settle in as fine family pets.

Because they do have three very distinct coat styles, a wide range of colours, and a remarkable range in size, they are able to serve a variety of tastes. This coupled with their good nature and responsiveness has kept them consistently among the most popular of all breeds.

Dachshunds are so extremely popular that the mass-producers have had a field day, and there are some perfectly awful specimens offered for sale every day. Stick to the best specialty breeders and make sure you have the dog you set out to own – a fine example of a truly outstanding breed.

Dalmatian

Land of origin: Yugoslavia

Original purpose: Coach-dog

Recent popularity ranking by K.C. registration: Moderate

HEIGHT: Dogs to 24 inches, bitches to 23 inches

WEIGHT: N.S.G.

COAT: Short, hard, dense, fine, sleek and glossy. Never woolly or silky

COLOUR: Very important in standards. Ground colour pure white. Black or liver spots as near uniform in size as possible. Patches a fault. Puppies born pure white

Amount of care coat requires: 1 2 3 4 5 6 7 8 9 10
 *

Amount of exercise required: 1 2 3 4 5 6 7 8 9 10
 * * * * * * * * * *

Suitability for urban/flat life: 1 2 3 4 5 6 7 8 9 10
 * *

The Dalmatian, wherever he came from (the point has been argued in print for more than a century), is a charmer with more ways to please an owner than we can probably record. In their long and varied careers these dogs have been shepherds, guard-dogs on border patrol, war-dogs as couriers and sentinels, ratters, bird-dogs, retrievers, draft-dogs, coach-dogs, general farm-dogs, and household pets. You ask it, and a Dalmatian will do it with élan. We know he was very popular in Dalmatia, part of former Austria-Hungary, in the last century, and hence the name.

The Dalmatian is an active animal – a spirited and willing animal who takes training more readily than many other breeds. He loves to run with horses (and horses seem to love being with Dalmatians).

Wherever the action is, there the Dalmatian wants to be. He isn't yappy, but he will bark with excitement as he runs back and forth. He is a good watchdog and is fine with children.

The Dalmatian is devoted to his master above all else and is good within the family circle. While not a particularly suspicious and certainly not a shy dog, he does like to get his facts straight when it comes to strangers. He takes his time and then generally makes a wise decision.

This is a clean dog, easily house-trained and requiring little care. He is hardy

and solid, and he loves to be in motion. For that reason he is a questionable choice for city life. Of course, there are city dwellers who lead active lives, taking long walks in the streets and heading out to a country place on weekends and holidays. A Dalmatian can enjoy that kind of life as long as he gets his workouts on schedule. People leading a sedentary life should resist the perfectly understandable temptation to own one of these splendid animals and should look elsewhere for a pet to share their quiet life-style.

There is an inherited tendency for deafness among Dalmatians, and the prospective owner should be cautious before confirming a purchase. The spots are extremely important in judging this breed and in the ideal those on the body should not be smaller than a penny or larger than a 50 pence piece. The spots on the head and face should be smaller than on the body and should be separate and distinct with as little running together as possible. A well-put-together Dalmatian is a beautiful animal. People have apparently thought so since ancient times.

Dandie Dinmont Terrier

Land of origin: Scotland and England

Original purpose: Fox and badger hunting

Recent popularity ranking by K.C. registration: Moderate

HEIGHT: To 11 inches

WEIGHT: To 18 pounds

COAT: Double – twice as much crisp outer hair as soft undercoat. Hair on head, including topknot, silky. Important judging and appearance point

COLOUR: Pepper or mustard – many intermediate shades in both colour groups. Pepper from dark bluish black to light silver grey. Mustards from reddish brown to pale fawn. Head may be creamy white

Amount of care coat requires:	1	2	3	4	5	6	7	8	9	10
		*	*	*	*	*	*			

Amount of exercise required:	1	2	3	4	5	6	7	8	9	10
		*	*	*	*	*	*			

Suitability for urban/flat life:	1	2	3	4	5	6	7	8	9	10
	*	*	*	*	*	*	*	*	*	*

The Dandie Dinmont has the distinction of being the only dog named after a fictional character. Dandie Dinmont was a farmer in Sir Walter Scott's novel *Guy Mannering*. The farmer Dinmont kept six rough-coated terriers who had been developed in the border country, and they became known, because of the great popularity of the novel, as Dandie Dinmont's dogs.

The Dandie Dinmont is a wonderful little character with great purpose and assertiveness. Once a hunting terrier, he is now a companion animal who is characteristically devoted to his master and who is fine with family members. Not mean or petty, the Dandie Dinmont can be reserved and cautious with strangers.

This is not the typical terrier; he has none of the terrier's square shape. He is a low-to-the-ground little roughneck with a large head and great, dark appealing eyes. They should be hazel and have deep lustre. The Dandie Dinmont's coat requires care on a regular basis, or it will be a mess and have to be stripped. It takes months for a coat to grow back once it has been pulled. The coat is crisp but not really wiry, and the head fur is soft and silky. That topknot is a must.

Although a hunting dog, the Dandie Dinmont is very adaptable and will do well in a flat. The size, of course, is perfect, and he makes a good watchdog, although he is not yappy and foolish. Anyone contemplating this breed should plan on two basic requirements – coat care and exercise. He is fine on a farm, in a suburban household, or in a city flat, but the Dandie Dinmont does require both these attentions from his human family if he is to be healthy and happy and keep his appealing good looks.

The training of the Dandie Dinmont should start early and continue on a regular basis. The dog can be headstrong and even overly assertive if allowed to go unchecked as a puppy, but this is an intelligent breed that will respond to training by a strong but sensitive owner. A well-behaved Dandie Dinmont is much more pleasant to have around than one who is wild and uncontrolled, but that is true of all breeds. The Dandie Dinmont is not a very popular breed in this country (that is apt to change at any time), and the breed standards have been well maintained by specialty breeders. It is a good idea to deal directly with them when seeking your puppy.

Deerhound

Land of origin: Scotland

Original purpose: Hunting, particularly deer

Recent popularity ranking by K.C. registration: Moderate

HEIGHT: Dogs 30 inches or more, bitches 28 inches or more

WEIGHT: Dogs to 105 pounds, bitches to 80 pounds

COAT: Harsh and wiry, to 4 inches long on the body and neck. Softer on head, breast and belly. Not woolly. Thick, close lying, ragged, crisp to touch. Some strains have silky mixed with harsh

COLOUR: Dark blue-grey is preferred. Also greys and brindles, yellow, sandy red, red fawn with black ears and muzzle. White is considered bad, so the less the better.

Amount of care coat requires: 1 2 3 4 5 6 7 8 9 10
                                    * *

Amount of exercise required: 1 2 3 4 5 6 7 8 9 10
                            * * * * * * * * *

Suitability for urban/flat life: Unsuited

The great Deerhound of Scotland is a true giant among dogs. He is in a class with the Irish Wolfhound (to which he may be related), the Borzoi, the Great Dane and other massive breeds. Once restricted in ownership to earls and lords of higher rank, said to have been the ransom of kings and the cause of wars, the Deerhound is a part of the wild and romantic past of the Highlands. Stories about him are legion, and whether all or only partly true, they suggest a history that may be the single most noble in canine annals.

The Deerhound is an ideal companion. Although huge, he is even-tempered, calm and some people say polite. He seems to understand his size and is careful not to inadvertently hurt anything smaller than himself. Not snappy, silly or mean, he is a fine companion for children, although a toddler should be watched around an exuberant Deerhound pup. The Deerhound thrives on love and attention. As a watchdog, of course, his mere presence is enough to discourage anyone, and it need hardly be stressed that no one should ever encourage a Deerhound to be aggressive or more suspicious than he naturally is around strangers. He likes to be absolutely certain in his own mind that the incoming stranger is a welcome addition to the household. The Deerhound takes companionship and friendship seriously.

It should be kept in mind that although the Deerhound is a gentle and sensible animal, he is also a hunter, and for that task he has been bred for centuries. He was designed to bring down animals as large as 250-pound stags. It probably would not take much to get him to assume that role again. Gentle with other pets at home, a Deerhound can play havoc with other people's cats. Though a superb companion, a Deerhound who misbehaves can be a gigantic pain in the neck.

The Deerhound obviously needs exercise. Cramped quarters without an opportunity to walk for miles and run until exhausted are not the style for this animal. One can suppose that there are still huge, barnlike flats in existence, and imagine their owners or renters as physical people who walk miles every morning and night, so we cannot say that this breed is wholly unsuited to flat life; Deerhounds are too fond of people and too adaptable for that. But certainly exercise should be a major consideration when thinking about this breed. The non-physical owner cannot unmake the breeding, planning and perfecting of centuries. The great, massive hound of Scotland will never really be a creature of pavement and traffic lights.

Doberman

Land of origin: Germany

Original purpose: Guard duty

Recent popularity ranking by K.C. registration: 9th

HEIGHT: Dogs to 27 inches, bitches to 25½ inches

WEIGHT: N.S.G.

COAT: Smooth, short, hard, thick and close. There may be an invisible grey undercoat on neck

COLOUR: Black, red, blue and fawn. Sharply defined rust markings above each eye and on muzzle, throat, chest, legs, feet and below tail. Small white marking on chest (under ½-inch square allowed). Fawn colour is known as Isabella

Amount of care coat requires: 1 2 3 4 5 6 7 8 9 10
                                ★

Amount of exercise required: 1 2 3 4 5 6 7 8 9 10
                              ★ ★ ★ ★ ★ ★ ★ ★ ★ ★

Suitability for urban/flat life: 1 2 3 4 5 6 7 8 9 10
                                  ★ ★

The Doberman is one breed whose history is well known. In the 1890s, Louis Dobermann of Apolda, Germany, developed the breed using old short-haired shepherd stock mixed with Rottweiler and terrier – specifically, it is believed, the Black and Tan Terrier. The dog he was apparently trying for was the dog he got. The Doberman has been from the beginning a superlative guard-dog of noble appearance.

A medium-sized dog with an extremely alert bearing, the Doberman is as handsome as a dog can be. Intelligent, swift, a consummate athlete, he combines the trainability of the old shepherd stock, the inner fire of the terrier and the positive attitude of the Rottweiler. Louis Dobermann's mixture managed to preserve the best of each type he used.

The Doberman is an active dog, and long, long walks are mandatory for his health and happiness. Many Dobermans are kept in flats, and their rise in popularity has been meteoric. The reason for this great popularity lies in the fact that it is believed to be a deterrent dog. An amateur criminal probably will give a wide berth to a home where a Doberman is known to live, but a

professional can incapacitate any dog on earth. The use of Dobermans as crime deterrents by amateur owners is not to be encouraged.

The supremely handsome and incredibly loyal Doberman is a controversial dog. One hears that he is a gentle, affectionate and reliable pet, and also that he is a born killer and can never be trusted. The answer lies in the middle.

The Doberman is an aggressive dog. The K.C. standards include the following statement: 'Shyness or viciousness must be heavily penalized'.

It is true that the Doberman is more nervous than many other breeds – not always, certainly, but often. It is also true that the breed is intelligent and will take training readily from someone who knows what he is doing. The Doberman is too much of an undertaking for many people, especially casual or first-time owners. For owners who can accept the responsibility, the Doberman is one of the great breeds of the working-dog group.

Drentse Partridge Dog

Land of origin: Holland

Original purpose: All-round gun-dog

Recent popularity ranking by K.C. registration: Rare

HEIGHT: To 24 inches

WEIGHT: N.S.G.

COAT: Shortish, with feather

COLOUR: N.S.G.

Amount of care coat requires:	1	2	3	4	5	6	7	8	9	10
		★	★	★						

Amount of exercise required:	1	2	3	4	5	6	7	8	9	10
	★	★	★	★	★	★	★	★	★	★

Suitability for urban/flat life:	1	2	3	4	5	6	7	8	9	10
		★	★	★						

This breed resembles a large Springer Spaniel and is almost unknown outside its native Holland. It is a working all-round gun-dog – especially pointing and retrieving – and fares well in field-trial competitions. Possibly under-rated as a breed, it seems of good temperament and adapts well to life as a house dog, though it is large in size and liberal exercise is its top priority.

The breed is related to the Munsterlanders. The coat is moderately long with feathering on the legs, chest and tail; a reasonable amount of grooming attention is therefore required to prevent matting of the feathers and ears. The coat colours are brown or orange markings on a white background. One of the breed characteristics is that the tail is wagged in a circle, especially when on the track of game.

Elkhound

Land of origin: Norway

Original purpose: Hunting big game

Recent popularity ranking by K.C. registration: Moderate

HEIGHT: Dogs to 20½ inches, bitches to 19½ inches

WEIGHT: Dogs to 50 pounds, bitches to 43 pounds

COAT: Thick and hard, rather smooth-lying. Longer outer coat and light, soft, woolly undercoat

COLOUR: Grey with black tips on long covering coat. Grey tones vary, but white or yellow are not desirable

Amount of care coat requires:	1 2 3 4 5 6 7 8 9 10
Amount of exercise required:	1 2 3 4 5 6 7 8 9 10
Suitability for urban/flat life:	1 2 3 4 5 6 7 8 9 10

For the owner who envisages himself the master of a mighty wolflike beast of enormous power, the Elkhound offers special possibilities. This great hunting dog of the North is not very large, less than half the weight of a real wolf, but he has many outstanding qualities and characteristics.

The Elkhound accompanied the Vikings on their forays. He hunted with them, he herded flocks outside their villages, and he guarded man and animal alike against wolves and bears. Almost a legend now, the Elkhound is one of the oldest and most romantic of breeds.

This is a northern breed, an animal well suited to rugged weather and rugged terrain. He is a bold dog, impressively powerful and packed with seemingly endless energy. He has a superb sense of smell, and his hearing is reputed to be better than that of many other breeds. He is a hunting dog and one devoted to his master. He learns quickly and takes all kinds of training well, but he is also stubborn. An Elkhound will have no difficulty in picking out an inappropriately soft hand. A wishy-washy owner will have a bad time of it and probably will not be able to master the dog.

The Elkhound can be aggressive with other animals – but this happens rarely with human beings, unless they are strangers who threaten. Because he

is such a powerful and assertive animal and will enter into any kind of situation, the Elkhound requires not only early and careful training but everlasting control as well. He is not a dog to be allowed to wander through a suburban neighbourhood unattended.

Since he is a natural guardian of all that he loves, the Elkhound makes a perfect watchdog. He should never be taught to attack, and any tendency in that direction must be discouraged, but here is the answer for those who want an aggressive-sounding, alert and purposeful dog who will sound the alarm in the night.

The Elkhound is a handsome animal; he has great dignity and purpose. An ideal companion for those he knows and trusts, he tends to take life seriously. He does not take friends, devotion, insults or intruders lightly. He was put here with a job to do, and he spends the better part of each day attempting to fulfil his mission. He should be purchased only from the best available private kennel's stock. A mass-produced Elkhound could be dangerous, or at least unpleasant.

English Setter

Land of origin: England

Original purpose: Hunting

Recent popularity ranking by K.C. registration: 29th

HEIGHT: Dogs to 27 inches, bitches to 25 inches

WEIGHT: Dogs to 66 pounds, bitches to 62 pounds

COAT: Flat, without curl, not soft or woolly, and of medium length. Thin, regular feathers on legs and tail

COLOUR: Black, white and tan; black and white; blue belton; lemon and white; lemon belton; orange and white; orange belton; liver and white; liver belton; or solid white. Heavy patches of colour not as desirable as flecking all over

Amount of care coat requires: 1 2 3 4 5 6 7 8 9 10

Amount of exercise required: 1 2 3 4 5 6 7 8 9 10

Suitability for urban/flat life: 1 2 3 4 5 6 7 8 9 10

Very few dog fanciers would disagree with the claim that the English Setter not only is one of the handsomest dogs but also has one of the sweetest dispositions of all dogs and is a splendid performer in the field. No wonder that he has always had a loyal following.

No one knows all the steps that had to be taken to create the English Setter, but we believe he was derived several hundred years ago from Spanish land-dogs – dogs that came to be called spaniels after their place of origin. The English Setter has done nothing but improve, until today his beauty and dignity symbolize the striving for perfection in the dog world.

English Setters have few peers as family dogs. They are affectionate and loyal and are exceptional all-round companions. They love children and demand a great deal of affection in return. They are fine, smooth-working dogs that work and play well with other animals.

The Setter's coat requires some brushing every day to keep its fine appearance; this is an easy task and need not take more than a few minutes. It is shameful to let the coat go, since it is such an important element of the dog's appearance. English Setters are naturals when it comes to showing, and when they set up they are breathtaking. For this reason, and because they are so easy

to manage, they have long been favourites in the show-ring. Few dogs have been painted as often or by so many different artists.

There is one catch that the prospective owner should take into account. The English Setter needs an enormous amount of exercise, and he does not always thrive in the city. He really should be exercised or allowed to exercise for hours every day, and that is usually not practical in an urban setting. Even the mild, sweet disposition of the Setter can fray and show signs of going sour if he is held in the city and denied his true nature. This should be considered very seriously, because a lot of people do find Setters stylish, and some pet shops will sell them with the assurance that they are ideal flat dogs. They distinctly are not.

English Toy Terrier

(BLACK AND TAN)

Land of origin: England

Original purpose: Ratting

Recent popularity ranking by K.C. registration: Moderate

HEIGHT: To 12 inches

WEIGHT: To 8 pounds

COAT: Thick, smooth and of glossy appearance

COLOUR: Black and tan. N.B. No white hairs allowed

Amount of care coat requires: 1 2 3 4 5 6 7 8 9 10
                                        *

Amount of exercise required: 1 2 3 4 5 6 7 8 9 10
                                    * * *

Suitability for urban/flat life: 1 2 3 4 5 6 7 8 9 10
                                    * * * * * * *

This breed is often referred to as the Toy Manchester Terrier. These dogs were originally devised for ratting, and in looking at the breed one can immediately see a close resemblance to Italian Greyhounds and Whippets which, of course, show splendid manoeuvrability in their working life. They were known to acquit themselves well in the ratting sport, i.e. working in a rat pit. The English Toy Terrier is extraordinarily easy to care for, requiring the minimum of attention, but, like most Terriers, tends to be a one-person dog, and may well resent outsiders. It may, therefore, be a bit of a mixed blessing in a social household, and may tend to be snappy as well as vociferous.

Eskimo Dog

Land of origin: Siberia

Original purpose: Sled-dog

Recent popularity ranking by K.C. registration: Moderate

HEIGHT: Dogs to 27 inches, bitches to 24 inches

WEIGHT: Dogs to 105 pounds, bitches to 90 pounds

COAT: Medium short with some feathering, especially of the tail; very dense

COLOUR: N.S.G.

Amount of care coat requires: 1 2 3 4 5 6 7 8 9 10
                                  * * * *

Amount of exercise required: 1 2 3 4 5 6 7 8 9 10
                                  * * * * * * * * * *

Suitability for urban/flat life: 1 2 3 4 5 6 7 8 9 10
                                  * * *

This husky-type dog is one of several varieties found as working sled-pullers in the Arctic and Antarctic regions. It is related to the Samoyed and Malamute and is sometimes referred to as the Greenland Dog. In addition to pulling sled transport, they are harnessed to pull fishing-boats ashore. As a breed they are more strong-willed than most and, being large and powerful, it is essential that they are taught to obey commands and are disciplined from puppyhood. They are suspicious of strangers but are extremely hardy, making good outdoor-living watchdogs.

Estrela Mountain Dog

Land of origin: Portugal

Original purpose: Guard-dog and herder

Recent popularity ranking by K.C. registration: Rare

HEIGHT: Dogs to 30 inches, bitches to 28½ inches

WEIGHT: N.S.G.

COAT: N.S.G.

COLOUR: N.S.G.

Amount of care coat requires: 1 2 3 4 5 6 7 8 9 10
                                              * * * *

Amount of exercise required: 1 2 3 4 5 6 7 8 9 10
                                              * * * * * * * *

Suitability for urban/flat life: Unsuited

This is a large, powerful and stubborn breed functioning well as a flock-protector in the Portuguese Estrela Mountains. It has not long been in the U.K. It is very much a specialist's dog, unsuited to most owners and households and certainly not for the city life. These dogs require to be kept under the strictest control for they are almost impossible to train reliably. Because of their natural power and basic aggression they prove a real threat to other dogs, livestock and possibly also to humans.

In recent times dogs of this type have been considered in the U.K. as potential flock protectors (their original function), where with training they could be entrusted to guard sheep and cattle at pasture from the ravages of uncontrolled worrying dogs (and foxes), in addition to rustlers. However, this type of flock-guard animal is not a natural and untrained dogs could be as inclined to worry livestock as any other dog.

Finnish Spitz

Land of origin: Finland

Original purpose: Hunting

Recent popularity ranking by K.C. registration: Moderate

HEIGHT: Dogs to 20 inches, bitches to 18 inches

WEIGHT: Dogs to 36 pounds, bitches to 29 pounds

COAT: Short, dense undercoat; long ruff and leg feathers (especially males)

COLOUR: Basically reddish-brown or red-gold with lighter shadings and some black hairs

Amount of care coat requires: 1 2 3 4 5 6 7 8 9 10
                                               * * * *

Amount of exercise required: 1 2 3 4 5 6 7 8 9 10
                                       * * * * *

Suitability for urban/flat life: 1 2 3 4 5 6 7 8 9 10
                                * * * * * *

This is the national dog of Finland. Originally bred for hunting, especially game birds, it still functions well in the field. The breed shows well and is rated highly for its appearance. It has cat-like ability to groom itself. It was introduced to the U.K. in 1920. This breed is hardy and settles well into family life in all ways, providing basic discipline is instilled in puppyhood and adequate exercise given at all times.

The Spitz family tree includes Chows, Elkhounds, Keeshonden, Samoyeds, etc. They are not as a rule naturally friendly towards strangers, and they have a potential as puppies to be rather boisterous, though this can be controlled by adequate exercise and sufficient play periods with the humans in the household or with other dogs in the family. The coat is fairly long and dense and requires attentive grooming. This is so especially in the Spring and Autumn when the majority of dogs will moult excessively and create extra work for the housewife, unless the dogs are especially carefully combed and brushed out of doors to minimize casting of hair in the house.

Foxhound

Land of origin: England

Original purpose: Hunting

Recent popularity ranking by K.C. registration: Moderate

HEIGHT: Dogs to 23 inches, bitches to 22 inches

WEIGHT: N.S.G.

COAT: Short, dense, glossy and hard – typical of hounds

COLOUR: Black, white, tan, yellow; not important as long as basic hound colours are present

Amount of care coat requires: 1 2 3 4 5 6 7 8 9 10
                                          *

Amount of exercise required: 1 2 3 4 5 6 7 8 9 10
                            * * * * * * * * * *

Suitability for urban/flat life: Unsuited

The Foxhound's studbooks go back to the eighteenth century and have been well kept, for the breeding has been in the hands of masters of hounds. Any owner of a Foxhound today should be able to trace that dog back to 1800 or before.

The well-boned, sturdy and reliable Foxhound on the average tends to be somewhat stouter than his American counterpart to whose origins he contributed so much. The head is large but not gross. The neck is long and clean and should extend at least ten inches from the base of the skull to the shoulder. This is not a small dog. He is symmetrical in appearance and should have a bright and eager look. Willingness is a prime characteristic of the breed.

Because Foxhounds have typical hound coats, they are clean and easily kept. They do shed, but that is seldom a problem unless the animals have been allowed to develop dry coats, a condition that is easily corrected.

He is affectionate and loyal to his master and to his family. He is wary of strangers and wants to be sure of his ground before allowing too many liberties. He has a fine voice, of course, and can make a good watchdog.

All the Foxhounds – American, English and their French counterparts – are trailing field-dogs and have no tolerance for flat living. It isn't the flat that matters so much as the life-style of urban families. The Foxhound likes to curl up in front of a fire as much as the next dog does, but that comes after a lot of

time acquiring aching muscles. All weather conditions suit the Foxhound, and miles and miles of sniffing the world is what he craves. You cannot take a fine field-dog, coop him up for weeks on end, and expect the classical Foxhound to show through. You will end up with a different kind of animal.

City dwellers who do not spend a great deal of time hiking or jogging in the country should think twice or more about this breed. One other thing: scent hounds like the Foxhounds get too interested in an exciting smell for their own good. They should be kept on leads anywhere near traffic, since they will put their nose down and go. They won't stop and look when they come to the kerb, and many, indeed, have come to grief as a result. Generally a most unsatisfactory breed for a pet dog.

Fox Terrier

(SMOOTH AND WIRE)

Land of origin: Wales and England

Original purpose: Hunting and companionship

Recent popularity ranking by K.C. registration: Moderate

HEIGHT: Dogs to 15½ inches, bitches to 14½ inches

WEIGHT: Dogs to 18 pounds, bitches to 16 pounds

COAT:
Smooth variety – smooth, flat, hard, dense and abundant
Wire variety – broken, hard and wiry but not silky or woolly. The more wiry the better

COLOUR: Basically white with black or black and tan markings. Not very important except red, liver and brindle are not desirable

Amount of care coat requires:

	1	2	3	4	5	6	7	8	9	10
Smooth:	★									
Wire:	★	★	★	★	★					
Amount of exercise required:	★	★	★	★	★	★	★	★	★	★
Suitability for urban/flat life:	★	★	★	★	★	★	★	★	★	★

There are, of course, two Fox Terriers, the Smooth and the Wire. They probably arose from totally different stocks, and the Wire is undoubtedly the older form, although the Smooth became known first in the show-ring. It was once common practice to cross these two forms, and although that is no longer done, the dogs are for our purposes identical except for coat style. They do have virtually the same personality; they are the same size and are judged by all the same point standards, again except for coat.

The Fox Terrier, Wire or Smooth, is a clown. Play is the thing, night and day without let-up. Anyone contemplating this breed should be prepared to participate, to toss balls and to have a marvellous little busybody butting into his life at every turn. The Fox Terrier is devoted, loyal, a fine watchdog and very good with family members. He is apt to be stand-offish with strangers. He

Smooth Fox Terrier   *Wire Fox Terrier*

seldom walks but goes at everything at full gallop. He can be protective, and that has to be controlled.

Although once a hunting dog (when the hounds had run the rabbit or fox to ground, the Fox Terrier was sent in for the kill), he is now chiefly a companion animal. The instinct to kill is still there, however, and that should be taken into consideration. A Fox Terrier can learn to live in a multi-animal household, but the puppy should be introduced carefully and with constant supervision.

The Fox Terrier can live anywhere people can – farm to urban metropolis – and as long as his human family is near, he will be happy. Since the breed is very active to begin with, it stands to reason that an example denied proper exercise will really act up. Improperly worked Fox Terriers become absolutely silly with their springy legs and boundless good humour. That energy *has* to be worked off, and a bouncing rubber ball is one good way of doing it *if* there is a place to do it. Although eminently trainable, the stylish Fox Terrier may not always respond as quickly as you want him to when you say, 'Come'. It is therefore essential to keep him on a lead in the city lest a tragedy occur. Many a Fox Terrier has spotted a cat or another dog he was unable to resist, and a Fox Terrier in the middle of a mad dash may not check for cars and buses.

The Fox Terrier is a long-lived animal, fine with children, at home in any setting where there is love and the chance to participate. There are plenty of bad examples of the breed around, and care should be taken about source and blood-lines. A good example is as fine a pet as a dog can be.

French Bulldog

Land of origin: England and France

Original purpose: Companionship

Recent popularity ranking by K.C. registration: Moderate

HEIGHT: N.S.G.

WEIGHT: Dogs to 28 pounds, bitches to 24 pounds

COAT: Moderately fine, short and smooth. Skin soft and loose

COLOUR: Solid brindle, fawn, white, brindle and white, and any colours *except* black and white, black and tan, liver, mouse or solid black

Amount of care coat requires:	1	2	3	4	5	6	7	8	9	10
	★									

Amount of exercise required:	1	2	3	4	5	6	7	8	9	10
	★	★	★							

Suitability for urban/flat life:	1	2	3	4	5	6	7	8	9	10
	★	★	★	★	★	★	★	★	★	★

If there is such a thing as a perfect flat dog, the French Bulldog could be it. He certainly would be in the finals when the choice was made. This is a neat, clean, compact dog who sheds hardly at all, is easily trained, has nice manageable habits and doesn't need or really want too much exercise.

The French Bulldog has nearly caused international incidents: the English laugh at the name, recognizing in the breed a miniature of the English Bulldog that didn't suit the English fancy and was exported to France; the French, in a kind of desperate casting about, claim him as an original. The English are undoubtedly right, but that's history, and it doesn't much matter. What does matter is that the French Bulldog is an outstanding companion animal under the right circumstances.

The ideal situation for this breed is a flat or house with a single person. The French Bulldog does not like to share and is not keen on strangers. This breed is also less than perfect with children. That is not to say that a French Bulldog would not settle down and become a good family dog – the family including a parcel of youngsters – because a great many have. It is just that if one were to seek the ideal setting, it would be with one person in need of getting and giving boundless affection and one French Bulldog in the same situation.

The overall impression one gets from one of these little companions is of a muscular, alert animal of good substance and intelligence. And all that is true.

If a person wants to show a dog, this is a good breed to consider. There aren't too many of them around, so the competition is not overwhelming, and the dog is easy to transport because of his small size. His coat requires virtually no care, so there is not a lot of get-ready-time. Pick up your dog and walk into the ring ready to go.

A single person seeking both love and involvement might find owning and showing a French Bulldog just about a perfect outlet. None of this should discourage other categories of owners, though, for this dog also will be happy on a farm. He may not do a lot of work, but he will be happy as long as he has access to his special person.

German Long-haired Pointer

Land of origin: Germany

Original purpose: Pointing and gun-dog

Recent popularity ranking by K.C. registration: Rare

HEIGHT: To 25 inches

WEIGHT: N.S.G.

COAT: Soft, shortish coat with feathers on chest, ears, legs and tail

COLOUR: N.S.G.

Amount of care coat requires:	1 ★	2 ★	3 ★	4	5	6	7	8	9	10
Amount of exercise required:	1 ★	2 ★	3 ★	4 ★	5 ★	6 ★	7 ★	8 ★	9 ★	10
Suitability for urban/flat life:	1 ★	2 ★	3	4	5	6	7	8	9	10

Sadly this breed is losing popularity to its short-haired and wire-haired counterparts. It is an efficient field-dog, resilient and intelligent. It makes a good household dog with an excellent temperament and aptitude for children. At first sight, it resembles a Setter more than a Pointer, having been derived from European Spaniels and the Gordon Setter.

As with all long-coated dogs, fanatical attention must be paid to coat-care and a thorough grooming at least once, and preferably twice, a day with comb as well as brush is essential. Long coats also create problems with bathing, which may be required if the coat becomes unduly muddy or smelly, and long hair is problematical when it comes to the times of the regular twice-yearly moult. The larger game-dogs have too much energy for many households – in the hunting season a twelve-hour working day may be the norm – and if this is not successfully run off it may result in boredom and resulting diversion into chewing, barking or other annoying tendencies.

German Shepherd Dog

(ALSATIAN)

Land of origin: Germany

Original purpose: Farm work, herding, guard work

Recent popularity ranking by K.C. registration: 1st

HEIGHT: Dogs to 26 inches, bitches to 24 inches

WEIGHT: N.S.G.

COAT: Double and of medium length. Outer coat should be dense, straight, harsh and close lying. Never silky, soft, woolly or open

COLOUR: Most are permissible, but not white. Black and tan, grey or black are common

Amount of care coat requires: 1 2 3 4 5 6 7 8 9 10
Amount of exercise required: 1 2 3 4 5 6 7 8 9 10
Suitability for urban/flat life: 1 2 3 4 5 6 7 8 9 10

The highly popular German Shepherd was derived over a period of several hundred years of native herding and from general farm-dogs in Germany and surrounding areas. From the beginning of this century his worldwide popularity has grown steadily. He is the most popular pure-bred dog in the U.K.

The German Shepherd is first, last and always a working dog designed to serve man in any way needed. A herding dog, a guard-dog for livestock, a police-dog, a military dog, a dog to lead the blind and pull carts – this sturdy, intelligent animal has never been outclassed by any task or any other breed. He is the pre-eminent working dog, and his popularity clearly reflects that fact.

A shy or nervous German Shepherd is not to be forgiven. A really nervous German Shepherd is a dangerous animal and should not have access to innocent bystanders. It is also unfortunately true that many inexpert people keep these animals as deterrent dogs. Too many accidents obviously happen as a result.

The German Shepherd can be taught just about anything, and one thing often taught this animal, most unfortunately, is to attack. Private citizens have no more right to an attack-trained German Shepherd than they have to a Luger in a shoulder-holster. Laws are enacted to regulate the sale of guard-dogs.

142

A German Shepherd raised as a pet and well trained is as fine a canine companion as anyone could possibly want. Intelligent, alert, a perfect watchdog, careful with strangers but not petty or mean – he is loyal unto death to his family and will do anything to protect family children. That does not have to be built in, it is already there.

The German Shepherd requires a lot of exercise to maintain condition, and his coat should be brushed regularly to keep its sheen. The breed is very susceptible to hip dysplasia, with about a 65 per cent heritability factor.

It is not easy nor is it inexpensive to locate a fine example of this breed. When you succeed, you have a superb dog. When you fail (and the exploiters win), you have a mess! Only the very best breeders should be consulted, and no German Shepherd should ever be purchased from a puppy factory.

German Short-haired Pointer

Land of origin: Germany

Original purpose: All-purpose hunting

Recent popularity ranking by K.C. registration: 40th

HEIGHT: Dogs to 25 inches, bitches to 23 inches

WEIGHT: N.S.G.

COAT: Short and thick, tough and hard

COLOUR: solid liver or liver and white (grey) only

Amount of care coat requires:	1	2	3	4	5	6	7	8	9	10
	*									

Amount of exercise required:	1	2	3	4	5	6	7	8	9	10
		*	*	*	*	*	*	*	*	*

Suitability for urban/flat life:	1	2	3	4	5	6	7	8	9	10
	*									

The handsome German Short-haired Pointer carries a number of blood-lines, only a few of which we know about with certainty. An old German bird-dog is there, a Spanish Pointer and a scent hound, perhaps even the great Bloodhound himself. There is terrier there, too. The Germans who bred this animal up from obscurity, drawing on dogs from all over Europe, outdid themselves. This is one of the better pets among the heavy field-dogs.

The German Short-haired Pointer is a supremely active animal and generally is unsuited to flat or city life. He is full of energy and always ready to go – and *go* does not mean simply to the kerb and back. This is an animal that has to move!

The German Short-haired Pointer is a loving companion and constant friend. He is not petty or mean, ill-tempered or moody, and he gets along with his master's family. If cooped up, however, his whole manner can change; in the city he can become crazed and act beyond control. He becomes yappy and foolish and seems to lose his intelligence along with his dignity. The German Short-haired should always be dignified – and will be if trained and worked. You certainly don't have to be a hunter to use this combination upland-lowland dog – this trailer, pointer and retriever in one package – but you have to like long walks in the clean, crisp air.

German Wire-haired Pointer

Land of origin: Germany

Original purpose: All-purpose hunting

Recent popularity ranking by K.C. registration: Moderate

HEIGHT: Dogs to 26 inches, bitches from 22 inches

WEIGHT: N.S.G.

COAT: Extremely important feature: protective undercoat full and dense in winter and all but invisible in summer. Outer coat straight, harsh, wiry, rather close lying; $1\frac{1}{2}$ to 2 inches in length

COLOUR: Liver or liver and white. Nose dark brown. Head brown, occasionally with white blaze. Ears brown. Any black is a serious fault

Amount of care coat requires: 1 2 3 4 5 6 7 8 9 10
                                      * *

Amount of exercise required: 1 2 3 4 5 6 7 8 9 10
                                       * * * * * * * * * *

Suitability for urban/flat life: 1 2 3 4 5 6 7 8 9 10
                                       * *

When the Germans decided they wanted the perfect all-purpose hunting dog, they took their justifiably famous Short-haired Pointer and combined him with Terrier, Poodle and other blood-lines to evolve the striking German Wire-haired Pointer, one of the finest hunting dogs in the world today.

The German Wire-haired Pointer is everything you could desire in a field-dog – a flawless retriever, a pointer, a steady, solid and determined friend and companion animal. His coat, one of the breed's most striking and important features, provides protection against all weather; it is virtually water-repellent, so there need be no hesitation about using the dog to retrieve in icy waters. The coat also protects against briars and thorns in the roughest terrain. There is even a bushy mass to protect the eyes. In winter the coat is thick, but it thins considerably by summer. It is easy to care for and naturally clean – the dog shakes dirt off the way he does water. Coat condition is obviously an important factor and is carefully considered by all judges.

The German Wire-haired Pointer is one of those dogs really not at all suited to city life. He was bred for the field, and only in the open will he display his exceptional qualities.

This breed makes almost ideal companion animals for their owners, though cross or ill-tempered examples should not be tolerated. While not unfriendly or aggressive, the dog is aloof and slow to accept strangers.

The German Wire-haired is an exceptional breed when living in special, planned-for circumstances. In other situations – if forced to fit into an inappropriate lifestyle – the good qualities he is known for may vanish. Some people try to take outstanding working or sporting dogs and remould them. It usually does not work, and only rarely will the family be satisfied. In a country setting, of course, dogs like the German Wire-haired Pointer make fine family pets.

This special and highly developed breed should never be obtained from anyone but a specialty breeder who can show you not only the parents' conformation show ribbons but their field-trial awards as well. Although handsome, rugged and even noble in his canine way, the German Wire-haired Pointer was made to perform, and that should be clearly evident when you examine a prospective puppy's background.

Giant Schnauzer

Land of origin: Germany

Original purpose: Cattle-driving

Recent popularity ranking by K.C. registration: Moderate

HEIGHT: Dogs to 27½ inches, bitches to 25½ inches

WEIGHT: N.S.G.

COAT: Hard, wiry, very dense; soft undercoat and harsh outer coat

COLOUR: Solid black or pepper and salt

Amount of care coat requires: 1 2 3 4 5 6 7 8 9 10
                                                 * * * * * * * *

Amount of exercise required: 1 2 3 4 5 6 7 8 9 10
                                                 * * * * * * * *

Suitability for urban/flat life: 1 2 3 4 5 6 7 8 9 10
                                                 *

Most people do not seem to realize that the Giant, Standard and Miniature Schnauzers are three distinct breeds, not just up-and-down versions of each other. Both the Standard and the Giant Schnauzers are working dogs.

The Riesenschnauzer or Giant is not as old a breed as the Standard (which was painted by Dürer the year Columbus sailed for the New World) but is older by a good margin than the terrier we call the Miniature Schnauzer.

All the Schnauzers, apparently, were developed in either Württemberg or Bavaria, and the Giant probably was developed in and around Bavaria from smaller dogs obtained from Stuttgart. He was made into a powerful drover to help get cattle to market. There is a strong belief today that the Flemish driving dog, the Bouvier des Flandres, and the black Great Dane were used with original Schnauzer stock to obtain the Giant we have today. The belief contains more than a little conjecture, however.

By World War I the Giant was in use by the police, and has been ever since. His progress in this country has been slow because the German Shepherd has been so extremely popular and the two dogs do overlap in use and appeal. The Giant Schnauzer is also much tougher than the average Shepherd, much more a real dog person's dog.

The Giant Schnauzer is a handsome dog of great strength and endurance. He is regal, standing very straight in a robust chest-first kind of way. He should

never be shy or nervous, although he is characteristically very aggressive toward other animals. That should be kept in mind.

The Giant Schnauzer has been bred from the beginning to serve man, and that means he takes training very well and is extremely loyal. He is a guard-dog, a watchdog, a working dog every inch of him. He is not a dog to be taken lightly or owned casually.

The Schnauzer's coat needs care. It needs pulling, trimming and hard brushing. Only then will that splendid look be in evidence. The Giant Schnauzer is a dog that needs a great deal of exercise and should be owned by a family with at least one fairly athletic member. He can be a house dog, even a flat dog, but long, long walks are in order every day and good runs whenever possible. Training is also mandatory, and anyone seriously considering this superior breed had better plan on some evenings at obedience school at the beginning. A well-trained Giant Schnauzer is a proud possession. One ill-trained or out of control is a great liability.

Glen of Imaal Terrier

Land of origin: Ireland

Original purpose: Working terrier (fox, badger)

Recent popularity ranking by K.C. registration: Rare

HEIGHT: To 14 inches

WEIGHT: Dogs to 35 pounds, bitches to 33 pounds

COAT: Semi-long-haired; thick protective coat

COLOUR: N.S.G.

Amount of care coat requires:	1 2 3 4 5 6 7 8 9 10
Amount of exercise required:	1 2 3 4 5 6 7 8 9 10
Suitability for urban/flat life:	1 2 3 4 5 6 7 8 9 10

This dog originated in County Wicklow, and is still comparatively rare outside Ireland. It is very much an efficient working dog, but given adequate exercise or liberty adapts splendidly to flat or house life, where it makes an excellent pet and children's companion. This may well be an up-and-coming breed of great potential.

The original purpose (for which it is still used in Ireland) was for fox and badger flushing. The breed has a medium length coat of blue-brindle or wheaten colour. They are rare dogs in the show ring, being rather more prized by their own breed clubs. The size and general shape resembles that of a standard dachshund.

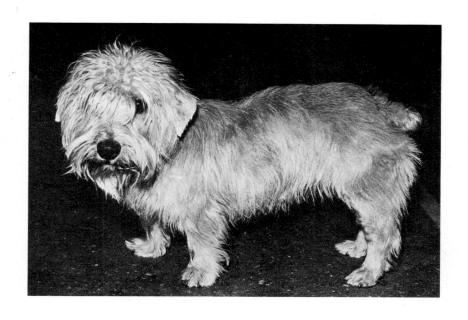

Gordon Setter

Land of origin: Scotland

Original purpose: Gun-dog

Recent popularity ranking by K.C. registration: Moderate

HEIGHT: Dogs to 26 inches, bitches to 24½ inches

WEIGHT: Dogs to 65 pounds, bitches to 56 pounds

COAT: Shiny, soft, slightly waved or straight, but not curly. Long hair on ears, under the stomach and on chest, tail and legs

COLOUR: Black with tan to red mahogany or chestnut markings. There may be black 'pencil lines' on the toes. Lighter markings are important; they should appear over the eyes, on the muzzle and throat, on the chest and inside of the hind legs, under the tail and on the feet. No red or tan hairs should be mixed in with the black. A *little* white is allowed on the chest.

Amount of care coat requires: 1 2 3 4 5 6 7 8 9 10

Amount of exercise required: 1 2 3 4 5 6 7 8 9 10

Suitability for urban/flat life: 1 2 3 4 5 6 7 8 9 10

This exceptionally handsome field-dog dates from the early 1600s in Scotland, but it wasn't until the fourth Duke of Gordon took the breed under his guidance a century and a half later that it really came into prominence. It has been admired and praised by dog fanciers ever since.

It is hard to tell why the English and Irish Setters have been more popular than the Gordon, unless it is because they are both a little faster in the open. That is the only advantage they have over the Gordon though, for this is a nearly perfect companion animal for the man afield.

A Gordon in good condition is one of the handsomest of dogs, silky and shiny with the distinctive pattern of black and red that sets it apart from all other sporting breeds. This breed tends to be more stable than the Irish Setter – rather more like the English Setter in temperament.

There is a saying that no one ever knew a Gordon Setter who would bite a child, and that is a lot closer to fact than fiction. Although active, Gordons are sensible, even-tempered and affectionate. They don't usually throw themselves

at strangers and are happier with their own human family. They demand a great deal of attention, which can be a problem when there is more than one dog. Gordons can be jealous; this is often the cause of dog-fights in which the Gordon participates. In fact, Gordons apparently would like it very much if all other dogs and people just vanished and left them alone with their immediate family, which is not to say that Gordons are unfriendly or quarrelsome, just that they have a preferred way of living: privately and stage centre within their household.

Because of the breed's high style, some people do make city dogs out of Gordons. The dog can adapt because of his great affection for people, but the city Gordon Setter just isn't the same animal as the country Gordon. City life can make him tense, silly and sometimes hard to control. The smooth, natural world of open field and cool, clean air is the ideal setting for an animal who wants to please, responds easily to training and provides nearly perfect canine companionship. The dog held in the city will require intensive obedience-training and a great deal of walking. The Gordon Setter is not a dog just to be led from flat door to kerb and back; less than two miles a day may not be cruel, but it certainly is unkind. This is an animal who was bred to move, and only in movement can one appreciate the bold, strong driving quality of his gait and character.

Great Dane

Land of origin: Ancient and unknown; Germany for last century or so

Original purpose: Boar-hunting, bull-baiting, bodyguard

Recent popularity ranking by K.C. registration: 19th

HEIGHT: Dogs to 30 inches, bitches to 28 inches

WEIGHT: Dogs to 120 pounds, bitches to 100 pounds

COAT: Short, thick, smooth and glossy. It should not stand off the body or be dull

COLOUR: Great variety – brindle (golden yellow with black), fawn or clean golden yellow with black mask, steel blue, glossy black, harlequin (pure white with evenly distributed black markings)

Amount of care coat requires: 1 2 3 4 5 6 7 8 9 10
                               *

Amount of exercise required: 1 2 3 4 5 6 7 8 9 10
                               * * * * * *

Suitability for urban/flat life: 1 2 3 4 5 6 7 8 9 10
                                 * * *

The Great Dane is a true giant, one of the largest and most majestic dog breeds in the world. His history is not really known (a dozen mutually exclusive versions have appeared in print), but we do believe that his original purpose was to hunt boar. A dog of great power, courage and endurance was needed for this dangerous sport, and that is what was bred into this German 'mastiff'. Actually, the dog we call the Great Dane may have been at the sport in something like his present form in the days of the Pharaohs.

The ferociousness that must have gone into the original boar hunters is no longer apparent in the Great Dane. The dog we know is a gentleman, soft in manners, usually quiet and very affectionate with his master and family. He is lovely with children if properly raised and not mean or petty with strangers, although he certainly is impressive as a watchdog. Needless to say, a dog of this size should not be encouraged to be aggressive.

Some people, of course, keep Great Danes in city flats – presumably, in many cases, to discourage burglars. That is a foolish plan, for anyone close enough to be hurt by a dog is close enough to totally incapacitate him.

The Great Dane really needs comparatively little exercise but he can become stiff from improper exercise, resulting in poor muscle and bone development.

Anyone keeping this giant in the city should plan on miles of walking every day, or pay someone to do it for him. No day should be skipped.

The Great Dane is sociable and fine within the family circle. When young he can be a bit wild, and small children can be sent flying like ninepins. That should be kept in mind. As the Great Dane matures, he does so as a well-controlled, self-possessed animal who seems aware of his giant status. Aggressive or poorly managed Great Danes cannot be tolerated. The potential for really serious damage is far too great.

Unfortunately, Great Danes are not long-lived, and nine or ten good years with their families must be considered fortunate. Since older animals are subject to heart ailments and painful joint disorders, a quiet life is in order.

The Great Dane is one of the most handsome and regal of all dogs. He is a fine family pet, a good companion and protector of the home. He is, though, a giant; he needs room and an impressive quantity of food. He also needs obedience-training, often at the professional level. A prospective owner should take all these factors into account.

Greyhound

Land of origin: Probably ancient Egypt or Assyria

Original purpose: Almost certainly hunting, coursing game

Recent popularity ranking by K.C. registration: Moderate

HEIGHT: Dogs to 30 inches, bitches to 28 inches

WEIGHT: N.S.G.

COAT: Short, smooth and very firm

COLOUR: Not counted in judging. Often grey, white or fawn. Can be solid or marked

Amount of care coat requires:	1*	2	3	4	5	6	7	8	9	10
Amount of exercise required:	1*	2*	3*	4*	5*	6*	7*	8*	9*	10*
Suitability for urban/flat life:	1*	2*	3*	4	5	6	7	8	9	10

No one will ever know the exact origin of the Greyhound. This extremely ancient breed may have started in Assyria or Egypt. Carvings on ancient tombs show dogs almost identical in appearance to the Greyhound we know today, or at least dogs who were the ancestors of our modern speed demon.

All through recorded history the Greyhound has cropped up, always as a coursing or sporting dog. The name Greyhound itself is of unknown origin. It could come from 'Graius', which means 'Grecian', since the ancient Greeks thought very highly of this swift animal. The name also could come from the Old English words 'grech' or 'greg', meaning 'dog'. Grey may have been a prevailing colour at one time, and that would logically have given the breed its present name. We are unlikely ever to know.

Besides being the fastest dog in the world, the Greyhound is one of the fastest of all four-footed animals. He has been bred for thousands of years to chase other animals. All manner of quarry have been pursued, but hare was probably the natural target of this streak of canine lightning. Today, sadly, the breed is used on professional racing circuits, and the cruelties involved in that industry are too well known to list here. It is a sad fate for a superb breed of dog.

If ever there was a breed that was capable of causing controversy, it is the

Greyhound. He is a clean dog, an easy dog to maintain with just about no coat care required. One the other hand, he does require a lot of exercise, as should be perfectly obvious, and most owners are unwilling to take the time.

As for disposition, here the opinions run from A to Z. This is a highly strung breed, no doubt about that, and some owners have found Greyhounds to be far too much to handle. Some people say they are unreliable around children. Other owners, however, have found them to be affectionate and totally reliable. I think the answer may lie in different strains. There are Greyhounds bred solely for the track and others bred for show and for pet use. Dogs from the latter lines are more likely to be pleasing in the home.

Anyone buying a Greyhound should do so with great care; avoid track 'lines' and stay close to the best specialty breeders around. No one should think of owning a Greyhound unless he is either active himself or blessed with at least one very athletic family member. Since before the pyramids were built the Greyhound has been bred to move, and move he should if he is to retain his original qualities.

Griffon Bruxellois

Land of origin: Belgium

Original purpose: Companionship and killing of stable vermin

Recent popularity ranking by K.C. registration: Moderate

HEIGHT: N.S.G.

WEIGHT: To 11 pounds

COAT:
Rough style – wiry and dense, the harder the better. Never to look or feel woolly; never silky. Also not shaggy
Smooth style – like a Boston Terrier, no sign of wiry hair

COLOUR: Reddish brown, black and reddish brown mixed, black and reddish brown markings, or solid black. Often dark mask or whiskers. Black not allowed in smooth form. White a serious fault in either variety except age frosting on muzzle

Amount of care coat requires:

	1	2	3	4	5	6	7	8	9	10
Rough:	1	2*	3*	4*	5	6	7	8	9	10
Smooth:	1*	2	3	4	5	6	7	8	9	10
Amount of exercise required:	1	2*	3*	4*	5	6	7	8	9	10
Suitability for urban/flat life:	1*	2*	3*	4*	5*	6*	7*	8*	9*	10*

The Griffon Bruxellois has been around since at least the fifteenth century and possibly longer. He was a cross between the Affenpinscher and a Belgian street dog. Later the Pug and a breed known as the Ruby Spaniel were crossed in. At one time he was larger than the dog we know today and was used to control rats and mice around stables. It is believed that the Griffon was virtually a household fixture in French and Belgian homes. Long bred for companionship, it is in that capacity we know him today.

The Griffon Bruxellois is seen in two varieties: the rough and the smooth. The smooth, of course, harks back to the infusion of Pug blood. Both forms are delightful companions, intelligent, outgoing and affectionate. They are not close or mean in their dealings but open and willing. They are neat and take up little space. And they make good watchdogs.

Like many toys, the Griffon Bruxellois is quite capable of being a little mule, a bully, lording it over everyone in the house. How he behaves depends on

how he is handled as a puppy. Without thwarting him or destroying his personality he can be made to behave – especially on a leash, which he generally hates – and his barking can be controlled. He will try tricks to avoid having to be well mannered, and he is clever enough to be challenging to anyone but the owner alert enough to know when he is being duped.

The pert, saucy little Griffon Bruxellois does well with or without outdoor exercise, although he enjoys a fair romp. Care must be taken around traffic because he cannot be depended upon to have good traffic sense. He travels well and prefers to be taken along rather than be left at home. He must not be left in a closed car during warm weather, since he can expire from heat exhaustion in minutes without ventilation. It is a tragic accident that happens more times than one would expect.

The Griffon Bruxellois is a toy-lover's dog in all respects – impudent, assertive, lovingly responsive and razor-sharp. A dog to admire and, sad to relate, to spoil absolutely rotten. Most owners of this breed do.

Hamilton Stovare

Land of origin: Sweden

Original purpose: Hunting

Recent popularity ranking by K.C. registration: Rare

HEIGHT: Dogs to 23½ inches, bitches to 21 inches

WEIGHT: N.S.G.

COAT: Dense

COLOUR: Neck, back and tail should be black on upper aspects; also sides. Rest predominantly brown. Muzzle, breast, tail tip and feet should be white

Amount of care coat requires:	1	2	3	4	5	6	7	8	9	10
	*									

Amount of exercise required:	1	2	3	4	5	6	7	8	9	10
	*	*	*	*	*	*	*	*	*	*

Suitability for urban/flat life:	1	2	3	4	5	6	7	8	9	10
	*	*	*	*	*					

This dog is reputed to be an ideal dog (of its type) for home-dwelling. Unlike most hounds, it is kept singly (or in pairs) rather than in a pack. Its purpose is to flush game – especially in coniferous forests, and it is named after the founder of the Swedish Kennel Club, Count Hamilton. It is a largish hound but, in view of its origins, may be more intelligent and trainable than its other contemporaries. It needs much exercise, however, and may cause annoyance to neighbours by baying, as do most hounds.

The breed originated by the crossing of the English Foxhound with one of the many Scandinavian/German hound varieties. As a basic working variety, some reservation may be expressed about the conversion of this dog to domestic life. As with many hounds, there is a distinct tendency towards destructiveness when confined, especially if exercise is insufficient to tire the dog sufficiently.

Hovawart

Land of origin: Germany

Original purpose: Companion, guarding

Recent popularity ranking by K.C. registration: Rare

HEIGHT: To 27 inches

WEIGHT: To 90 pounds

COAT: Long-haired, slightly waved

COLOUR: Mid-blond, black, black and tan

Amount of care coat requires: 1 2 3 4 5 6 7 8 9 10
                                         * * * * *

Amount of exercise required: 1 2 3 4 5 6 7 8 9 10
                                         * * * * * *

Suitability for urban/flat life: 1 2 3 4 5 6 7 8 9 10
                                         *

This is a very old German breed derived for no specific purpose. However, the German 'Hovawart' means 'houseguard'. This is a large breed recently reintroduced to popularity in Europe by out-crossing with Leonbergers and Newfoundlands. The breed is an instinctive guarder and will fight other dogs with minimal stimulation. Its nature with adults and children alike is good, and loyalty is a major virtue.

Being large, it needs very firm handling and training from early puppyhood. Safely confined gardens and estates and exercise on leash are also prerequisites.

The breed resembles a large collie in all but colour and is similar in build to the Hungarian Kuvasz. The dog is of sufficient size and strength to prove a fierce adversary in a fight. For this reason it is not a variety to be entrusted to children to walk unless accompanied by an adult or unless the dog is well disciplined.

Hungarian Kuvasz

Land of origin: Tibet and Hungary

Original purpose: Guarding, and then some herding

Recent popularity ranking by K.C. registration: Rare

HEIGHT: Dogs to 29½ inches, bitches to 27½ inches

WEIGHT: Dogs to 115 pounds, bitches to 93 pounds

COAT: Rather long on neck but shorter on sides. Slightly wavy

COLOUR: Pure white only is desirable. No markings. Occasionally seen yellow saddle is serious fault

Amount of care coat requires:	1	2	3	4	5	6	7	8	9	10
	★	★	★							

Amount of exercise required:	1	2	3	4	5	6	7	8	9	10
	★	★	★	★	★	★	★	★	★	★

Suitability for urban/flat life:	1	2	3	4	5	6	7	8	9	10
	★	★								

The handsome white Kuvasz is another great guard-dog out of central Europe. He undoubtedly came to Hungary from Tibet and was known throughout the Eastern countries (including the Middle East) for many centuries. In Hungary he flourished to become the darling of kings and nobles.

The Kuvasz is said to have an uncanny ability to detect an enemy of his master even before the master himself realizes there is danger. The breed is fiercely loyal and protective. It is said of this great dog that he is either a friend or an enemy for life. In the Middle Ages the Kuvasz was undoubtedly much larger than our present standard. Kuvaszok must have been very intimidating to commoners, who were forbidden to own them.

The dogs were used in packs for hunting from the fifteenth century on. Eventually they got into the hands of the common people and were used as guards and perhaps as herders of cattle and sheep. By that time the breed had evolved to about where we know it today.

The Kuvasz is probably related to the Komondor, for they do have traits in common. Both are great outdoor animals, and both are extremely loyal to a very small and select core of people. People thinking of the Kuvasz as a pet might consider carefully, if this is to be their first dog, whether or not they are up to the task. They are generally not. The Kuvasz is not a casual dog for

the casual owner, nor is he a dog to be allowed to reign in the household.

This extremely handsome, very intelligent dog must be trained early and well and maintained that way, under constant supervision. A Kuvasz that gets the least out of hand is not only a nuisance but a potential menace. This is a dog for the firm, the strong and the devoted among really experienced dog-owners. There should never be any contest; the man must prevail and call all the signals. The very protective traits of the Kuvasz are things that must be kept in check, of course. No dog can be called upon to *always* know a friend from an enemy.

Hungarian Puli

Land of origin: Hungary

Original purpose: Shepherding

Recent popularity ranking by K.C. registration: Moderate

HEIGHT: Dogs to 18 inches, bitches to 16 inches

WEIGHT: Dogs to 33 pounds, bitches to 29 pounds

COAT: Unusual, weather-resisting, double. Outer coat long, never silky. May be straight, wavy, or somewhat curly. Undercoat soft, woolly, dense; mats into cords. Seen either combed or uncombed with hair hanging in neat even cords

COLOUR: Solid colours only, dark preferred. Black, shades of grey, and white. Blacks are rust or weathered. Some mixing in greys but overall effect must be of solid-coloured dog

Amount of care coat requires:	1	2	3	4	5	6	7	8	9	10
	*	*	*	*	*	*	*	*	*	*

Amount of exercise required:	1	2	3	4	5	6	7	8	9	10
	*	*	*	*	*	*	*	*		

Suitability for urban/flat life:	1	2	3	4	5	6	7	8	9	10
	*	*	*	*	*	*				

The Puli is another of the superior shepherd's dogs from Hungary, where they have been in use for at least a thousand years. No one knows where they came from or what their ancestral stock might be. There is a strong argument for the Tibetan Terrier, since the two breeds bear a resemblance, and the Hungarian dogs generally are believed to have come from the East. Arguments that the breed arose from stock from Lapland and Iceland are less convincing. It is a problem that will not be solved, for no records were kept, and the movement of dog breeds and groups of breeds apparently was constant over thousands of years.

The Puli is an agile, active outdoor dog who is as much a herder today as he ever was in history (the breed is said to have run across the backs of sheep, even to have ridden them!). A Puli shows his best qualities when being worked. Tough, extremely intelligent and readily trained by anyone who knows what he is doing, this breed is not for the casual or indifferent owner. A Puli is more than just careful with strangers; he tends to be openly suspicious. He makes, therefore, a first-rate watchdog. He must be regulated, though, lest watchfulness

becomes aggressiveness. There is no doubt that this is a special breed for special purposes.

The coat of the Puli (the plural form is Pulik) is another special characteristic. It tends to cord like that of the Komondor and is protection against all weather. The Puli never has to come inside.

If he is to match himself in dog-handling skills to the dog he buys, the first-time owner (or one with very limited patience) should go slow with this breed. Unless managed well and really appreciated for his superior abilities to learn and respond, the Puli will not only be wasted on such an owner but become a nuisance. This breed is headstrong, assertive and very expert at what it does – handling other animals and guarding the master's territory. It is thought to be one of the most intelligent of all breeds.

Hungarian Vizsla and Hungarian Wire-haired Vizsla

Land of origin: Hungary

Original purpose: Gun-dog

Recent popularity ranking by K.C. registration: Moderate

HEIGHT: Dogs to 25 inches, bitches to 23½ inches

WEIGHT: To 66 pounds

COAT: Short, dense and smooth. Lies flat, no undercoat

COLOUR: Solid rusty-gold or dark sandy-yellow. Dark brown and pale yellow not desirable

Amount of care coat requires: 1 2 3 4 5 6 7 8 9 10
*

Amount of exercise required: 1 2 3 4 5 6 7 8 9 10
* * * * * * *

Suitability for urban/flat life: 1 2 3 4 5 6 7 8 9 10
* * * * *

The Magyar hordes swarming into central Europe ten centuries ago brought with them a hunting dog that was probably already an old breed. We believe that dog gave rise to the hunting dog of Hungary known today as the Vizsla. This is a fast, tensely mounted animal of boundless energy and willingness. He wants to work, he wants to please and he wants reward in the form of praise.

This graceful animal is an aristocrat, not unlike a thoroughbred horse with its neat, perfected conformation and smooth, even power. The Vizsla is also extremely headstrong and determined to have it out once and for all with his master. Someone, man or dog, is going to be boss. Sanity with a Vizsla in the home requires that this issue be settled early on. A Vizsla who has not been properly trained for life in a home is a monumental pest. Left alone he just might decide to go sailing through a plate-glass window in order to have some fun outside. He'll keep on running up your glazier's bill, too, until the rules are outlined for him and his stay-at-home manners learned.

The Vizsla can be fine with his master's family, though he may be very slow to take to strangers, and he can be aloof, to say the least. Shyness, however, would be considered a fault.

Hungarian Vizsla   *Hungarian Wire-haired Vizsla*

As is often the case with large, smooth-coated field-dogs, the Vizsla is a doubtful choice for urban or even suburban living and not really the dog for people who are sedentary in habit. One way or another, the Vizsla is going to get the workout he needs to stay in shape and burn up his endless energy reserve. If you don't work him in the field, then he is going to be bumptious and a nuisance. Of course, you don't have to be a hunter, but you do have to like very long walks. A Vizsla needs to run and explore and respond to cool, even, but very forceful commands.

You cannot fault the Vizsla on his qualities as a field-dog. He is intelligent, responsive, perfected for the job he was designed to do. The Vizsla is one of the special-purpose dogs for special kinds of committed dog-owners.

The Hungarian Wire-haired Vizsla is in all respects like the smooth-coated variety, with the exception of the longer wiry-coat texture. It is rare by comparison with the smooth Vizsla.

Ibizan Hound

Land of origin: Probably Egypt, then Spain

Original purpose: Coursing, hunting

Recent popularity ranking by K.C. registration: Moderate

HEIGHT: To 28 inches

WEIGHT: To 50 pounds

COAT: Short all over, shortest on head and ears – only slightly longer at back of thighs and under tail

COLOUR: White and red, white and lion, or solid white, red or lion. Solids very desirable but rare

Amount of care coat requires:	1 2 3 4 5 6 7 8 9 10
Amount of exercise required:	1 2 3 4 5 6 7 8 9 10
Suitability for urban/flat life:	1 2 3 4 5 6 7 8 9 10

No one knows the real history of this very ancient breed. By the time of King Tutankhamun (1366 to 1357 B.C.) it already was immortalized in stone. Specimens may have been brought to Egypt from some other land long before the time of the boy king. For at least four thousand years they have survived around the periphery of the Mediterranean, but in recent years the greatest concentration has been found on the Balearic Islands off the coast of Spain. They are known by many names, but the concentration on the island of Ibiza seems to have labelled them at least as far as the English-speaking world is concerned. In Spain they are known variously as Podenco Ibicenco, Ca Eivissenc, Mallorqui, Xarnelo, Mayorquais, Charnegue and Chien de Baleares. On the island of Malta they are called Rabbit Dogs and on Sicily, Cirnecco dell'Etna. The name Ibizan Hound has taken hold in the United Kingdom, though, and probably will not change.

People who know this breed well speak of the Ibizan Hound as being exceptionally quiet and clean. He is responsive to his human companions but is reserved with strangers. He is particularly sensitive to change and will take his time to think things through, and that includes the arrival of new people

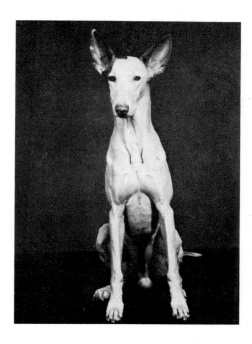

on the scene. He is not awkward in the way some sight hounds may be. He is, rather, sensible as well as sensitive, and steady in his habits.

The Ibizan Hound is, like the Greyhound, the Saluki and the Afghan Hound, a dog of grace and dignity. He is fast and sleek and particularly adept at both high and broad jumps. He is, then, above all else an athlete – and a fairly large one, too. He must have exercise, like all the true coursing hounds. It would not be proper to keep this dog in a flat unless he was assured of very long walks and an occasional trip to a safe area where he could be allowed to run.

The Ibizan Hound is not a sharp breed, but he is a careful, determined friend to his master and family. It is too soon to tell how he will evolve in the United Kingdom now that his popularity is likely to rise. His mysterious and almost certainly unknowable beginnings are bound to add to his attractiveness. It is claimed that it was the Ibizan Hound (obviously known then by a different name) that was the model for the god Anubis, the guardian of Egyptian dead. He may be one of the few breeds, perhaps the only one, that was actually worshipped.

Iceland Dog

(ICELANDIC SHEEPDOG)

Land of origin: Arctic

Original purpose: Sheepdog

Recent popularity ranking by K.C. registration: Rare

HEIGHT: To about 19 inches

WEIGHT: N.S.G.

COAT: Very dense undercoat and topcoat long forming mane, brush and feathering

COLOUR: N.S.G.

Amount of care coat requires: 1 2 3 4 5 6 7 8 9 10
                               * * * *

Amount of exercise required: 1 2 3 4 5 6 7 8 9 10
                             * * * * * * * *

Suitability for urban/flat life: 1 2 3 4 5 6 7 8 9 10
                                 * * *

This dog resembles its close relatives the Finnish Spitz and the Norwegian Buhund. It is an all-round farming dog, and as such needs plenty of exercise.

Rarely seen in the U.K., this is a specialist fancier's dog. There is no reason why the breed should not work as herders perfectly satisfactorily, but there is little to commend them over the indigenous Collie breeds in the British Isles; indeed, they may prove more headstrong and difficult to train than our Collies, judging by the behavioural patterns of their near relations – the Spitz varieties.

Potential owners should be aware that the low numbers of this breed in the U.K. will create difficulties in the selection of suitable mates should breeding be contemplated, and at all times the herding dogs must be seen in their original function of almost limitless energy (twelve-hour working day) and their natural inclination to obey only one master (their 'shepherd'). Hence their great exercise potential, which makes them hardly suited for city life and requires caution in advising them as family pets.

Irish Setter

Land of origin: Ireland

Original purpose: Gun-dog

Recent popularity ranking by K.C. registration: 16th

HEIGHT: N.S.G.

WEIGHT: N.S.G.

COAT: Of moderate length and flat. Feathering long and silky on ears and forelegs. Ideal is free from wave or curl

COLOUR: Mahogany or rich chestnut red. *Any* trace of black is a serious fault. Very small amount of white allowed on chest, throat or toes

Amount of care coat requires: 1 2 3 4 5 6 7 8 9 10
                      * * * * *

Amount of exercise required: 1 2 3 4 5 6 7 8 9 10
                      * * * * * *

Suitability for urban/flat life: 1 2 3 4 5 6 7 8 9 10
                      * * * *

Once a red and white dog (and still seen that way), the Irish Setter is now a rich red mahogany animal of great and enduring beauty. Certainly one of the handsomest of dogs, the red Irishman may have been in part undone by his splendour. It was originally a field-dog and there was none better. But in recent years it has been a show animal, and many people familiar with the breed think this is a sad waste of talent.

We are not sure where the Irish Setter came from. It seems certain that some spaniel and English Setter, perhaps Gordon Setter and Pointer, were involved. Any trace of black today (which would go back to the Gordon) is considered a fault.

Wherever it came from and however it is used, the Irish Setter is a stunning animal and a terrible clown. A pet dog through and through, it is affectionate and extremely demonstrative. But it can be a problem when not obedience-trained. It is capable of taking over a household where there is not a firm and knowing hand, but equally capable of learning anything that reasonably can be expected of an upland dog. One or the other, a model of decorum, or a dunce and a nuisance – it will depend on the owner.

There is a difference of opinion as to where and how the Irish Setter is best maintained. In my own opinion, the red Setter, although adaptable and loving under any circumstances, is too active for flat life. It needs an enormous amount of exercise, and that every day. In a flat there is no way in which this can be achieved. A walk is not the same as a run. I have seen some perfectly splendid examples of the breed as awkward as a dog can be from over-confinement. It is sad to see one of these splendid field-dogs leaping and lunging for want of proper exercise.

Irish Setters tend to stray, and in the suburban setting they should be carefully supervised. They are also terrible thieves, so don't be surprised if you wake up some morning to find that your Irish Setter has brought home an Oriental carpet or a family Bible. They are also born clowns and will never leave you short of stories to tell. Endearingly beautiful, active and affectionate, in the right setting and in the hands of the right owner, the Irish Setter cannot be beaten.

Irish Terrier

Land of origin: Ireland

Original purpose: Hunting

Recent popularity ranking by K.C. registration: Moderate

HEIGHT: To 18 inches

WEIGHT: Dogs to 27 pounds, bitches to 25 pounds

COAT: Dense and wiry, rich but not soft or silky. Skin barely shows when hair is parted with fingers. Curly or kinky coats very objectionable

COLOUR: Solid coloured; bright red, golden red, red wheaten or wheaten. *Small patch of white on chest is allowed but not desirable. Black hair found in puppies should not last into adulthood*

Amount of care coat requires:	1 2 3 4 5 6 7 8 9 10
Amount of exercise required:	1 2 3 4 5 6 7 8 9 10
Suitability for urban/flat life:	1 2 3 4 5 6 7 8 9 10

The Irish is one of the oldest of the terrier breeds, and his origins are a matter of conjecture. He so strongly resembles the Irish Wolfhound in shape and character that there is a temptation to think of him as the great hound bred down in size – far down to be sure. The Irish Terrier, however, is an authentic terrier type in both appearance and nature.

The energetic, racy red terrier from Ireland is a perfect companion animal. Once it gives its love, it is assigned until death. There is no hardier dog than this and none more adaptable – as long as his master is at hand. A large country estate is fine with an Irish Terrier, but so is a flat or a small suburban house. What matters is that the right people live there as well.

With the children of the household the Irish Terrier is a perfect playmate, but it is also apt to be protective, and that is something that has to be held in check. Not every child who comes running into the garden to tackle or wrestle the owner's child is an enemy – but an Irish Terrier may not always be able to make that distinction. This is one breed for whom 'no' must mean 'NO!'

This Irishman has been used as a land and water retriever, and at both jobs it not only excels but thoroughly enjoys itself. It is a born hunter and is death

on vermin, but here again the red terrier may not always agree with the neighbourhood's definition of vermin. That, too, must be held under some kind of control. What it amounts to is that if you avail yourself of one of these superior terriers, you are going to have to make some of the decisions and pass the news along to your dog. An Irish Terrier should be trained early and well and constantly given refresher courses.

During World War I the Irish Terrier was famous as a patrol- and courier-dog and proved utterly fearless in all situations. No one can reckon how many men survived that holocaust as a direct result of this noble element in the Irish Terrier's character.

Show-dog, ratter, big-game hunter, war-dog, companion, household guard, and playmate – all these describe the Irish Terrier. The breed is still as good as it is because of the efforts of the fanciers who love it above all others. Turn to them for help if you decide to buy one of these splendid dogs for your own family and home. Be sure to give your Irish Terrier a great deal of exercise; he both needs and deserves it.

Irish Wolfhound

Land of origin: Ireland

Original purpose: Hunting, coursing wolves and other large game

Recent popularity ranking by K.C. registration: Moderate

HEIGHT: Dogs 31 inches and over, bitches 28 inches and over

WEIGHT: Dogs 120 pounds and over, bitches 90 pounds and over

COAT: Rough, hard and wiry. Longer on face

COLOUR: Grey, brindle, red, black, white and fawn

Amount of care coat requires: 1 2 3 4 5 6 7 8 9 10
                  * * *

Amount of exercise required: 1 2 3 4 5 6 7 8 9 10
                  * * * * * * *

Suitability for urban/flat life: 1 2 3 4 5 6 7 8 9 10
                  *

The mighty Irish Wolfhound is one of the tallest and most powerful of all dogs. His origins are lost to us, although he was known and revered around the time of Christ. Records dating back to the third century A.D. suggest that the Celts may have brought him with them to Greece five hundred years earlier.

This great hound was developed for the hunt, to course wolves and even the elk of ancient Ireland. He is said to be able to run down a wolf and make the kill unaided. When coursing was the sport of kings, this regal dog was considered an appropriate gift from one king to another. There is a story of a war fought for the possession of a single specimen of the breed.

The last of these dogs in their original form faced extinction about the time of the American Civil War. An officer in the British army – a Scot – set out to collect the few that remained in Ireland and rebuild the breed along ancient lines. He finally succeeded, and today's Irish Wolfhound closely resembles his ancestors.

Despite his being bred for violent purposes, the Irish Wolfhound is a gentle and reliable animal. He is well aware of his size and power and is extremely courageous. He is also intelligent and an excellent companion. He is not suited to city life, and even a small suburban home might be crowded with an animal of this size trying to find a place to relax. This is clearly a country dog, an estate dog or a dog for the farm. He is good with children and will take a lot of

punishment without displaying bad temper. He will be a deterrent to burglars, of course, and his presence can impart a feeling of security. Because of his enormous size and strength, it would be unthinkable to train him to attack. The look of him is enough.

The Irish Wolfhound is not an inexpensive dog to buy or keep. He requires a lot of food and a lot of room. A good example of the breed may cost a lot and should be purchased only from a reputable breeder. Like all hounds, the Irish Wolfhound does not like pulling up roots. Once he has settled into a home, he wants to stay there – for life – guarding it and sharing it with its human inhabitants. This is a splendid breed of dog for special situations only. He is for the home where there is the need and the means to own the largest dog in the world, and one of the most noble.

Italian Greyhound

Land of origin: Italy, but very ancient

Original purpose: Companionship and rabbiting

Recent popularity ranking by K.C. registration: Moderate

HEIGHT: N.S.G.

WEIGHT: To 10 pounds (ideally 6–8 pounds)

COAT: Short, glossy like satin, soft

COLOUR: Any colour and markings, except that dogs with tan markings where they would appear on black and tan dogs of other breeds cannot be shown

Amount of care coat requires: 1 2 3 4 5 6 7 8 9 10
*

Amount of exercise required: 1 2 3 4 5 6 7 8 9 10
* * * * * *

Suitability for urban/flat life: 1 2 3 4 5 6 7 8 9 10
* * * * * * * * * *

This lovely little dog, who can be traced back to ancient times, has been the companion of kings and queens for almost as long as there has been written European history. He is nothing more than the ancient Greyhound bred down selectively and then refined. He differs little from the Greyhound except in size and personality.

The stories are legion about the roles this breed played in the lives of royal households. A king knelt weeping in the garden as he dug away the earth with his hands to lay to rest the dog who had sat on the throne with him. More than one king has been said to have gone to war with an Italian Greyhound on the saddle in front of him. This dog was first seen in England about three hundred years ago and was an immediate favourite in England and Scotland. What lay behind this popularity, particularly among the privileged and super-privileged who could have owned any animal they chose?

The Italian Greyhound is one of the most pleasant of all dogs. Mild-mannered, sweet and affectionate, he is never snappy or nasty, even though his size makes him exceedingly vulnerable. He is fine-boned, and like his relative, the Whippet, he is unable to assume an awkward pose. Often pictured in paintings by the masters and in fine china and porcelain, the Italian Greyhound always looks as if a work of art has suddenly come alive. It probably is the

sweetness of his disposition and his beauty that has charmed the artistic and the discerning.

Owners of the breed insist that although one no longer has to be of noble blood to own an example, the owner is elevated to nobility, in a sense, by this dog. That is worth thinking about.

Italian Greyhounds do not like cold weather and should be protected from it. They are perfect home and flat pets and are very easy to maintain with their short coats and natural good manners, manners naturally as good as the disposition that goes with them. They can be a little stubborn when it comes to house-training, though.

Graceful, elegant, refined, beautiful and exceedingly pleasant, the Italian Greyhound is a dog to admire. His continuing popularity among the discerning is easy to understand.

Italian Spinone

Land of origin: France, then Italy

Original purpose: Gun-dog

Recent popularity ranking by K.C. registration: Rare

HEIGHT: Dogs to 25½ inches, bitches to 23½ inches

WEIGHT: N.S.G.

COAT: N.S.G.

COLOUR: N.S.G.

Amount of care coat requires: 1 2 3 4 5 6 7 8 9 10
   * * *

Amount of exercise required: 1 2 3 4 5 6 7 8 9 10
   * * * * * * * *

Suitability for urban/flat life: 1 2 3 4 5 6 7 8 9 10
   * * *

These dogs are excellent workers in the field, particularly over marshy or wooded country. Their ancestry includes European Pointers and Griffons. They are large dogs with unlimited exercise potential, and this should be borne in mind by would-be owners. In other respects it is an easily trainable, affectionate, soft-mouthed retrieving breed. It is extremely hardy, and has guard-dog possibilities.

While it appears that this breed is an all-rounder, it should be clearly understood that it is basically a gun-dog, and as such there are few natural workers – all require training to the hunting field or gun, and some much more than others. Also it is quite likely that they may not satisfactorily train using methods normally employed for the indigenous British gun-dog species.

Anyone contemplating a Spinone would be well advised to spend some time observing them working in Europe and seeking counsel from an experienced Spinone-trainer before embarking on what could prove an expensive and disastrous exercise.

Japanese Akita

Land of origin: Japan

Original purpose: Heavy hunting

Recent popularity ranking by K.C. registration: Rare

HEIGHT: Dogs to 24 inches, bitches to 21 inches

WEIGHT: To 110 pounds

COAT: Double, with outer coat being somewhat on the harsh side

COLOUR: All colours permitted. White should not account for more than one-third of total

Amount of care coat requires:	1	2	3	4	5	6	7	8	9	10
		*	*							

Amount of care coat requires: 1 2 3 4 5 6 7 8 9 10
                                           * * *

Amount of exercise required: 1 2 3 4 5 6 7 8 9 10
  * * * * * * * *

Suitability for urban/flat life: 1 2 3 4 5 6 7 8 9 10
  * *

The Akita or Akita-inu is the heavy-duty work-dog of Japan. Named for the province of Akita on Honshū Island, this breed was used to hunt bear, boar and deer and as a protector of life and limb. There are two other similar breeds in Japan – the Nippon-inu and the Shiba-inu – but they are somewhat smaller.

Four thousand years ago the inhabitants of Japan had a dog known to archaeologists as the peat dog. No doubt the Akita is a descendant of that animal. Also sometimes referred to as the Japanese Spitz, the Akita has a general Spitz-like appearance but is larger and stronger. The Akita has been likened to the Chinese Chow Chow, and it is possible that the two have some ancestry in common, since commerce with the mainland followed the period when the peat dog was a part of every band, clan and household. When highwaymen wandered the Japanese countryside, the Akita and his forebears no doubt played a very important role as watchdogs, a task this animal readily takes to still.

We have the Akita today because of military personnel stationed in Japan. A number of Akitas survived the war, and servicemen were impressed with the breed's intelligence and his adaptability as both pet and guard-dog. They began bringing examples back with them, and today the Akita enjoys full breed status from the Kennel Club.

People who have come to know this new breed speak highly of his intelligence, his responsiveness to training, and his desire to please his master. Essentially a good-natured animal, this dog is still large, powerful and assertive. There can be little doubt that an Akita who has been obedience-trained is much more desirable as a neighbour than one who has not.

Every indication suggests that the Akita will grow in popularity. It is to be hoped that breeders here will be as firm in their resolve to hold to the standards as their Japanese counterparts have been for centuries. Because of their hunting background and their fearless quality, Akitas are best maintained under tight control. They can be quite aggressive towards other dogs and should be owned only by people with some prior experience with large, tough-minded dogs. The Akita is not a casual pet.

Japanese Chin
(JAPANESE SPANIEL)

Land of origin: Japan

Original purpose: Probably companionship

Recent popularity ranking by K.C. registration: Moderate

HEIGHT: N.S.G.

WEIGHT: To 7 pounds

COAT: Profuse, silky, long and straight preferred. Totally free from wave or curl.
Tendency to stand out. Thick mane or ruff. Profuse feathering; very plume-like tail

COLOUR: Black and white or red and white. Reds range from sable, brindle, and
lemon to orange. White to be clear. Good distribution required

Amount of care coat requires: 1 2 3 4 5 6 7 8 9 10
                                          * * * * * *

Amount of exercise required: 1 2 3 4 5 6 7 8 9 10
                                          *

Suitability for urban/flat life: 1 2 3 4 5 6 7 8 9 10
                                          * * * * * * * * * *

The Japanese Chin, formerly the Japanese Spaniel, probably originated in
China and only reached Japan after being established in his present form.
Literally stolen from Japan by visiting sailors, these dogs came to be sold at
high prices all over the world. Commodore Perry was presented with some
legally, and he in turn presented a pair to Queen Victoria. The avenues of
distribution of this breed were not recorded because they were so often
contraband.

There are actually several different coat styles for these gay little dogs – the
profuse coat, the shorter coat and even a coarser-textured coat – but all carry
the high style and grand good looks of this ancient companion toy.

The Japanese Chin, still a relatively rare breed in this country, is a perfect flat
dog. He does shed, and his coat does require some brushing, but the dog
himself is companionable, intelligent and most affectionate and responsive. He
does not require much exercise and is in general easily kept. A lively little
animal, he wants very much to be a part of everything his family is involved
in, including meals. He wants most of all to be spoiled, and many owners of
this breed want them for just that purpose – spoiling.

Often, we must admit, this and other finely bred toys were created and are maintained along such elegant bloodlines expressly for spoiling. They never grow up and are what I refer to as 'neotonous', eternally childlike and perpetually naughty enough to serve their own purpose: to call attention to themselves.

Elderly people, single people and couples without children may find these characteristics in a dog to be exactly what they have wanted all along, and they often are the ones to favour them. Like most toys, the Japanese Chin travels well and enjoys going along on house visits, to parties and on other simple outings. The Japanese Chin is as fragile as most toys are and should not be exposed to extremes. Being locked in a closed car is very often a death sentence and must be avoided at all costs. It is far better to leave your Japanese Chin at home if you know you are going to be making stops where he cannot accompany you.

Japanese Spitz

Land of origin: Scandinavia originally, then Japan

Original purpose: Herding (?) and companionship

Recent popularity ranking by K.C. registration: Rare

HEIGHT: Dogs to 16 inches, bitches to 14 inches

WEIGHT: N.S.G.

COAT: Long, fluffy coat, short on lower legs and face

COLOUR: Fawn to white

Amount of care coat requires:	1	2	3	4	5	6	7	8	9	10
	★	★	★	★	★	★				

Amount of exercise required:	1	2	3	4	5	6	7	8	9	10
		★	★	★						

Suitability for urban/flat life:	1	2	3	4	5	6	7	8	9	10
	★	★	★	★	★	★	★			

This breed resembles a larger edition of the Pomeranian (another Spitz-derived breed). It is a comparatively new breed outside Japan, and is quite rare in the U.K. It is said to enjoy its freedom of exercise, though adapting well to life as a house-dweller in town and country. In common with many Spitz types, it tends, however, to be a one-man dog and can be tricky with strangers.

This dog tends also to be yappy and to show an inbuilt sharpness or snappiness. It is not a breed that can be well recommended for family households, especially where there are young children who have no natural apprehension of dogs. They could make good companions for the single person or for the elderly couple. Being small in size, their food consumption and other 'running costs' are minimal.

Keeshond

Land of origin: Holland

Original purpose: Barge-dog and as watchdog

Recent popularity ranking by K.C. registration: Moderate

HEIGHT: Dogs to 18 inches, bitches to 17 inches

WEIGHT: N.S.G.

COAT: Abundant, long, straight, harsh and off-standing. Thick downy undercoat. On legs, smooth and short except for feathering. On tail, profuse and plume-like. Never silky, wavy or curly, and not parting on back

COLOUR: Mixture of grey and black. Undercoat pale grey or cream. Outer-coat hairs black tipped. White markings not allowed. Dark spectacle markings on face typical and desirable

Amount of care coat requires:	1	2	3	4	5	6	7	8	9	10
	*	*	*	*	*	*	*	*		

Amount of exercise required:	1	2	3	4	5	6	7	8	9	10
	*	*	*	*	*					

Suitability for urban/flat life:	1	2	3	4	5	6	7	8	9	10
	*	*	*	*	*	*	*	*	*	*

The Keeshond (the plural form is Keeshonden) has a complex and colourful history. In the period just before the French Revolution, the followers of the Prince of Orange, known as the Partisans, were vying with a group known as the Patriots to become the dominant political force in Holland. The leader of the Patriots was a man called Kees de Gyselaer of Dordrecht. He owned a dog, also called Kees, an example of a breed we know today as the Keeshond. The dog became the symbol of the Patriots, a party of working-class people.

In time the Prince of Orange prevailed, and a lot of people apparently felt it best not to have living symbols of the opposition around the house. The Keeshond did not so much fall from favour as vanish for safety reasons. Once seen on all the small barges moving along the canals and in almost every farmhouse, the Keeshond soon became something of a rarity. About 1920 the Baroness van Hardenbroek took an interest in the breed and found enough good examples still left to re-establish it in Holland and, since then, around the world.

The Keeshond is another perfect house dog. Handsome, small and companionable, he is generally quieter and perhaps more sensible than the

other Spitz-like breeds to which he is related. All the relationships have not been worked out, but it is likely the Keeshond has common ancestry with the Pomeranian, Samoyed, Norwegian Elkhound and Finnish Spitz.

The splendid little Hollander depends a great deal on his handsome coat for his high style, and there is daily work involved in keeping it in good condition. The hair is brushed against the grain to keep it off-standing. Since washing tends to soften hair and make it floppy, the Keeshond is seldom, if ever, bathed.

The Keeshond is a loyal, loving family dog and a good watchdog, and he is easy-going with other animals. He does not take immediately to strangers but will accept those who do not appear to be threatening to his home and family. He should be walked regularly, of course, but the Keeshond does well in the suburban home and the flat. This dog has an engaging personality and a lot of style. Mass-producers and retailers have tended to make something of a mess of this breed, producing outsized and unpleasant-looking specimens, so the prospective Keeshond owner should head for the specialty breeder. The Keeshond seldom disappoints the new owner who has taken the time and trouble to learn about the breed and to seek a fine specimen. Charming in the show-ring and never failing to attract attention, they are equally desirable as family pets.

Kerry Blue Terrier

Land of origin: Ireland

Original purpose: General utility herding and hunting

Recent popularity ranking by K.C. registration: Moderate

HEIGHT: N.S.G.

WEIGHT: To 37 pounds

COAT: Soft, dense and wavy. Never harsh, wiry or bristly

COLOUR: Important: from deep slate to light blue-grey. Quite uniform. Darker areas on muzzle, head, ears, tail and feet

Amount of care coat requires: 1 2 3 4 5 6 7 8 9 10

Amount of exercise required: 1 2 3 4 5 6 7 8 9 10

Suitability for urban/flat life: 1 2 3 4 5 6 7 8 9 10

The Kerry Blue Terrier is an animal of enormous style and character. He is a substantial dog with temper and temperament. Whether shown 'in the rough' as he is in his native Ireland, or in a refined shape as he is in the U.K., he is handsome and regal.

It is sometimes claimed that the Kerry Blue (he came from County Kerry) is descended from the Soft-coated Wheaten Terrier. Whatever his origin, there is little he has not done in the way of dog's work. He has been used as a water retriever, a trailing dog, a herder, and a general farm utility dog. He has even been trained to a limited extent for police work in the British Isles.

The Kerry Blue Terrier is hardy, can tolerate any weather and is long-lived. At eight years, when some other breeds are nearing the end of their lives, this terrier is still a young animal.

The Kerry Blue is not keen on strangers and can be a little unpredictable at times. He has been known to bite, but this tendency can be offset by early and intense obedience-training. Certainly, it is essential that an owner establish at the beginning that there is a chain of command within the household and that the dog is not at the top. The Kerry Blue Terrier would like that position and will try to take it. This is a breed that can explode with other animals, and owners are obligated to keep their pets under firm control – on a leash. If a

Kerry Blue Terrier decides he doesn't like another dog he passes in the street, it may take a lot more than a voice command to get the two apart.

The Kerry Blue Terrier is a very devoted friend and can be fine with his owner's family. He will be stubborn if allowed to be, and there again early training is essential.

None of this is to say that the Kerry Blue Terrier isn't a fine pet as well as a watchdog or show-dog in the right household, but he is the kind of dog who can prove to be more than the new owner reckoned on. He is so assertive, strong-willed and loaded with character that inexperienced dog owners should be warned about what they are getting into. The Kerry Blue Terrier is simple for a real dog person, but it takes some years of experience to earn that title.

His long life, his high style, his great character and personal power have made the Kerry Blue Terrier something of a cult dog with people well acquainted with the breed. He remains something of an enigma to almost everybody else.

King Charles Spaniel

Land of origin: Probably Japan

Original purpose: Companionship

Recent popularity ranking by K.C. registration: Moderate

HEIGHT: N.S.G.

WEIGHT: To 14 pounds

COAT: Soft, long, silky and wavy. Tendency to curl is a fault. Profuse mane down front of chest. Feathering also profuse

COLOUR: King Charles – rich black and glossy mahogany tan
Ruby – Whole-coloured, rich chestnut-red
Blenheim – chestnut and white, broken-coloured
Prince Charles – tri-colour (white, tan and black)

Amount of care coat requires: 1 2 3 4 5 6 7 8 9 10
                                           * * * *

Amount of exercise required: 1 2 3 4 5 6 7 8 9 10
                                           *

Suitability for urban/flat life: 1 2 3 4 5 6 7 8 9 10
                                           * * * * * * * * * *

The King Charles Spaniel has been known in England for several hundred years and has long been a favourite of royalty. Tradition has it that Mary, Queen of Scots, went to the block with her favourite at her side. The breed is certainly not English in origin, however. It may be an ancient Chinese breed that was exported to Japan and later to Spain and only then to England. That routing must always remain speculative. It is undoubtedly Asian though.

This Spaniel is lovable and good-natured. He gets along with children, better, in fact, than most other toys. He is eminently spoilable, and that is how he is most often encountered – eminent and spoiled absolutely rotten, which is when he is at his best.

Because he does not really require outdoor exercise and because he is a pretty little creature when properly fussed over and cared for, he is a favourite of a special kind of owner. He is equipped to fulfil many needs. The breed is also well known on the Continent.

Fine examples of this breed are not easily purchased. Anyone breeding this dog well will be extremely careful about whom he sells to.

Komondor

Land of origin: Hungary

Original purpose: Guarding flocks and herding

Recent popularity ranking by K.C. registration: Moderate

HEIGHT: Dogs from 26 inches, bitches from 23½ inches

WEIGHT: Dogs to 135 pounds, bitches to 110 pounds

COAT: Unique. Dense, weather resistant, double. Woolly, soft and dense undercoat with long, coarse outer coat. Outer coat tends to cord and hang in characteristic ropes

COLOUR: White only. Any other colour disqualifies

Amount of care coat requires: 1 2 3 4 5 6 7 8 9 10
Amount of exercise required: 1 2 3 4 5 6 7 8 9 10
Suitability for urban/flat life: Unsuited

The Komondor has been bred in Hungary in the form we know today for over a thousand years. He probably arrived there from central Asia a thousand years before that. The Komondor (plural form is Komondorok) is one of the oldest breeds in Europe and probably the best guard-dog of all. He was also used as a shepherding dog. The Komondor had the sole responsibility of driving away or killing wolves, bears, foxes and any other animals that appeared to endanger the master's flocks. At this task the powerful and purposeful Komondor excelled.

As a puppy the Komondor is playful and typical, but as he matures, he hardens into a guard-dog with undying loyalty and resolve. He is cautious with strangers and only slowly accepts even apparent friends of the household. The one-time or first-time visitor is watched quietly but without relaxation. Anyone who seems to threaten the tranquillity of the household might expect to get a chunk taken out of him!

The Komondor is serious but good with the family of his master. He is not especially nervous or snappy, and he is intelligent. Training is easy and should start early. It is practically impossible to call on a Komondor for more than he can deliver. His ability to learn and his determination to please and protect are apparently without limit.

The Komondor lives naturally in the open, in very harsh climates, and outside quarters are a good idea for him even as a pet. There is no weather that will bother him, since he lives virtually encased in an impervious corded coat of white hair. It forms into hanging ropes, and the breed characteristically looks unkempt. That coat, though, is one of the more protective and efficient in the world of dogs.

Tough, hardy, alert, the Komondor needs a lot of exercise to stay in good condition. With the fear of crime as great as it is, some people have begun to think of the Komondor as a good guard in a flat. That is unwise for several reasons. A flat is not a proper setting for so large an outdoor animal, and a guard-trained or even a naturally protective Komondor is much more than the average pet-owner can handle.

Lakeland Terrier

Land of origin: England

Original purpose: Fox-hunting

Recent popularity ranking by K.C. registration: Moderate

HEIGHT: To 14½ inches

WEIGHT: Dogs to 17 pounds, bitches to 15 pounds

COAT: Double – soft undercoat with a hard, wiry outer coat

COLOUR: Blue, black, liver, black and tan, blue and tan, red, red grizzle, grizzle and tan, or wheaten. Light tans very much preferred over mahogany-like tones

Amount of care coat requires: 1 2 3 4 5 6 7 8 9 10

Amount of exercise required: 1 2 3 4 5 6 7 8 9 10

Suitability for urban/flat life: 1 2 3 4 5 6 7 8 9 10

The Lakeland Terrier, a product of the Lake District, was once known as the Patterdale Terrier. He is one of the oldest of the English working terriers and is typical of that type of dog. He is utterly fearless, impossible to tire, game and full of fire. He was used to chase foxes and otters to ground and is a deadly adversary. The desire to hunt is as strong in today's dog as it was a century or two ago.

The Lakeland is not common, but that is probably due to the fact that he is a working terrier and is not as often reduced to being a plain companion animal as other small terrier breeds. He is more stable than many other terriers, calmer and a good deal more sensible. He is also good-natured and especially good with children whom he knows. He is devoted to his master but slow to take up with strangers. Before entering into an in-depth relationship, the Lakeland wants to *know* that it is a good move. The Lakeland seems to shy away from shallow relationships with people, preferring all or nothing.

The Lakeland is strong on land and in the water, probably the strongest of all terriers in his weight class. He works with and therefore generally can live with other dogs; he has been used with Otterhounds and Foxhounds.

Young Lakeland Terriers were highly prized in the Lake District a century or more ago and were kept for breeding purposes. It was some time before

examples were really known outside this small, somewhat secluded region. The tendency to keep the dog at home was strengthened by the fact that the northern districts – counties like Northumberland, Cumberland and Westmorland – had their own working terriers and seldom needed to draw upon the outside. Perfecting was done from within, and attention was paid to performance, not to colour or conformation. Many of those old working terrier breeds are lost to us today, and, indeed, we don't even know their names. The Patterdale survived, however, to become the powerful and congenial animal we have today. It is a breed to be held in esteem.

Lancashire Heeler

Land of origin: England

Original purpose: Cattle herding, rabbiting

Recent popularity ranking by K.C. registration: Rare

HEIGHT: N.S.G.

WEIGHT: N.S.G.

COAT: Ultra-short coat

COLOUR: N.S.G.

Amount of care coat requires:	1	2	3	4	5	6	7	8	9	10
	★	★	★							

Amount of exercise required:	1	2	3	4	5	6	7	8	9	10
	★	★	★	★	★	★	★			

Suitability for urban/flat life:	1	2	3	4	5	6	7	8	9	10
	★	★								

This breed is fairly common in north-west England, where it was used for herding cattle and hunting small vermin – particularly rabbits. Only recently registrable by the U.K. Kennel Club, these dogs are described as being very active, small, strong workers, low-set in profile. They are considered to be affectionate but protective, and though small in stature are obviously much more suited to farm life than to flat- or city-dwelling.

While this breed has been established for a considerable length of time, they are still definitely outdoor dogs and may well be snappy towards strangers and children. They are, however, compact in size, easy to keep groomed, inexpensive to feed and boundless in energy. They could make amusing working pets for the family living in or on the borders of the real countryside.

Large Munsterlander
and Small Munsterlander

Land of origin: Germany

Original purpose: All-purpose gun-dog

Recent popularity ranking by K.C. registration: Moderate

HEIGHT: Dogs to 24 inches, bitches to 23 inches

WEIGHT: Dogs to 65 pounds, bitches to 55 pounds

COAT: Resembles that of a Setter – medium length with longer feathers

COLOUR: N.S.G.

Amount of care coat requires:	1*	2*	3*	4*	5	6	7	8	9	10
Amount of exercise required:	1*	2*	3*	4*	5*	6*	7*	8*	9	10
Suitability for urban/flat life:	1*	2*	3*	4*	5*	6	7	8	9	10

This breed is one of the most recently developed, with the exception of its country of origin, Germany, where it is well established. In build and coat it resembles a Setter, though the head is more reminiscent of a Spaniel.

As a breed they make good family pets from every point of view, though exercise requirements may be greatly in excess of the average dog walker.

At one stage, this breed was referred to as a Long-haired German Pointer.

The Small Munsterlander, occasionally referred to as the Moorland Spaniel, is in all general features similar to the Large, though obviously it is lighter in weight and should not exceed 22 inches in height.

Leonberger

Land of origin: Europe

Original purpose: Stock-guarding and draught-dog

Recent popularity ranking by K.C. registration: Rare

HEIGHT: Dogs to 30 inches, bitches to 27½ inches

WEIGHT: N.S.G.

COAT: A very thick, dense coat to give protection against the elements

COLOUR: Varies from yellow to reddish-brown with shading

Amount of care coat requires: 1 2 3 4 5 6 7 8 9 10
                                    * * * * * * * *

Amount of exercise required: 1 2 3 4 5 6 7 8 9 10
                               * * * * * * *

Suitability for urban/flat life: Unsuited

This is a very large dog of striking good looks. Originally bred in Germany, it derived from crossing Newfoundlands with Pyrenean Mountain Dogs. As one might imagine, these dogs need a lot of space and a generous amount of exercise. They are reputed to be lively and bouncy dogs with above-average intelligence. They have in the past been used to pull carts in Europe and as guard-dogs, so it is not unreasonable to envisage that they will make first-class watchdogs at home.

They have been seen in this country for quite a number of years now, though breeding in the U.K. is limited.

The breed originated in Leonberg, Germany, where an alderman named Essig created the breed to resemble the heraldic lions on the town's coat of arms. The breed is very handsome in appearance and could be likened to a long-haired Alsatian (German Shepherd Dog), although the two are not related. The now extinct Alpine Mastiff is also in the ancestry of the Leonberger.

Lhasa Apso

Land of origin: Tibet

Original purpose: Companionship, formerly goat guard

Recent popularity ranking by K.C. registration: 38th

HEIGHT: To 10 inches

WEIGHT: N.S.G.

COAT: Heavy, straight, hard and dense. Not woolly or silky. Long

COLOUR: Golden, sandy, honey, dark grizzle, slate, smoke, parti-colour, black, white or brown. Golden or lionlike colours are considered best. Dark tips to ears and beard very good

Amount of care coat requires:	1	2	3	4	5	6	7	8	9	10
	*	*	*	*	*	*	*	*	*	*

Amount of exercise required:	1	2	3	4	5	6	7	8	9	10
	*	*	*							

Suitability for urban/flat life:	1	2	3	4	5	6	7	8	9	10
	*	*	*	*	*	*	*	*	*	*

The Lhasa Apso, one of the four breeds that we know came from the mountains of Tibet, was the small companion animal kept inside the house to warn of intruders. Outside was the fierce Tibetan Mastiff. The Lhasa Apso, because he was the inside dog, naturally became a pet. He is bred for that role today and is rapidly increasing in popularity. Aiding his rise in favour is the fact that he is a perfect city companion and has great style and charm.

Lhasa Apsos are devoted to their masters and mistresses and to their families. They are forever suspicious of strangers, a characteristic that harks back to their early role as watchdogs. Strangers coming into the home should let them be, and allow them to make any overtures. Pushing yourself on a strange Lhasa Apso is one way of forcing an issue and making him snappy.

Because the Lhasa Apso is such a demanding pet, this is not always the best breed to have around young children. He will be in direct competition for the role of baby of the house and will tend to be jealous and resentful. This is a strong-minded, purposeful little animal, not a pushover in any category. The owner should establish at the start who is to be master of the house. The Lhasa Apso is perfectly willing to take over and become a splendid despot, and if that happens only the owner is to blame.

The coat of the Lhasa Apso, one of his shining highlights, does require care, considerable care, and enough time should be left each day to bring it up to full glory and keep it there. The Lhasa Apso will compensate for the time you spend on his coat by not demanding long walks in nasty weather. Although his typical Tibetan coat (all Tibetan dogs apparently have the heavy coat and the up-curled tail seen in this breed) will enable him to withstand any weather you are likely to encounter, the dog does not crave long walks and is happy around the house.

The Lhasa will take training readily and will always strive to please family members. He is playful and affectionate and loyal. He has risen so suddenly in popularity in the last few years that it is wise to be careful when making a purchase. Make sure you are getting a really good puppy from a truly good line or you will inherit a bundle of bad manners and disappointing conformation.

Lowchen

Land of origin: Possibly France

Original purpose: Companionship

Recent popularity ranking by K.C. registration: Rare

HEIGHT: To 13 inches

WEIGHT: To 9 pounds

COAT: Long and wavy, but not curly. Fine and silky. Is clipped in the traditional lion clip

COLOUR: Any colour combination permissible

Amount of care coat requires:	1 2 3 4 5 6 7 8 9 10
Amount of exercise required:	1 2 3 4 5 6 7 8 9 10
Suitability for urban/flat life:	1 2 3 4 5 6 7 8 9 10

This breed was originally called the Little Lion Dog, as was the Pekingese. It is, however, strictly speaking, of the Bichon family, and it is traditional to clip these dogs, as with Poodles, in the lion cut. The overall appearance is one of a maned animal with a tufted tail. Grooming usually has to be left to the experts, but daily brushing and combing is essential.

They are happy, lively little dogs by reputation. Surprisingly, the breed is a very old one, since it was known in the sixteenth century, and is supposed to have been painted by Goya. As yet its numbers in Britain are few, and it would certainly be regarded more frequently as a show-dog rather than a household pet.

Maltese
(MALTESE TERRIER)

Land of origin: Malta

Original purpose: Companionship

Recent popularity ranking by K.C. registration: Moderate

HEIGHT: To 10 inches

WEIGHT: N.S.G.

COAT: Long, flat and silky. No kinkiness, curls or woolly texture allowed

COLOUR: Pure white. Some tan or lemon on ears allowed but not desirable

Amount of care coat requires:	1 ★	2 ★	3 ★	4 ★	5 ★	6 ★	7 ★	8 ★	9 ★	10 ★
Amount of exercise required:	1 ★	2 ★	3	4	5	6	7	8	9	10
Suitability for urban/flat life:	1 ★	2 ★	3 ★	4 ★	5 ★	6 ★	7 ★	8 ★	9 ★	10 ★

The Maltese, although often thought of as a terrier, is actually a form of tiny spaniel. He is one of the most ancient of pure-bred dogs and certainly one of the oldest of the toy breeds. For the romantic dog-owner, the Maltese holds special attractions. He was a favourite of the upper classes in ancient Greece and Rome and was the beloved of titled ladies in the time of Elizabeth I. All through history, writers have spoken of this breed with reverence and a little awe. Five hundred years ago fine examples of the breed were selling for what even today would be considered enormous sums – the equivalent of the annual income for an entire village of working-class people.

The Maltese is a child, and no one should entertain the thought of buying this breed without that foremost in mind. The lovely flowing coat needs hours of care and constant attention, and the dog himself never really grows up. He is loving, even adoring, and loaded with personality, but he characteristically is a fussy eater with a tricky digestive system. He can be frail. The Maltese wants (and usually gets) his own way. He wants to be the centre of attention and doesn't like sharing his love sources with anybody or anything else. He is, then, a nearly perfect dog for a single person or a couple who will not have children to compete with their dog. Because of his small size he is very

appropriate in the flat, although he is a dog who wants to be exercised a reasonable amount of time each day. Care should be taken in bad weather, though, and paper training as an emergency alternative is to be recommended. The Maltese prefers being warm and dry and makes no pretence of being a retriever or herding dog. This is a dog designed for the lap and the silken pillow almost thirty-five hundred years ago, and he seems to know it in every fibre of his body.

The Maltese generally will not treat strangers or even known outsiders the way he will treat his master. He can even be snappy with people he does not know, although that isn't much of a threat to human safety and well-being. It is, though, a reflection of the spirit and nature of this remarkable little animal with so much of the history of Western culture built into him.

Manchester Terrier

Land of origin: England

Original purpose: Ratting

Recent popularity ranking by K.C. registration: Moderate

HEIGHT: Dogs to 16 inches, bitches to 15 inches

WEIGHT: To 22 pounds

COAT: Short and smooth. Should be thick, dense, close and glossy. Never soft to the touch

COLOUR: Well-defined jet black and rich mahogany tan. White considered very bad and will disqualify if over ½ inch in any dimension

Amount of care coat requires: 1 2 3 4 5 6 7 8 9 10

Amount of exercise required: 1 2 3 4 5 6 7 8 9 10

Suitability for urban/flat life: 1 2 3 4 5 6 7 8 9 10

The breed probably first emerged in Manchester when a coarse Black and Tan Terrier was crossed with a Whippet to produce a superior gaming dog for the rat pits and for practical use along the waterfront. (Today's Manchester Terrier was also once called the Black and Tan, but is, under any name, far more refined than that older parent breed.)

The Manchester in either size is a superior companion animal. He is like a fine racehorse – trim, neat and with the look of perfection about him. Not only is he affectionate, responsive and intelligent, but he is also clean, virtually odourless and fits well into any family situation. He is fine in a flat and will be satisfied with a limited amount of outdoor exercise. He would still make a good ratter on the farm, but he is almost exclusively a companion animal today.

The Manchester Terrier is a good watchdog and a very understanding friend. Only the finest breeders should be trusted, for this is a breed that must not be mass-produced, nor should its standards be abused.

Maremma Sheepdog

Land of origin: Europe

Original purpose: Stock-guarding

Recent popularity ranking by K.C. registration: Rare

HEIGHT: Dogs to 28½ inches, bitches to 27 inches

WEIGHT: Dogs to 99 pounds, bitches to 88 pounds

COAT: Dense, thick wavy coat with shorter hair on the head, limbs and feet. Slight feathering on the backs of legs

COLOUR: White, with small amounts of pale shading permissible

Amount of care coat requires: 1 2 3 4 5 6 7 8 9 10
                                 * * * * * * * *

Amount of exercise required: 1 2 3 4 5 6 7 8 9 10
                              * * * * * * *

Suitability for urban/flat life: Unsuited

As with many stock-guarders, this is a dog that needs to be regarded with great caution. The breed is not renowned for obedience, nor is it said to tolerate discipline well. Unlike the German Shepherd Dog, it has not worked as a shepherding dog. It is very old-established, dating back to Biblical times, and is thought to have derived from the Hungarian/North Italian region.

Quantity of exercise is less important than frequent walks, as befits a breed originated for guarding purposes.

In view of the specialized nature of this breed, it is strongly advisable that would-be owners should make contact with an experienced breeder.

Mastiff

Land of origin: England for 2,000 years, before that a mystery

Original purpose: Guarding, hunting, war

Recent popularity ranking by K.C. registration: Moderate

HEIGHT: Dogs to 30 inches, bitches to 27½ inches

WEIGHT: N.S.G.

COAT: Outer coat tends towards coarseness, with undercoat short, close-lying and dense

COLOUR: Apricot, silver-fawn, or dark fawn-brindle. Fawn-brindle dogs to have fawn as background with brindle evenly distributed as dark stripes. Face the darker the better, but always darker than body

Amount of care coat requires: 1 2 3 4 5 6 7 8 9 10
                                        *

Amount of exercise required: 1 2 3 4 5 6 7 8 9 10
                                * * * * *

Suitability for urban/flat life: Unsuited

No one knows (and probably never will) where the Mastiff came from or how he was spread across the face of the world. There are lots of theories and some pretty fascinating bogus history, but it is conjecture at best. When Caesar invaded the British Isles in 55 B.C., the Mastiff was there alongside his British masters fighting against the Roman legions. As might be expected, examples of the breed were carried back to Rome.

The giant Mastiff (generically, the word mastiff implies a whole family of giant dogs) was bred for violence. He was a guard-dog thousands of years ago, he was a war-dog, a hunting dog for the largest game and he was used in the pit in the most horrific of blood sports. It is more than a little strange that such a dog has developed into a generally docile animal.

In a setting large enough for this animal (a flat is hardly right), he is a perfect pet. He is great with children, fine with almost anyone and usually not quarrelsome with strangers, although he may be cautious until he has assured himself that all is well. He can be protective, which presents a problem because of his size. By nature obedient and responsive, the Mastiff will take training well and will be serious about the things he is asked to do.

Because he is so massive and so powerful, the Mastiff must be under control at all times. There are examples who are short with other animals, and they must be watched and, if possible, have trained out of them any sign of aggression. Other examples will be surrogate parents to the whole world and are provocation-proof.

It should be noted that the Mastiff and the Bullmastiff are two different breeds. The latter is a cross between the Mastiff and the English Bulldog. In error, many people use the names interchangeably. The Mastiff is much the larger of the two.

The Mastiff requires little coat care, but does need exercise if he is to stay in good condition and not become stiff and lame. In situations where he must be tightly controlled, long walks are in order. He is best, of course, on a farm or a large estate, where he may exercise himself. These giants are rugged, hardy and, needless to say, very intimidating as watchdogs.

Mexican Hairless

Land of origin: Asia or Turkey; eventually Mexico

Original purpose: Religious dog (?)

Recent popularity ranking by K.C. registration: Moderate

HEIGHT: To 19 inches

WEIGHT: To 35 pounds

COAT: Hairless, except for little mat on top of skull

COLOUR: N.S.G.

Amount of care coat requires: Nil

Amount of exercise required: 1 2 3 4 5 6 7 8 9 10
                 * * *

Suitability for urban/flat life: 1 2 3 4 5 6 7 8 9 10
                 * * * * * * * * * *

Although one of the oldest-known breeds, numbers have now declined to a point of concern for its survival. It makes a good house-dog in that it is virtually odourless, and of course does not cast its coat. It is unaggressive and generally quiet; rather than bark, it whines and vocalizes like a Basenji. These dogs do need frequent bathing and some skin care, since they sweat 'from all pores' (unlike virtually all other breeds which sweat 'through their tongues'), and in view of their lack of hair insulation, thrive best in warm or heated environments. Their normal body temperature is considerably higher than haired breeds to compensate for heat loss. The breed is said to be originally vegetarian (fruit and vegetable) but is easily converted to conventional dog foods.

Mexican Hairless are believed to be related to the Chinese Crested Dogs and were thought to have been introduced to Mexico (where conservancy breeding has now started) from Asia or Turkey by nomadic traders (Turkey also has a hairless dog variety of Toy Greyhound). The Mexican Hairless enjoyed religious worship from the Aztec tribesmen, due to its supposed healing properties.

Miniature Pinscher

Land of origin: Germany

Original purpose: Probably companionship

Recent popularity ranking by K.C. registration: Moderate

HEIGHT: To 12 inches

WEIGHT: N.S.G.

COAT: Smooth, short, hard, straight and lustrous; uniform over body

COLOUR: Red, lustrous black with sharply defined rust markings, solid brown, or chocolate with rust or yellow markings

Amount of care coat requires: 1 2 3 4 5 6 7 8 9 10
                               *

Amount of exercise required: 1 2 3 4 5 6 7 8 9 10
                               * * *

Suitability for urban/flat life: 1 2 3 4 5 6 7 8 9 10
                               * * * * * * * * * *

Despite many statements to the contrary, the Miniature Pinscher undoubtedly has been around a few centuries longer than the Doberman, but he is not, as so many people believe, a bred-down version of the latter.

The breed was little known before 1928. From about 1929 on, the little toy has grown in popularity, and probably will continue to do so.

The Minpin, as he is often called, is a lively little devil with a high-stepping style that marks him everywhere he goes. He is a natural showman and is a favourite in the ring. He is a show-off and an assertive character.

The Miniature Pinscher is best owned by people who are at least as strong-willed as he is. He is affectionate and loyal and a real participator. He is also, given the chance, a bully and a brat. Having one of these handsome little dogs around is like having a gifted child: you have to know how to handle the situation or it quickly will get out of control. But the Minpin does respond well to authority.

Some people feel the Miniature Pinscher is better in a home without children, since he is clearly a child himself. Others have had quite different experiences and claim he is fine with children, indeed with any people as long as he considers them family. He is a perfect watchdog and will never let a

stranger come near without giving voice. He is, in fact, a noisy little toy, always quick to express a point of view.

For the individual or family looking for a clean, compact, strong-willed little dog of character and high style, the Miniature Pinscher may be just about the perfect choice. There are more restful breeds, though, and more than a few easier to train and control. Here is a breed that should be matched to a personality need. When that is right, this is an outstanding breed of dog.

Miniature Schnauzer

Land of origin: Germany

Original purpose: Companionship

Recent popularity ranking by K.C. registration: Moderate

HEIGHT: Dogs to 14 inches, bitches to 13 inches

WEIGHT: N.S.G.

COAT: Double – hard, wiry outer coat and a close undercoat. Usually plucked – length usually not less than ¾ inch

COLOUR: Salt and pepper, black and silver, or solid black. Tan shading is allowed

Amount of care coat requires: 1 2 3 4 5 6 7 8 9 10
                                 * * * * * * *

Amount of exercise required: 1 2 3 4 5 6 7 8 9 10
                                 * * *

Suitability for urban/flat life: 1 2 3 4 5 6 7 8 9 10
                                 * * * * * * * * * *

The Miniature Schnauzer was derived in part from the larger forms of Schnauzer by carefully crossing the smallest available specimens with Affenpinschers. It was recognized as a distinct breed by the end of the nineteenth century.

The Miniature Schnauzer strongly resembles the larger dogs, but he is the ideal small house- or flat-dog. He is long-lived, intelligent and affectionate. He seems to naturally adore children, and children generally adore him! Whatever is available in the way of space, love and attention, he will take. He loves to play, he seems to be made of springs and he never tires. Indoors or out he insists on being a part of everything that is going on around him. He sulks when omitted.

His popularity is based on his easy keeping qualities and his good disposition. He does like long walks but can survive without them when the weather is bad (he can take the weather, but his master can't always keep up); he is easily trained for any regimen. He is naturally happy and healthy, but is perfectly willing to become a first-class food fad if that is what you want him to be. He responds to what is offered and takes advantage of all opportunities. If you want to feed him chopped chicken livers on imported biscuits, that is fine with

him, as will kennel meal be if that is what you have to offer. This is a smart little animal, and a lot of owners feel the need to spoil them.

Because the Miniature Schnauzer is so popular, there have been an awful lot of suspect breeders. Hence, anyone wanting an example of this breed as it was meant to be is going to have to avoid the obvious pitfalls. This is a superlative companion animal, and there are fine breeders all across the country willing to place their puppies in good homes. What the buyer gets is what the buyer is willing to seek out; take the trouble to evaluate and to know what you are getting.

Neapolitan Mastiff

Land of origin: Italy

Original purpose: Guarding, war-dog, tracking

Recent popularity ranking by K.C. registration: Rare

HEIGHT: Dogs to 28½ inches, bitches to 27 inches

WEIGHT: Up to 150 pounds (both sexes)

COAT: Short-haired

COLOUR: N.S.G.

Amount of care coat requires: 1 2 3 4 5 6 7 8 9 10
                                 * *

Amount of exercise required: 1 2 3 4 5 6 7 8 9 10
                                 * * *

Suitability for urban/flat life: Unsuited

This is an enormous, solid breed of dog, of which only a handful are in the U.K. They are reputed to have excellent temperaments, but they are extremely strong, will automatically guard property and people, but are unlikely to attack except when ordered to do so.

As with many large breeds, the amount of exercise required does not relate to the size; but, all in all, these dogs would be quite unsuited to town life. Being large and powerful, much damage to humans and property can easily be wrought by an ill-tempered or ill-disciplined Mastiff, so that visitors can be at considerable risk.

This breed, in common with other Mastiff varieties, is not suited therefore to all households or lifestyles. Furthermore, they are big eaters and one should budget for several pounds of food daily to satisfy the appetite. Some concern has been expressed about potential skin trouble and hind-leg weaknesses in this breed.

Newfoundland

Land of origin: Canada

Original purpose: Sea rescue work

Recent popularity ranking by K.C. registration: Moderate

HEIGHT: Dogs to 28 inches, bitches to 26 inches

WEIGHT: Dogs to 150 pounds, bitches to 120 pounds

COAT: Outer coat moderately long but not at all shaggy. Flat and usually straight, although some wave is allowed. It should not curl. The undercoat is soft and dense, and much of it is lost in the summer

COLOUR: Black, with or without a little white on chest and toes and sometimes the tip of tail. Also bronze and shades of brown. White and black dogs are called Landseers.* Beauty in colour and marking is highly rated in judging

Amount of care coat requires: 1 2 3 4 5 6 7 8 9 10
                               * * * *

Amount of exercise required: 1 2 3 4 5 6 7 8 9 10
                               * * * * * * *

Suitability for urban/flat life: 1 2 3 4 5 6 7 8 9 10
                               *

* Dogs with the small white details on chest, toes and tail tip are still considered black. The rare Landseers are truly pinto-like.

The Newfoundland is a giant of a dog, in appearance and nature every inch a 'teddy bear'. Named after the island off the east coast of Canada, the Newfoundland is undoubtedly descended from dogs brought there by European fishermen and later developed in England.

The Newfoundland is a working-dog in fact as well as in classification (this is not the case with some breeds). This was a dog who was expected to help the islanders haul their nets, pull carts and carry loads, and he became a legend in life-saving. The number of men, women and children the Newfoundland is said to have pulled from icy seas is endless. How much is fact and how much romance is hard to say. It is about the same situation we have with Saint Bernards and their mountain rescue stories. Some of the lore is known to be true, some is questionable, but the whole truth does not really have to be known.

The Newfoundland is a lover of a dog: he worships his master and his family. He is sensible with strangers and openly friendly once shown that his

family is safe. Although not a nervous or even suspicious dog, the Newfoundland is very protective; with a dog of such size, that counts for something.

Fortunately, the Newfoundland is easy-going with other animals and, indeed, seems to want to have another dog or two around. He is in fact social and sensible in all matters and therefore ideal in a family situation.

Despite his heavy coat, the care of a Newfoundland is not a problem. A good work-over once a week will keep the coat from matting. If it is neglected, though, it can be a mess to straighten out.

The Newfoundland was built for water. He is a powerful swimmer and certainly more than strong enough to drag a man from the sea. No weather and no water temperature will bother this great dog, who seems to flourish in the worst possible weather. In fact, about all that worries this dog is disapproval or lack of human response.

The Newfoundland in spirit and size is one of the all-time great breeds. Owners remain owned and seldom will allow themselves to be without the companionship, sense of security and feeling of style, taste and pure unabashed love that this dog provides.

Norfolk and Norwich Terriers

Land of origin: England

Original purpose: As pets, companions, and for some hunting

Recent popularity ranking by K.C. registration: Moderate

HEIGHT: To 10 inches

WEIGHT: N.S.G.

COAT: Close-lying, hard and wiry. Distinct undercoat, outer coat straight. No curl, and not silky

COLOUR: Shades of red, wheaten, black, tan and grizzle. Small white markings on chest only allowed

Amount of care coat requires: 1 2 3 4 5 6 7 8 9 10
                               *

Amount of exercise required: 1 2 3 4 5 6 7 8 9 10
                             * * * * *

Suitability for urban/flat life: 1 2 3 4 5 6 7 8 9 10
                                 * * * * * * * * *

These Norwich and Norfolk Terriers are among the smallest of terriers in size and among the largest in spirit. The gait, stance and personality of each reflect true English terrier blood and support the supposition that both Border Terrier and Irish Terrier blood went into the making of these breeds. The Norwich and Norfolk Terriers are not old breeds, but they do have some special qualities. Developed in England in the 1880s, the original version quickly became a fad dog with undergraduates at Cambridge University. There are still some people who believe the breed (now breeds) should be known as Cantab Terriers in honour of this early support. But, actually, at that time their forerunner was known as the Jones Terrier; it wasn't until after World War I that the name Norwich Terrier came into use.

By 1964 breeders in England had achieved two breeds, Norwich and Norfolk. They are now two separate breeds for purposes of registration and showing. The dogs are virtually identical except for the ears (the Norwich is prick-eared, the Norfolk lop-eared), and for the Norfolk having a slightly longer neck. It will be interesting to see if that difference stands and what other differences, if any, emerge.

The Norwich and Norfolk are incredibly responsive to their environment and their family. They can be exclusively attached to one person if that is what

Norfolk Terrier

Norwich Terrier

is expected of them, but they can also be family dogs. They are all personality and quickly capture the heart of anyone who comes to know them. They want to be in on absolutely everything that is going on around them. For the family with or without children, the Norwich or Norfolk can be the almost ideal breed. Each is small and neat and travels well, and is assertive enough to handle himself in almost any situation. Their hard, always straight and wiry coat requires little care. It doesn't retain dirt, and these dogs are cleaner than most.

Although perfectly fine in a flat if well exercised, these breeds are best suited for the country or suburbs. They naturally love horses and farm life. Both live with other animals, cats included, but it should be remembered that some of the earliest examples were used for hunting. The Norwich and Norfolk love a good chase and will bedevil small wildlife if given an opportunity to do so. Too small to become a real stock-killer, they should be trained to guard small farm-animals rather than pursue them. This is the kind of training a Norwich or a Norfolk can take, since they are loyal, great little watchdogs, and take to obedience-training as if it were the grandest pastime on earth. Some enthusiasts believe that the Norwich has the softer disposition of the two. Now that the breeds are free to go their separate ways, it will be interesting to see how the two develop.

Norwegian Buhund

Land of origin: Norway

Original purpose: Herding

Recent popularity ranking by K.C. registration: Moderate

HEIGHT: Dogs to 17¾ inches, bitches rather less

WEIGHT: N.S.G.

COAT: Close, harsh and smooth

COLOUR: Wheaten, black, red and sable. White blazes are permitted, as are black masks and ears and tail tips

Amount of care coat requires: 1 2 3 4 5 6 7 8 9 10
                * *

Amount of exercise required: 1 2 3 4 5 6 7 8 9 10
             * * * * * * * * *

Suitability for urban/flat life: 1 2 3 4 5 6 7 8 9 10
             * * * * * * *

The Buhund, like the Border Collie, is a natural herder; it is reputed to make an excellent playmate for children, and it does need a lot of exercise.

The breed is one of Norway's national dogs and it is still worked in that country as an all-purpose farm-dog, but particularly to control sheep and cattle. This breed is closely related to the other Arctic Spitz varieties, such as the Keeshond and the Iceland Dog. It is not a large breed, but has great strength and persistence.

The coat is very dense, providing natural insulation against the inclement weather of its native Norway. As a result, its periodic coat-casting may prove daunting to owners, and this may not be adequately reduced even with the most thorough grooming.

The breed is slowly becoming popular in Britain, but is unlikely to overtake the more frequent Elkhound or Samoyed.

Old English Sheepdog
(BOBTAIL)

Land of origin: England

Original purpose: Driving livestock

Recent popularity ranking by K.C. registration: 12th

HEIGHT: Dogs to 25 inches, bitches to 24 inches

WEIGHT: N.S.G.

COAT: Profuse but not excessive; hard-textured, not straight, but shaggy and never curly. Not soft or flat. Undercoat forms waterproof pile

COLOUR: Shades of grey, grizzle, blue or blue merle with or without white markings. No brown or fawn allowed

Amount of care coat requires:	1	2	3	4	5	6	7	8	9	10
	*	*	*	*	*	*	*	*	*	

Amount of exercise required:	1	2	3	4	5	6	7	8	9	10
	*	*	*	*	*	*	*	*		

Suitability for urban/flat life:	1	2	3	4	5	6	7	8	9	10
	*	*								

The Old English Sheepdog is English, without doubt, but not quite as old as his name might imply. The breed probably emerged in the latter half of the eighteenth century, although the groundwork was laid somewhat earlier. The ancestry of the breed is not known. Many people insist on Collie as the foundation stock, while others opt for a Russian dog known as the Owtchar. If it was Collie, it was probably what we now know as the Bearded Collie.

The dog was a sheepdog, again as the name implies, but not so much a herding animal as a drover. The dog's task was to help drive sheep and probably other livestock to market. The peculiar ursine gait, a wonderful ambling shuffle, speaks of great stamina. The Old English Sheepdog lives inside a protective shield of a coat and should not be stripped of that coat unless it becomes hopelessly matted. Unfortunately, this is a common occurrence. So the Old English Sheepdog's coat does require maximum care. It should be brushed every day to help keep it clean and free from knots.

The Old English Sheepdog is not at his best in confinement, though he is a house-dog. Ideal on a farm, he will do well in a suburban home but not in a flat. He must get plenty of exercise in all kinds of weather. A dog that is closely confined and not exercised can become lame and may be awkward to deal

with. Such a bumptious pest is appealing for only a very short time. Naturally obedient and decidedly pleasant, the Old English Sheepdog will reflect the care and consideration with which he has been raised. Not meant to be chained or left alone in close quarters, he will be destructive and uncontrollable only if driven to it by conditions which he could be expected to tolerate poorly.

The Old English Sheepdog has rocketed in popularity in recent years, and there are an inevitable number of poor examples of the breed on the market. Get to know the parents of the dog you are considering. Only puppies from solid, pleasant and even-tempered stock should be considered. It is a shame to become disenchanted once your puppy has started to grow. And no one should consider the breed unless they have studied it well. This is a large, demanding working dog who requires extensive obedience-training. Only then will he keep his promise as a pet. He is not an ideal first dog.

Otterhound

Land of origin: Probably England and Wales; some argument for France

Original purpose: Hunting otters

Recent popularity ranking by K.C. registration: Moderate

HEIGHT: Dogs to 27 inches, bitches to 24 inches

WEIGHT: Dogs to 115 pounds, bitches to 100 pounds

COAT: Double; rough outer coat 3 to 6 inches long on back, shorter on legs. It must be coarse and crisp (hard). The undercoat is woolly and water-repellent. The coat is an important feature of this breed

COLOUR: Any colour or combination of colours is allowed

Amount of care coat requires: 1 2 3 4 5 6 7 8 9 10
                                     * * *

Amount of exercise required: 1 2 3 4 5 6 7 8 9 10
                                  * * * * * * *

Suitability for urban/flat life: Unsuited

The Otterhound is a dog little known in this country. Probably in use here by the reign of King John (1199–1216), he was bred in a straight line from a mixture of several different hounds (Harrier, Bloodhound and others) to kill otters. A somewhat coarse or rough-looking dog, he has been so perfected as a single-purpose animal that he has never become a popular pet. Otterhounds were almost always trained to work in packs, and their precise response to commands was legendary in the last century, when otter-hunting was in vogue. Those packs are now gone, as are most of the otters in England and Wales, and the breed is down almost to remnant level. The Otterhound is one of those dogs who could vanish in the years ahead unless other qualities are accentuated.

It would be a shame to lose what has taken almost ten centuries to perfect. In fact, the Otterhound shows qualities that should not be lost and could be adapted to other life-styles. He is loyal to his master, he has a very good nose, he is amazing in the water (he has webbed feet) and he can stand any weather and any water temperature. He would probably make a fine watchdog and should adjust well to an owner's family. But he is a tough fighter, and a brawl can quickly become a savage display. He therefore needs firm handling and constant supervision.

The Otterhound is a large dog, often well over 100 pounds, and his jaws are immensely powerful. His gait is easy and free, exhibiting great power and drive. He is a dog who never seems to tire, not letting up once he has a trail. He is out for blood and will not stop as long as he has a clue as to where the otter may be hiding.

Until breeders develop those qualities in the Otterhound that would make him attractive for today's owner, he is better suited to country life. An Otterhound and a city flat are not the right combination. Owners should keep in mind that if their pet can't find otters (which he probably can't), he may practise on other wildlife and a few neighbourhood cats. Otterhounds, like all powerful and headstrong animals, must be under full-time control. History has taught us that they respond well to training, so there is no excuse for an ill-behaved Otterhound.

Papillon
(BUTTERFLY DOG)

Land of origin: Probably Spain

Original purpose: Companionship

Recent popularity ranking by K.C. registration: Moderate

HEIGHT: To 11 inches

WEIGHT: N.S.G.

COAT: Abundant, long and fine, silky and flowing, straight and resilient. No undercoat. Ears well fringed. Profuse on chest and tail

COLOUR: White predominates. Patches may be any other colour except liver. Also tri-coloured. Colour must cover both ears and extend over both eyes. No solid colours allowed, including white

Amount of care coat requires: 1 2 3 4 5 6 7 8 9 10
                               * * * * * *

Amount of exercise required: 1 2 3 4 5 6 7 8 9 10
                               * *

Suitability for urban/flat life: 1 2 3 4 5 6 7 8 9 10
                               * * * * * * * * * *

The Papillon probably acquired his present form in Spain, for he is, it is believed, truly a dwarf spaniel. These dogs were traded to wealthy fanciers, particularly in Italy and France, and became favourites with members of royalty. They were painted by some of the greatest artists – Rubens, Watteau, Fragonard, Boucher and other fashionable portrait-painters of the court. Madame de Pompadour and Marie-Antoinette were fanciers, and in the early 1600s the future queen of Poland was known to own at least one dwarf spaniel.

The history of the Papillon is, then, one of elegance, privilege and a certain élan that belongs only to the truly élite. Although he is the only working toy— he is still, they say, a good little ratter – his general use has been to weigh down silk cushions and help dispose of delicacies. He has been used consistently for adornment and rarely fails to make an elegant setting even more elegant, a regal person even more impressive. The little butterfly of dogdom was meant to be spoiled.

The Papillon, although not exactly a Labrador Retriever, is not as delicate as he may appear to some people. He can stand some weather and will do well in

a flat, in a house or on the farm. He does prefer to be comfortable, though, and people who fancy this breed will probably feel better themselves if their pet is indoors at night and not out hunting and fending for himself.

Anyone who purchases an example of this breed should make a firm commitment to his coat. It does require care if it is to look its elegant best. This is not something that happens by itself. The dog is small and the task isn't large, just regular.

The Papillon likes exercise because he is an intelligent little busybody, but he does not require a great deal of it. The Butterfly Dog is affectionate and responsive to his family and is a very good little watchdog. He will not fail to announce strangers.

Pekingese

(LION DOG)

Land of origin: China

Original purpose: Ornamental companionship

Recent popularity ranking by K.C. registration: 17th

HEIGHT: N.S.G.

WEIGHT: Dogs to 11 pounds, bitches to 12 pounds

COAT: Long, with thick undercoat; straight and flat, not curly or wavy, rather coarse but soft. Profuse ruff; very heavy on tail and legs

COLOUR: All colours allowed: red, fawn, black, black and tan, sable, brindle, white, and parti-coloured. Well-defined black mask and spectacles with lines to ears desired. White on feet and chest of otherwise solid-coloured dog is not a parti-colour. Good distribution required

Amount of care coat requires:	1*	2*	3*	4*	5*	6*	7*	8*	9*	10
Amount of exercise required:	1*	2	3	4	5	6	7	8	9	10
Suitability for urban/flat life:	1*	2*	3*	4*	5*	6*	7*	8*	9*	10*

The Pekingese has long been a favourite with flat-dwellers who want a splendid little character to fuss over.

The Pekingese, the Little Lion Dog of China, dates back to ancient times, when they say it was a crime punishable by death to steal one. Slave girls were used as wet nurses to suckle these dogs, and special eunuchs were assigned to care for them. Whether they were actually sacred is not known, but they certainly were among the most spoiled dogs who ever lived. Specimens were stolen during the looting of China's imperial court in 1860, and some eventually reached Europe. But most were slaughtered by the Chinese, who did not want them to fall into the hands of Europeans. Out of all this romantic history comes the top push-faced toy in the world today.

Maintaining the coat of the Pekingese, his crowning glory, is a daily task, although not a big one. It must be seen to, however, or the Pekingese will soon look anything but elegant. This is an assertive, headstrong, wilful, possessive, positive, brave and forceful little character. He is not devoted to strangers and

will make a good watchdog. Very often children are not adored, although this dog will accept his place in a family and work out all necessary relationships. There will be no problem as long as the Pekingese is where he feels he must be: at the centre of the universe.

This is, of course, an ideal dog for the couple with limited space everywhere except in their hearts. This is a dog to cherish and share a life-style with. He is not to be left out or denied full recognition as a part of the family. He is the perfect animal to fuss over, and most Pekingese owners like to carry their pets with them. The pets think that is just wonderful.

Owning a Pekingese is like having a human infant with an adult's wiles. It is quite an experience and one that many people simply will not deny themselves.

'Sleeve' Pekes are freak miniatures occasionally thrown in a litter and weighing less than six pounds.

Petit Basset Griffon Vendeen

Land of origin: France

Original purpose: Hunting

Recent popularity ranking by K.C. registration: Rare

HEIGHT: To 15 inches

WEIGHT: N.S.G.

COAT: Extremely supple skin; wire-haired

COLOUR: N.S.G.

Amount of care coat requires:	1 2 3 4 5 6 7 8 9 10
Amount of exercise required:	1 2 3 4 5 6 7 8 9 10
Suitability for urban/flat life:	1 2 3 4 5 6 7 8 9 10

This is an intelligent hunting French breed, resembling a small Basset and showing the same qualities. It is an absolutely dedicated hunter, originally used for hunting wolf and now for hunting wild boar.

They are happy little dogs with a very typical loud bark. It is the only one of the specific breeds of Basset found in Britain that is currently registrable by the Kennel Club.

In view of its exercise potential, however, it is generally thought unwise to advise this breed in town life.

Pharaoh Hound

Land of origin: Egypt

Original purpose: Hunting

Recent popularity ranking by K.C. registration: Moderate

HEIGHT: Dogs to 25 inches, bitches to 24 inches

WEIGHT: N.S.G.

COAT: Short and glossy with feathering

COLOUR: Tan, or tan and white

Amount of care coat requires: 1 2 3 4 5 6 7 8 9 10
*

Amount of exercise required: 1 2 3 4 5 6 7 8 9 10
* * * * * * * *

Suitability for urban/flat life: 1 2 3 4 5 6 7 8 9 10
* * * * *

This is supposedly the original domesticated dog, and has been recorded as long ago as 4000 B.C.

As hunting dogs they were widely used in Ancient Egypt and are depicted on walls of caves and tombs. They are described as a medium-sized hound, and are enthusiastic and fast hunters, working both by scent and sight. They will hunt rabbit and hare splendidly. As with other favoured animals belonging to the Egyptian hierarchy, they were buried ceremonially in special tombs alongside their masters.

Pointer

Land of origin: Spain, then England

Original purpose: Pointing hare and later wing-shooting

Recent popularity ranking by K.C. registration: Moderate

HEIGHT: Dogs to 27 inches, bitches to 26 inches

WEIGHT: N.S.G.

COAT: Smooth and short, but dense and with a very definite sheen

COLOUR: Liver, lemon, black or orange – solid-coloured or any one in combination with white. Great variety seen

Amount of care coat requires: 1* 2 3 4 5 6 7 8 9 10

Amount of exercise required: 1* 2* 3* 4* 5* 6* 7* 8* 9* 10

Suitability for urban/flat life: 1* 2 3 4 5 6 7 8 9 10

The Pointer was developed in Europe during the Middle Ages, but no one is certain just where. One hears, from various supposed authorities, that France, Belgium, Germany, Spain and Portugal were all the original home of this breed. We simply aren't sure, but we do know that, from the mid 1600s on, England is where this breed flourished.

Originally Pointers were used in conjunction with Greyhounds. The Pointer found the hare, and the Greyhound ran it to ground. Later, when ballistics made wing-shooting possible, the Pointer became exclusively a bird dog. He is considered to be the ultimate dog in this field today.

Pointers are powerful, durable, clean-lined dogs of great poise and character. They do well in bench shows and excel in field trials. They are better suited to kennel life than are most large sporting dogs, for they require somewhat less human attention. Pointers will work well for a stranger more readily than will most other field-dogs. The Pointer has one thing on his mind: find that bird.

This breed is packed with nervous energy and requires an enormous amount of exercise. A Pointer that is cooped up is ready to explode when finally brought out into the open. There are exceptions, of course, but the Pointer is generally not as ideal a pet as are some of the other large sporting dogs. Pointers have quick tempers and really would rather be working than wasting their time on other things. Some have made excellent pets, but usually with a family

that works the dog in the field. How good they are in the average household is questionable. For a non-sporting family, one that cannot build a bond with the dog in the area the dog knows and loves best – field work – the Pointer may be less than ideal.

Pointer owners are, of course, devoted to their splendid breed. Because Pointers are so energetic and intent on their profession, they are not good city dogs – certainly not flat dogs. It has taken hundreds of years to perfect this masterpiece of upland wing-shooting, and it is a rare Pointer indeed who will respond well to any other life-style. None of this is to say that the Pointer is not an affectionate pet. He can be, but he is best suited to a master of a special type.

Pointing Wire-haired Griffon

Land of origin: Holland

Original purpose: All-purpose hunting

Recent popularity ranking by K.C. registration: Moderate

HEIGHT: Dogs to 23½ inches, bitches to 21½ inches

WEIGHT: N.S.G.

COAT: Unique in sporting dogs – downy undercoat and hard, dry, stiff outer coat like bristles on a wild boar

COLOUR: Steel grey, white with chestnut splashes, all chestnut, or dirty white and chestnut. Black a serious fault

Amount of care coat requires:	1	2	3	4	5	6	7	8	9	10
	*	*	*							

Amount of exercise required:	1	2	3	4	5	6	7	8	9	10
	*	*	*	*	*	*	*	*	*	

Suitability for urban/flat life:	1	2	3	4	5	6	7	8	9	10
	*									

This seldom seen hunting dog began his career in Holland late in the nineteenth century. One man, really, was responsible for developing the breed from a mixture of spaniels, setters, hounds and mixed-breed dogs. Because of a family quarrel the man, E. K. Korthals, eventually left Holland for Germany and then moved on to France. He took his dogs with him and kept up the breeding experiments for the rest of his life. In France they still refer to this dog as the Korthals Griffon.

The Pointing Wire-haired Griffon is a somewhat slow, very deliberate and skilful multi-purpose hunting dog. He is a pointer as well as a retriever. His harsh, rough coat makes him an ideal dog for cold climates, miserable weather and tough terrain like saltwater marshes. This is a steady, positive and intelligent breed of dog. He is also a particularly pleasant companion breed.

The Pointing Wire-haired Griffon is loyal to his master and good with children. He is calm and reasonable with strangers, although he can be slow to offer affection or to show enthusiasm. He is detached and perhaps cautious by nature when he is unsure of newcomers.

The Pointing Wire-haired Griffon, a rare dog, is not a flat or city dog. Confined, he cannot be relied upon to retain his naturally calm, intelligent way of dealing with life. He needs enormous amounts of exercise to stay well and

happy, and the more exposure he gets to rough terrain and hard living, the happier he seems to be. People attempting to remould Korthals's many years of hard work and skilful breeding in a single generation are in for a disappointment. This is one breed that will not be recast that easily. This is a dog for an active family – perhaps ideally an active single person. He thrives on miserable weather, rough water and long days that begin before sunrise. If you have that kind of abuse and misery to offer, you are going to have a happy dog. He will curl up by the fire at night and kick his legs in dreams that re-create the day, but he wants that day to be rough enough to try him.

A Pointing Wire-haired Griffon should not be difficult or ill tempered. There is a solid, workaday look about him, a pragmatic Dutch way of going about the day's labours.

Polish Sheepdog
(LOWLANDS [NIZINNY] AND TATRY MOUNTAIN [PODHALANSKI])

Land of origin: Poland

Original purpose: Shepherding

Recent popularity ranking by K.C. registration: Rare

HEIGHT: Nizinny to 20 inches, Podhalanski to 26 inches

WEIGHT: N.S.G.

COAT: The Lowland variety has a long soft coat (like the Old English Sheepdog). The Tatry Mountain dog has a very dense, moderately short coat

COLOUR: N.S.G.

Amount of care coat requires:
Nizinny: 1 2 3 4 5 6 7 8 9 10
Podhalanski: 1 2 3 4 5 6 7 8 9 10

Amount of exercise required: 1 2 3 4 5 6 7 8 9 10

Suitability for urban/flat life: 1 2 3 4 5 6 7 8 9 10

Both varieties are strong herding dogs rarely seen outside Poland. They are reputed to have, in general, good temperament, and as such would make suitable house-dogs, albeit with a sound guarding tendency. The Lowlands variety closely resembles an Old English Sheepdog and is reputed to be more docile than the Tatry Mountain variety, which looks similar to a Kuvasz or Retriever.

The long coat of the Lowland variety does create grooming problems and, as with the Bobtail, owners may feel tempted to have the dogs clipped once or twice a year to improve manageability of the grooming. This has always created controversy, and aficionados have a valid point in decrying this as sheer laziness. Why, they ask, get a long-coated dog in the first place if it is intended to have it clipped short?

Owczarek Nizinny

Pomeranian

Land of origin: Pomerania (Germany)

Original purpose: Companionship

Recent popularity ranking by K.C. registration: 36th

HEIGHT: N.S.G.

WEIGHT: Dogs to 4½ pounds, bitches to 5½ pounds

COAT: Double – short, soft, thick undercoat with a long, coarse, glistening outer coat. Off-standing and profuse. Always straight

COLOUR: Red, orange, cream and sable, black, brown and blue, white, sable, chocolate, plus others

Amount of care coat requires:	1	2	3	4	5	6	7	8	9	10
		*	*	*	*	*	*	*		

Amount of exercise required:	1	2	3	4	5	6	7	8	9	10
	*									

Suitability for urban/flat life:	1	2	3	4	5	6	7	8	9	10
	*	*	*	*	*	*	*	*	*	*

A very long time ago the diminutive toy we call the Pomeranian was a sled-dog, one of the group known as the Spitz dogs, essentially northern, full-coated dogs with a curled tail. Later, the breed was used for shepherding, although its exact history remains uncertain. Somehow the centre for breeding the Spitz seemed to be in Pomerania on the Baltic Sea, although possibly the ancestral dogs may have come from Iceland and Lapland. It was probably in Pomerania that breeding down started, although it is difficult to understand what may have originally motivated that development.

By the time the breed reached England in the middle of the last century, it was down considerably in size, although specimens probably weighed five or six times as much as they do now. It is said that some were still in the thirty-pound class. That is a far cry from the four- to five-pound toys we see today.

The Pomeranian now is strictly a companion dog. He is a spirited, brash, proud little strutter with some of that old northern Spitz fire still evident. He is a dog who is made to be spoiled, and both owner and dog, apparently, are happiest when that is the situation. The Pomeranian tries to take over; that appears to be his chief motivation in life. Many Pomeranian owners, amused by the brashness of this little charmer, seem pleased to relinquish command.

Some Pomeranians are fine with children, but as a general rule they are best

when they are the children of the household. They have a short temper when someone tries roughing them up, and are ideal for single people and elderly couples. They are fiercely loyal and are good little watchdogs.

The Pomeranian is an ideal flat dog. He requires little exercise, since even a brief walk with his short legs seems like miles to him. He likes to be comfortable and neat and will use a paper in a plastic tray, making walks in bad weather unnecessary. That is particularly important for those people who are limited in their outdoor activities and who do not like to go out in the city at night.

The Pomeranian's coat is glorious. The dog should not be bathed very often because that does soften his coat, which needs some care. Brushing is important to keep the coat off-standing and glistening.

Pretty as a picture, the little Pomeranian is just about the perfect dog for the right kind of home. He is demanding but rewarding to own, assertive yet loving and protective.

Poodle
(STANDARD, MINIATURE AND TOY)

Land of origin: France or Germany

Original purpose: Probably water retrieving

Recent popularity ranking by K.C. registration: Standard – moderate, Miniature – 22nd, Toy – 13th

HEIGHT: Standard – dogs and bitches over 15 inches, Miniature – dogs and bitches between 11 and 15 inches, Toy – to 11 inches

WEIGHT: N.S.G.

COAT: Naturally harsh in texture, extremely profuse and dense. Seen in a variety of clips

COLOUR: Solid only, never parti-coloured. Colours seen include blue, grey, silver, brown, café au lait, apricot, cream, black and white

Amount of care coat requires: 1 2 3 4 5 6 7 8 9 10
                                 * * * * * * * * * *

Amount of exercise required: Varies with size

Suitability for urban/flat life: Varies with size

No one really knows where the Poodle originally came from. It almost certainly is not from France, despite the fact that he is so often referred to as the French Poodle. It may have been from Germany, although even that is doubtful. The breed is probably of great antiquity.

Almost everywhere in the world that the breed is known, it is at the top of the popularity chart. Many reasons are put forward for this phenomenon, but the answer probably lies in intelligence. The Poodle is one of the most intelligent of all dogs. He seems able to learn anything, he makes a fine watchdog and he is an excellent water retriever. We are told that the exaggerated clips we see today are outgrowths of clips that facilitated the retrieving Poodle in water. The name Poodle is derived from the German slang word *pudeln*, which means, roughly, to splash around in the water.

The Poodle in his magnificent show clip is the brunt of many jokes, and the uninformed sometimes see it as an effete kind of status symbol. Were they to know! The Poodle in any clip is a superb dog – assertive, extremely responsive, loyal and intelligent beyond belief.

Because Poodles come in such a variety of colours and can be clipped in so

Standard Poodle

many ways, they serve any taste. That too, no doubt, has added to their popularity. They do not shed, although their hair is fast-growing and has no apparent maximum length. It keeps growing for as long as you let it. It does need regular clipping and styling – every four to six weeks – and that is a chore many people prefer to leave to the experts. It is not inexpensive, but the Poodle, owners feel, is worth the investment.

Poodles get along well with children, and with other dogs and cats. They fit in and respond to the people around them in an almost uncanny way. A Poodle in the family is truly like having an extra person on hand. There is nothing Poodles do not seem to understand. They are, as a result, immensely popular and probably will be for a long time to come.

Portuguese Warren Hound

(PODENGO PORTUGUÊS)

Land of origin: Portugal

Original purpose: Hunting and companion

Recent popularity ranking by K.C. registration: Rare

HEIGHT: Three size varieties – Small (Pequeno) 8–12 inches
Medium (Medio) 20–22 inches
Large (Grande) 22–27 inches

WEIGHT: N.S.G.

COAT: Smooth- or rough-coated

COLOUR: Usually fawn; also yellow, brown, off-black (with or without white spotting)

Amount of care coat requires: 1 2 3 4 5 6 7 8 9 10
                                  ★ ★ ★

Amount of exercise required: 1 2 3 4 5 6 7 8 9 10
                               ★ ★ ★ ★ ★ ★

Suitability for urban/flat life: 1 2 3 4 5 6 7 8 9 10
                               ★ ★ ★ ★ ★

This breed, while very popular in Portugal, is rare elsewhere. The smallest varieties are used in packs for hunting rabbits and hares, and closely resemble the Chihuahua. The large size, which hunts singly or in pairs, is very fast and can bring down deer; it is similar in appearance to the Ibizan Hound. These dogs make good indoor pets, but the larger hounds do need sufficient exercise.

The breed is elegant, short and squat. The head is fine and forms a triangular wedge shape. The dog is short-coated with slight pluming of the tail. The coat is brown to yellow in colour, or grey-black with or without white spots.

Portuguese Warren Hound – Medium

Portuguese Water Dog

Land of origin: Portugal

Original purpose: Fishing

Recent popularity ranking by K.C. registration: Rare

HEIGHT: Dogs to 22½ inches, bitches to 20½ inches

WEIGHT: Dogs to 55 pounds, bitches to 48½ pounds

COAT: May be long- or short-coated. The former is usually trimmed to a line clip like the Poodle, and the latter has a short curly coat

COLOUR: N.S.G.

Amount of care coat requires: 1 2 3 4 5 6 7 8 9 10
                                    * * * * * * * *

Amount of exercise required: 1 2 3 4 5 6 7 8 9 10
                                    * * * * * * * * * *

Suitability for urban/flat life: 1 2 3 4 5 6 7 8 9 10
                                    * * * * * *

This dog is very reminiscent, from many points of view, of the Standard Poodle. It is intriguing in that it is a sporting dog which, while capable of catching small game like rabbits and hare, justifies its name by protecting fishing nets and retrieving fish, and is equally at home in the water or on land.

The temperament of this dog is slightly suspect, especially with strangers, and, being one of the rarer breeds, cannot with enthusiasm be recommended as a family companion.

These dogs are rare in Great Britain, and while they were once used throughout Portugal, they are now seen mainly in the Algarve.

Pug

Land of origin: Turkey then France

Original purpose: Companionship

Recent popularity ranking by K.C. registration: Moderate

HEIGHT: N.S.G.

WEIGHT: To 18 pounds

COAT: Fine, smooth, short, glossy and soft to the touch. Neither hard nor woolly

COLOUR: Black, silver or apricot-fawn. The light-coloured dogs have black masks and ears and a dark line or trace on the back

Amount of care coat requires:	1 2 3 4 5 6 7 8 9 10
Amount of exercise required:	1 2 3 4 5 6 7 8 9 10
Suitability for urban/flat life:	1 2 3 4 5 6 7 8 9 10

We assume several things when we take up the Pug. First, we assume the breed originated in China a long time ago. This animal has the pushed-face and curled-tail look of a Chinese dog. We also assume the Pug was never intended for any task except loving, for that is where the Pug fits into human society. The Pug is a child who never grows up.

The Pug doesn't have a particularly strong odour, although like all push-faced dogs he does tend to gulp air, and that has predictable results in a closed room. He doesn't shed much, and he doesn't drool. This is altogether a pleasant little dog to have around. He is another of those dogs who make absolute prisoners of their owners. Pug owners tend to be Pug owners all their lives once they have tried the breed.

A Pug is good with children, although a small child might seem something of a challenge to him. Children, when they get a little older, from five or six on, seem to do better with this breed than in their earlier years. The Pug is jealous of other dogs, and small children seem to be included among them. A disgruntled Pug may decide to punish his owner by neglecting previously well-understood rules about toilet habits. Pugs, in fact, train well and easily and, once they catch on to the idea of reward at the far end, are not difficult. This dog, however, is always looking for an opening and will quickly take over and run the show if indecision and lack of assertiveness become apparent. For

example, a Pug is not a choosy eater as a rule, but let an owner start with the diced chicken breast and bonbon routine, and he will have a first-rate food fad on his hands. In brief, some Pugs, like some children, are a lot smarter than some parents, and it really isn't reaching too far out to suggest that people who avail themselves of a Pug come closer to parenthood than dog ownership.

The character of the Pug – smart, tidy, willing and loving – should be viewed in the light of the breed's development. He does exactly what he was designed to do perhaps a thousand or more years ago. He is only playing the role for which he was cast.

The Pug owner of today is joining a long line of famous and royal men and women who have preferred this breed. Many Pugs have sat beside the throne, and the trick with the Pug is to convince him that he doesn't belong *on* the throne. If you want to love with the absolute certainty of being loved back, you might want to think about the Pug.

Pyrenean Mountain Dog

Land of origin: Europe (Pyrenees Mountains)

Original purpose: Herding and guard work

Recent popularity ranking by K.C. registration: Moderate

HEIGHT: Dogs minimum 28 inches, bitches minimum 26 inches

WEIGHT: Dogs minimum 110 pounds, bitches minimum 90 pounds

COAT: Fine, heavy white undercoat; long, flat, thick outer coat with coarse hair. Straight or slightly wavy

COLOUR: All white or mainly white with badger, grey or tan markings

Amount of care coat requires: 1 2 3 4 5 6 7 8 9 10
                                         * * * * * * * *

Amount of exercise required: 1 2 3 4 5 6 7 8 9 10
                                         * * * * * * * *

Suitability for urban/flat life: Unsuited

The magnificent Pyrenean Mountain Dog is a breed of enormous antiquity. Of the mastiff group, he probably came to the Middle East thousands of years ago from central Asia. There his ancestors existed during the Bronze Age, almost four thousand years ago, and also around the Baltic and Black seas. Examples were carried across Europe and developed to the form we know today in the Pyrenees Mountains. Pyreneans have a long and noble history as guard-dogs, sheepdogs and bear- and wolf-fighters. They were favourites of the French court and other royal strongholds. There is a lot of history in this breed, and a lot of this breed in European history.

Pyreneans are giant dogs with more good qualities than we can catalogue. They are loyal unto death to their family; they will tackle anything that threatens them. They are very affectionate and responsive to human moods. They take to children naturally and are generally safe and reliable. They are incomparable baby-sitters. Gentle and considerate with strangers (although cautious at first), they are not usually quarrelsome. They get along with other animals and have to be driven into a fight. Once they are in combat, though, few animals can best them. In the Middle Ages they were really invincible.

Undeniably, Pyreneans are also among the handsomest of dogs. They are especially appealing as puppies, and once grown they move with enormous purpose and self-assurance. They do require exercise, and this must be kept in

Retriever (Chesapeake Bay)

Land of origin: United States

Original purpose: Water retrieving

Recent popularity ranking by K.C. registration: Rare

HEIGHT: Dogs to 26 inches, bitches to 24 inches

WEIGHT: Dogs to 75 pounds, bitches to 65 pounds

COAT: Thick and short, up to $1\frac{1}{2}$ inches long only, with a fine, dense and woolly undercoat. Coat is wavy in places but never curly

COLOUR: From dark brown to oatmeal. Solid colour preferred, but very small white spots on chest and/or toes allowed

Amount of care coat requires: 1 2 3 4 5 6 7 8 9 10
                                               *

Amount of exercise required: 1 2 3 4 5 6 7 8 9 10
                               * * * * * * * * * *

Suitability for urban/flat life: 1 2 3 4 5 6 7 8 9 10
                                   * *

The Chesapeake Bay Retriever is descended from two dogs rescued from a sinking British brig off the coast of Maryland in 1807. The dogs are believed to have been Newfoundland puppies named Sailor and Canton, and there are many guesses as to what was bred to these two dogs, or possibly to their offspring. Approximately eighty years later a definite type emerged – the dog we call today the Chesapeake Bay Retriever.

The Chesapeake is by all standards a superior dog. He is one of the greatest of all water retrievers and one of the hardiest. No weather will deter this dog from doing what he was born to do: go into the water and retrieve fallen game. Not only is he peerless with waterfowl, he is also a consummate companion.

The Chesapeake is a good watchdog and a responsive pet. He is fine when obedience-trained, since he is one of the most intelligent dogs and one of the most willing. Put him to any task and he will do it. Disposition is an extremely important factor in judging, for this is one breed of dog that is expected to be even-tempered, sensible and non-aggressive. Anything less than that is considered unworthy.

All of this is not to say that the Chesapeake is wishy-washy or without strong character. Just the opposite. This is a dog of great purpose and highly developed

skill. He is aloof to yapping nonsense, but gets on well with other animals who show an appropriate amount of respect.

The Chesapeake Bay Retriever, one of the few American breeds, has been used successfully as a guide-dog for the blind. He can survive in an apartment as long as he is surrounded by people who care about him and as long as he gets sufficient exercise. It is not fair nor is it even humane to have an active sporting dog like this living the life of a toy. The Chesapeake thrives on work, on being needed for a tough and demanding job. Above all, the Chesapeake wants and needs open water. If one of these splendid dogs is kept in the city, it should be by people who will exercise him every day and from time to time get him out to some river, lake or shoreline where he can retrieve sticks and display his real nature.

Retriever (Curly-coated)

Land of origin: England

Original purpose: Water retrieving

Recent popularity ranking by K.C. registration: Moderate

HEIGHT: To 27 inches

WEIGHT: To 80 pounds

COAT: Crisp curls all over the body, the tighter the better. Saddle or area of uncurled coat seriously faulted in judging

COLOUR: Black or liver; sparse white hairs on chest allowed

Amount of care coat requires: 1 2 3 4 5 6 7 8 9 10
                                 * * * *

Amount of exercise required: 1 2 3 4 5 6 7 8 9 10
                                 * * * * * * * * *

Suitability for urban/flat life: 1 2 3 4 5 6 7 8 9 10
                                 * * *

The arguments among dog people as to the real origin of the Curly-coated Retriever will go on as long as there are dog people to argue. It usually is stated that the breed comes down from the English Water Spaniel, popular in the 1500s. To that line is said to have been added a form of setting retriever. The Irish Water Spaniel is also said to be a foundation breed to which everything from Poodle to Newfoundland is supposed to have been added. However it may have come about, several hundred years ago the base was laid down, and by 1803 a breed could be described. Its first appearance in shows came in 1859.

The Curly-coated Retriever is a special-purpose dog with incredible stamina and skill. As a water retriever he is surpassed by few breeds, and is popular with duck hunters in Australia and New Zealand. Most people have never seen an example, and he can be confused with the Irish Water Spaniel by those who have seen only one or two of that breed. The Irish Water Spaniel has a distinctly rat-like tail, while the breed we're discussing has a tail covered with ringlets. Actually, there is little difference in popularity.

The Curly-coated Retriever is not really suited to flat or urban life. He is an action dog for foul weather and water. He needs and wants to swim. It is not easy to re-create those conditions in the living room. People who try to take this breed into a flat and reshape the dog will be dissatisfied. Walks along city

266

streets simply are not enough. The Curly-coated is a good companion for his owner and even for his family, but demands should not be made upon him by strangers. They should be quite satisfied with him when he is aloof.

Training should start early with this breed and continue over a long period of time. It is a serious matter for dog and master. This dog is clever, very clever, and will take over if allowed. Because he is a big animal, such assertiveness is intolerable, and snapping should be severely curtailed. Like many other really fine hunting breeds, the Curly-coated Retriever can be stubborn, or, rather, single-minded. Without that quality he would not be the great field performer he is.

Retriever (Flat-coated)

Land of origin: America/England

Original purpose: Water and upland retrieving

Recent popularity ranking by K.C. registration: Moderate

HEIGHT: N.S.G.

WEIGHT: 60 to 70 pounds

COAT: Dense, fine and flat

COLOUR: Black or liver

Amount of care coat requires:	1	2	3	4	5	6	7	8	9	10
	★	★	★							
Amount of exercise required:	1	2	3	4	5	6	7	8	9	10
	★	★	★	★	★	★	★	★	★	
Suitability for urban/flat life:	1	2	3	4	5	6	7	8	9	10
	★	★	★							

The Flat-coated Retriever is an exceptional dog, and is one of the few American breeds. He was derived from the Newfoundland and the Labrador Retriever. His main development, however, took place in England during the reign of Queen Victoria.

The solid, sturdy and well-muscled Flat-coated Retriever is a field-dog first and foremost, but he also can be an ideal family pet. Marvellous with children, he is loving and gentle with the whole family. He holds his peace with strangers, though he wants to know a lot about someone coming through the door before he offers friendship. Once one of these fine dogs does offer it, the arrangement is permanent. They are loyal and outgoing, stable and intelligent.

The Flat-coated Retriever lives for his master and takes training very well. He wants to learn and to please, and he loves being congratulated and rewarded. In this he is like a child, once his interest in a project is aroused. More cheerful than some of the other gun-dogs of his general size and configuration, he resembles the Golden Retriever and Labrador Retriever in his attitude towards human beings. Though not exactly a jolly clown, he is a pet and he does need attention.

A Flat-coated Retriever should be taken regularly to an open area where he can run and retrieve. He is particularly fond of water and should be allowed to swim – in any weather. His coat is easy to maintain, and he is easily kept.

Considering the popularity that the Golden and Labrador Retrievers enjoy, it just might be that the Flat-coated Retriever will have his day. The breed is now on the first rung of the popularity ladder. People wanting a dog of the retriever style, but also wanting something different, might think about starting the long, hard hunt to find a really good example of this rare breed. They could be getting in on the start of a whole new trend.

Retriever (Golden)

Land of origin: England

Original purpose: Water retrieving

Recent popularity ranking by K.C. registration: 4th

HEIGHT: Dogs to 24 inches, bitches to 22 inches

WEIGHT: Dogs to 80 pounds, bitches to 70 pounds

COAT: Dense and water-repellent. Good undercoat. Flat against body with some wave

COLOUR: Lustrous gold of different shades. Solid. No white markings allowed

Amount of care coat requires: 1 2 3 4 5 6 7 8 9 10
Amount of exercise required: 1 2 3 4 5 6 7 8 9 10
Suitability for urban/flat life: 1 2 3 4 5 6 7 8 9 10

It was in early nineteenth-century England that the retrievers first came into prominence. Four main types were developed almost simultaneously – the Curly-coated, the Flat-coated, the Labrador and the Golden. Setters, Water Spaniels and other sporting dogs were crossed with a light retrieving dog known as St John's Newfoundland to achieve these ends.

From the beginning the extraordinary qualities of the Golden Retriever were recognized. He is a truly superior hunting dog with a soft mouth and great intelligence. The Golden is hardy and can thrive in almost any weather. He will never shy from leaping into icy water to please his master and do the job he was bred to do. He is hurt and seemingly embarrassed when denied the opportunity to help, to carry, to bring you something in order to show his affection. His need to retrieve is legendary – he is never as happy as when he is fetching and carrying. The Golden is never mean or petty. He naturally loves children and other animals, cats and kittens included. He is loyal, almost unbelievably affectionate and so intelligent that he is becoming one of the most popular of all guide-dogs for the blind. All these qualities make him an ideal family dog and pet. The authors believe that the Golden Retriever comes very close to being the greatest of all breeds. Although other people may have different favourite breeds, almost no one has anything bad to say about this one.

The Golden Retriever is so much the perfect companion and family dog that there is very naturally a tendency to think of him as perfect for every set of circumstances. This is not quite true. The Golden Retriever is an outdoor animal, and although he will adapt to city life (he will adapt to *anything* as long as he has his family nearby), he requires exercise – lots and lots of exercise. No one should think of owning a Golden unless he is willing to walk the dog at least two hours every day, no matter what the weather. It isn't fair to treat this superb dog otherwise. He also should have frequent opportunities to retrieve, especially from water. He loves to swim all year round. Since retrievers are prone to a congenital malformation known as hip dysplasia, they should be obtained only from reputable breeders. Animals that show any signs of dysplasia should not be bred.

Retriever (Labrador)

Land of origin: Newfoundland and England

Original purpose: Water retrieving

Recent popularity ranking by K.C. registration: 3rd

HEIGHT: Dogs to $22\frac{1}{2}$ inches, bitches to 22 inches

WEIGHT: N.S.G.

COAT: Short, very dense and not wavy. Feels hard to the hand, and there are no feathers

COLOUR: All black, yellow or chocolate. Very small white spot on chest allowed. Eyes black to pale yellow; brown or hazel generally preferred

Amount of care coat requires:	1 ★	2 ★	3	4	5	6	7	8	9	10
Amount of exercise required:	1 ★	2 ★	3 ★	4 ★	5 ★	6 ★	7 ★	8 ★	9 ★	10 ★
Suitability for urban/flat life:	1 ★	2 ★	3 ★	4 ★	5 ★	6 ★	7 ★	8	9	10

It is no accident that the Labrador Retriever has become one of the most popular dogs, now consistently ranked among the top ten. He is a peerless pet as well as a superlative performer in the field, under the gun or in field trials. He can be used as a guide-dog for the blind or as a general watchdog. There are people who insist that the Labrador Retriever is the most even-tempered of all dog breeds.

The Labrador can be owned in almost any circumstances because he is so sensible, so steady and so adaptable. It is up to the owner, however, to be fair and give the dog a chance to be himself. There is no doubt that this splendid animal needs exercise, and it is unkind to keep one locked away all day and night without an opportunity to get out and go. It is also less than kind to maintain a Labrador in a city or a suburban house without a place to swim. Labradors were made for the water, and diving in after a stick is their greatest joy – whatever the weather. The coat does not require a lot of care, but daily brushing for a few minutes will help keep it glistening and healthy.

Labrador Retrievers are legendary with children as responsible baby-sitters and faithful guards. They are fine with strangers who do not appear dangerous to the household, and they are perfect with other animals.

Labradors will fight, of course, but only if pressed into it. They are never petty or mean, rarely sulky or moody. They are not always as demonstrative as Golden Retrievers, but their love of master, family and home is quite genuine. The very slight reserve does not suggest less love or less reliability. The Golden and Labrador Retrievers stand side by side as two of the most desirable dogs in the world.

Because 'Labs' are so popular, it is extremely important that they be obtained only from the best professional specialty breeders. There has been too much mass production, which is to be discouraged.

Because the Labrador Retriever can be trained to do anything, or *almost* anything, that any other dog can do, some have been trained as attack-dogs. This is nothing less than criminal, and a dog so trained should not be looked upon as a Labrador Retriever at all. He is no more reliable than any other potential killer. The prospective owner concerned about the safety of his or her home should not think an attack-trained Labrador is safer around a family than any other dog in that lamentable condition.

Rhodesian Ridgeback

Land of origin: Southern Africa

Original purpose: As combination hunting and guard watchdog

Recent popularity ranking by K.C. registration: Moderate

HEIGHT: Dogs to 27 inches, bitches to 26 inches

WEIGHT: Dogs to 80 pounds, bitches to 70 pounds

COAT: Short and dense, sleek and glossy. Should never be woolly or silky

COLOUR: Light to red wheaten. Small white markings permitted

Amount of care coat requires: 1 2 3 4 5 6 7 8 9 10
                                 *

Amount of exercise required: 1 2 3 4 5 6 7 8 9 10
                                * * * * *

Suitability for urban/flat life: 1 2 3 4 5 6 7 8 9 10
                                * * * *

This powerful guard- and hunting dog of southern Africa is a cross between a number of European breeds brought there by settlers and a native dog known to us only as the Hottentot dog. That native African animal, probably little more than half wild, had a strange ridge of hair on his back that grew backwards. Today's Rhodesian Ridgeback has inherited that unique characteristic, and hence the name.

The Rhodesian Ridgeback was bred to care for his master and his master's family. That meant standing off all comers, including armed human beings and predatory cats. The Ridgeback does not back down easily. He is reserved with strangers and usually will not give another dog a second look. Should a dog challenge the Ridgeback, however, that is something else again.

The Ridgeback can be a distinctly one-person animal, although certainly a gentleman with the rest of the family. He is a natural watchdog and can be extremely intimidating when suspicious. He takes any weather and can go for twenty-four hours without water. A combination of working and hunting dog, he will pull down fleet-footed game or flush birds, whichever is asked of him.

The Ridgeback tends to be hard-headed. He will accept a balance with his master, but however much he may love him, he still will try for the upper hand. Good, firm training starting early in puppyhood is required, and when it is accomplished, the reward is a good watchdog and family companion. This

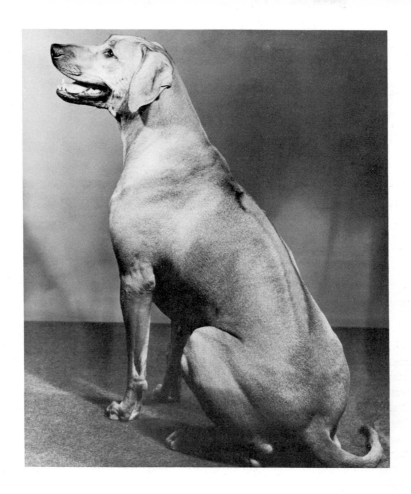

breed is too powerful, too bright and too active to be anything but totally obedient. A Ridgeback with bad manners is unthinkable around other people.

Some people do attempt to keep Rhodesian Ridgebacks as flat-living dogs: a bad idea except in the most unusual cases. A Ridgeback locked in a flat all day is unlikely to mature into the animal he was bred to be. In fact, some city-kept Ridgebacks become downright awkward and can be all but impossible to manage. Wherever the animal is raised, he should go to the best obedience class available with his master. Don't leave the training of one of these splendid animals to chance or 'instinct'. Every effort should be made to maintain quality of behaviour as well as form in this unique dog from Africa.

Rottweiler

Land of origin: Germany

Original purpose: Driving livestock, pulling carts, guard and police work

Recent popularity ranking by K.C. registration: 23rd

HEIGHT: Dogs to 27 inches, bitches to 25 inches

WEIGHT: N.S.G.

COAT: Short, coarse, flat. Undercoat does not show through

COLOUR: Black with tan to mahogany markings on cheeks, muzzle, chest, legs and over both eyes. Small white spot on chest or belly is allowed but not desired

Amount of care coat requires: 1 2 3 4 5 6 7 8 9 10

Amount of exercise required: 1 2 3 4 5 6 7 8 9 10

Suitability for urban/flat life: Unsuited

The Rottweiler has a noble and fascinating history. The ancestral form was carried through Alpine passes by Roman legions invading the centre of Europe. The dogs were used to drive the cattle needed to feed the troops in countries where raiding was not profitable. Some of these dogs were left behind in Rottweil in Württemberg in southern Germany. The breed hung on there into modern times, although it was virtually extinct around the turn of the century. The rebuilding of the breed began about 1910.

The Rottweiler has been used with great success as a drover, guard, beast of burden and police dog. He is highly intelligent and very willing, and he accepts virtually any training. Despite the hard usage to which the breed has been put throughout history, the Rottweiler today is affectionate, alert, and very good with his family. He is a natural watchdog and will be very cautious with strangers; with members of his family he tends to be a gentle, easy-going animal not given to temper or hysteria. He will tolerate other animals if they are raised with him and if he is made to understand that they are his master's property.

The Rottweiler is a rugged dog with stamina and a very purposeful approach to life. He is a serious animal and goes about things in an intelligent, deliberate manner. Training should start early and continue, for the breed's capacity to learn is apparently without limit.

Some people do keep Rottweilers in small suburban houses, and they will do well enough under those conditions if close to their family and if given plenty of exercise. They are better on a farm or large estate, though, for they are hard, outdoor animals. Exercise, wherever they live, is necessary for their good health. Too much confinement can make them tense and alter their disposition.

Some so-called 'trainers' have been turning out so-called guard- and attack-trained dogs, using the Rottweiler along with other large working breeds. These animals are to be avoided as they are potentially extremely dangerous.

Saint Bernard

Land of origin: Switzerland

Original purpose: Unknown – later, patrol and rescue work

Recent popularity ranking by K.C. registration: Moderate

HEIGHT: N.S.G.

WEIGHT: N.S.G.

COAT:
Short-haired – very dense, close-lying, smooth, tough, but not rough to touch
Long-haired – medium length, can be slightly wavy, not rolled, curled or shaggy

COLOUR: White with red or red with white, various shades; brindle with white markings. Brown-yellow equal value to shades of red. Faces desirable dark. Never without white; solid and other colours faulty

Amount of care coat requires:

Short-haired:	1	2	3	4	5	6	7	8	9	10
	★									
Long-haired:	1	2	3	4	5	6	7	8	9	10
		★	★	★	★	★	★			
Amount of exercise required:	1	2	3	4	5	6	7	8	9	10
		★	★	★	★	★				
Suitability for urban/flat life:	1	2	3	4	5	6	7	8	9	10
	★	★	★							

The Saint Bernard has a long and romantic history. Sometime after 1550, large working dogs were brought up to a monastery in the high Saint Bernard Pass in the Swiss Alps from the towns and villages below. They may have been obtained by the monks as companions or as watchdogs. The records have been lost that might reveal dates and reasons. We do not know the history of the breed before that, although it is often suggested that they were descended from the great Molossian dog from ancient Epirus (Greece), which in turn may have been descended from giant Asian breeds of the mastiff type. The dog imported by the monks, or rather brought up into the mountains, may have been the Talhund. All of this will probably forever remain theory and conjecture.

In time the dogs (not named Saint Bernard until the 1880s) came to do patrol work with the monks. They were used for testing trails and are said to have been able to predict storms and avalanches. They eventually were used to sniff out lost travellers. So much romantic literature was built on these stories that truth and fiction are difficult, if not impossible, to separate.

The Saint Bernard is a massive dog of enormous strength. He is traditionally calm and sensible and a fine pet in homes where there is plenty of room. But he is too large for confined quarters; he should get a great deal of exercise if his condition is to be maintained. Typical of large dogs, he is not very long-lived, and he appears far too often with hip deformities due to the careless breeding and mass-production engendered by his popularity.

In recent years the press has reported Saint Bernards turning sour and attacking people. This is so contrary to the character of this breed that it must again be laid at the feet of bad breeding and greed. The breed has been subjected to great cruelty, and there are very bad and even dangerous examples around.

Only the very finest specialty breeders should be trusted to supply a dog who can truly reflect the intelligent, quiet, sensible and affectionate nature of this superior breed. And potential owners should not allow themselves to be mesmerized by the 'cuteness' of a Saint Bernard puppy. That puppy very quickly becomes an absolute giant of a dog.

Saluki (Gazelle) Hound

Land of origin: Middle East

Original purpose: Coursing

Recent popularity ranking by K.C. registration: Moderate

HEIGHT: Dogs to 28 inches, bitches to 26 inches

WEIGHT: N.S.G.

COAT: Smooth, soft, silky, with slight feathers on the legs, at the back of the thighs and on the ears

COLOUR: White, cream, fawn, golden, red, grizzle, and tan, tri-colour (white, black and tan), black and tan

Amount of care coat requires:	1	2	3	4	5	6	7	8	9	10
	★	★	★							

Amount of exercise required:	1	2	3	4	5	6	7	8	9	10
	★	★	★	★	★	★	★	★	★	★

Suitability for urban/flat life:	1	2	3	4	5	6	7	8	9	10
	★	★	★							

The exotic Saluki may be the oldest breed of pure-bred dog in the world. Some people insist he is the dog the Sumerians knew and used almost seven thousand years before Christ – which would make him almost nine thousand years old. Whether or not he originated in ancient Sumer, the Saluki spread throughout the Middle East and parts of Asia. Before the birth of Western civilization the breed was already known as a coursing hound.

He is an incredibly fast dog, once used on gazelle and later on smaller game. He is also a dog of great stamina and endurance – no weather is too harsh and no terrain too rough. Like most coursing hounds, he has a so-so nose (at least that is the reputation most often heard) but fine eyesight and almost unbelievable speed. Owners should keep in mind that, being a coursing dog, he will worry wildlife and small domestic animals if not supervised. A bolting rabbit cannot be resisted and neither, on occasion, can a cat.

The Saluki never fails to attract attention, in the show-ring or on the end of a lead. He looks the part of the exotic hound, and his grace and free-flowing movement are distinctive and most attractive.

Although not demonstrative, the Saluki is a loyal friend who likes to work with and please his master. He is good with family, although small children and Salukis don't always make the happiest combination. Because there is a

certain flare, there is also a flashpoint. Children must be taught how to behave around dogs like Salukis, and Salukis must be taught how to behave around children.

The Saluki is headstrong, like any hound who has had his own head for thousands of years, so any new owner should make his position of command clear. The Saluki needs a reasonable amount of obedience-training. No one wants such a good-looking dog with that kind of venerable background rolling over and playing dead or begging, but neither does one want a Saluki who bursts through doors and breaks loose into heavy traffic.

It is questionable whether Salukis can ever get enough exercise living in an urban setting. Because of their high style and elegance, some people do keep them in the city, but they should be walked great distances and be taken regularly to a place where they can really let go.

Exotic, expensive, and very handsome, the Saluki is a special dog for special owners.

281

Samoyed

Land of origin: Siberia

Original purpose: Protection, herding reindeer, pulling sleds

Recent popularity ranking by K.C. registration: Moderate

HEIGHT: Dogs to 22 inches, bitches to 20 inches

WEIGHT: N.S.G.

COAT: Double. Undercoat soft, short, thick and very dense. Outer coat long, harsh, straight from body without curl. Should glisten

COLOUR: Pure white, white and biscuit, cream, and all biscuit. No other colours allowed at all

Amount of care coat requires: 1 2 3 4 5 6 7 8 9 10
                                 * * * * * * *

Amount of exercise required: 1 2 3 4 5 6 7 8 9 10
                                 * * * * * * * * * *

Suitability for urban/flat life: 1 2 3 4 5 6 7 8 9 10
                                 * * * *

The magnificent Samoyed is an extremely ancient dog whose true origins are lost in the mists of the Arctic. Apparently, for thousands of years he has been the companion of the Samoyed peoples, who have roamed the northern reaches of Asian Russia. A dog of the tundra, he is hardy and durable and extremely useful in many ways.

No one is sure how the Samoyed was first used. He was utilized variously to herd reindeer and to guard the flocks and herds against wolves, bears, perhaps even tigers. He was used to guard the wandering nomads too, and later the villages and other permanent settlements. He has been used right up to the present time for pulling sleds, and indeed there has not been a major Arctic or Antarctic expedition utilizing sled-dogs that hasn't had the Samoyed out in front with the best of them. The Samoyed, naturally a jolly animal, puts himself into the sled game as readily as he does any other. More than anything else, he wants to be part of the action whatever the cost in exertion or even danger to himself.

Several characteristics distinguish this truly splendid breed. He is an extremely intelligent dog, perhaps the most intelligent of all sled-dogs. He is beautiful – some people say the single most beautiful of all dogs, although we

would have to view that as subjective. No one, though, can deny the pure splendour of a Samoyed in fine coat.

The great Samoyed by his very nature gets on well with people and other animals. He is a natural with children and is rarely mean or nasty. The standard called for in the Kennel Club breed standard seems to say it all. Under disposition it says: 'Intelligent, alert, full of action, affectionate. Unprovoked aggressiveness to be severely penalized'.

Despite the fact that the Samoyed is a northern dog and is happiest in cold climates, and even though he is a very active dog, he can survive in a flat with a properly loving family. He should be exercised a great deal and especially when the weather is harsh. It is never too cold for a Samoyed, and there is never enough running and ploughing through snow. The coat, of course, is the breed's crowning glory and must be seen to. Brushing, dry cleaning and only occasional bathing are the techniques whereby a Samoyed maintains his position at the top level of canine splendour.

Schipperke

Land of origin: Flemish Belgium

Original purpose: Barge guard

Recent popularity ranking by K.C. registration: Moderate

HEIGHT: N.S.G.

WEIGHT: To 16 pounds

COAT: Abundant, longer on neck, forming ruff or cape. Undercoat short and dense. Outer coat somewhat harsh to touch

COLOUR: Solid black only

Amount of care coat requires: 1 2 3 4 5 6 7 8 9 10
                            * *

Amount of exercise required: 1 2 3 4 5 6 7 8 9 10
                  * * * * * * *

Suitability for urban/flat life: 1 2 3 4 5 6 7 8 9 10
                  * * * * * * * * *

The Schipperke, a dog from the Flemish areas of Belgium and to some extent northern France, is not of Spitz derivation, although this has been suggested. He is bred down from the Belgian Sheepdog and is a version of the sheepdog known as the Leauvenaar. The name Schipperke (pronounced 'skip-er-key') is Flemish for 'little captain' and refers to his use as a watchdog on barges that plied the rivers and canals of northern Europe.

Generally an outstanding pet, the Schipperke is a born watchdog. Though not argumentative or snappy, he is very curious about everything that is going on around him. He checks out things and people and will be quick to let you know if he finds anything amiss. He is a vivacious dog, intelligent, loyal and very responsive to his own family and their likes and needs. He has one outstanding specialty, though: children. He is naturally drawn to them and watches them constantly. He is not only their companion but also their guardian. His small size makes him an ideal house pet.

The bobbed tail and foxy face of this lively little outdoor dog is most distinctive, and the breed just can't be confused with any other. He does well on the farm, where he makes a good ratter, and he has been used to hunt small game; he will be equally fine in the suburbs and the city. In a flat there is an obligation to provide exercise. The Schipperke needs walks several times a day, and in the country a good romp is deeply appreciated.

The Schipperke's coat is deep and sheds water. It will take any weather and does shed out in the summer. It is easy to care for, and a good brushing a couple of times a week will keep it in order.

The Schipperke, while never a fad dog in this country, has a devoted following. People who get to know the many fine qualities of this breed tend to stick with it. It is a long-lived breed, and more than a few individual dogs have been known to reach seventeen or eighteen years. Schipperkes are strong, durable, healthy and easy to keep.

Schnauzer

Land of origin: Germany

Original purpose: As companion, ratter, hunter, guard and herder

Recent popularity ranking by K.C. registration: Moderate

HEIGHT: Dogs to 19 inches, bitches to 18 inches

WEIGHT: N.S.G.

COAT: Tight, hard, wiry and thick. Soft, close undercoat and harsh outer coat

COLOUR: Pepper and salt or pure black. Many shades of pepper and salt from dark iron to silvery highlights. Black as strong as possible. Black rarer in this country

Amount of care coat requires:	1	2	3	4	5	6	7	8	9	10
	*	*	*	*	*					

Amount of exercise required:	1	2	3	4	5	6	7	8	9	10
	*	*	*	*	*	*	*	*	*	*

Suitability for urban/flat life:	1	2	3	4	5	6	7	8	9	10
	*	*	*	*						

The Schnauzer is known in this country in three sizes – the Giant, the 'Standard', and the Miniature – and each is considered a separate breed. They are all shown in the same group (Utility). Of the three breeds, the Miniature is by far the most popular.

The Schnauzer has long been known in Germany and was painted by Dürer, Cranach, Reynolds and many other artists, usually as part of a noble portrait. They were companion animals as well as ratters, hunters, guards, retrievers – almost anything a dog could be called upon to do. They are among the most intelligent of all dogs, and this has apparently always been the case.

It is believed that the Schnauzer originated from crosses of a black German Poodle and a grey Spitz-type dog. The original stock may have been Pinscher with these other types crossed in. The breed is old enough for these facts to be indeterminable.

Standard Schnauzers are solid, square, highly active animals with great affinity for human beings and human activities. As house pets they are participators. They make the best of all possible worlds out of every situation and have the ability to endear themselves and attract attention. They love to play and they love to work, and they enter into everything with boundless enthusiasm. They are rugged and tough and will take on all comers. They are excellent watchdogs although not overly suspicious.

Standard Schnauzer

Their fine form must be seen to at least twice a year by someone with professional grooming skills, but their day-to-day care is not oppressive. They are, as they say in the horse world, easy keepers.

Standard Schnauzers are fine house dogs and can be kept in a flat if given plenty of exercise. They are so fast and so quickly caught up by an idea that care must be taken to keep them on a lead anywhere near traffic. They are, none the less, eminently trainable in all things appropriate to the companion dog. Early and intensive obedience-training is necessary.

Scottish Terrier
(ABERDEEN TERRIER)

Land of origin: Scotland

Original purpose: Sporting after small game

Recent popularity ranking by K.C. registration: 39th

HEIGHT: To 11 inches

WEIGHT: To 23 pounds

COAT: Rather short (about 2 inches) – dense undercoat with very hard outer coat. Should be *very* wiry to the touch

COLOUR: Steel or iron grey, brindled or grizzled, black, wheaten or sandy. White markings not desired, but *small* amount on chest allowed

Amount of care coat requires:	1	2	3	4	5	6	7	8	9	10
	★	★	★	★	★	★	★			

Amount of exercise required:	1	2	3	4	5	6	7	8	9	10
	★	★	★	★	★					

Suitability for urban/flat life:	1	2	3	4	5	6	7	8	9	10
	★	★	★	★	★	★	★	★	★	★

The arguments are endless over the origins of this rather old Scottish breed. Some say the Scottish Terrier is the original Skye Terrier, who is not to be confused with the dog we know by that name today. Other historians have different ideas. In fact, the details of the Scottie's evolution in the Highlands are uncertain, for records were seldom kept. We do know the breed comes from the Highlands; it is respectably old and has long been highly regarded.

The Scottish Terrier, or, as it is commonly addressed, the 'Scottie', is a game, close-to-the-ground, working terrier who must have been a holy terror on vermin. He is, like all dogs of this line, without a semblance of fear. He is also hardy and will take any terrain, any weather and any number of hours afield. He will back away from nothing as long as he can still draw a breath.

The Scottie is a dour character, as befits his origin, and takes loyalty to his master and mistress seriously. If they have children, he will behave well as long as he is raised with them. He is very slow to accept strangers at all, much less take up with them, and he is never happier than when he is alone with his own family. The rest of the world, man and animal alike, could vanish, and the Scottie wouldn't care a bit. Some people find this aloofness (for that is the best

description) one of the Scottish Terrier's most attractive characteristics, and indeed it does make one respect the breed.

The Scottie should be trained early and well. Because he can threaten strangers and can be a scrapper, the Scottie should learn how to obey instantly. Strangers should be advised to give the dog time and let him make the overtures.

Young Scotties are extremely appealing and very demonstrative. Few breeds have more charming youngsters. That jumping and licking display tends to disappear in the adults, and one should not be misled. The adult Scottie is a square, solid, determined and intelligent dog; he remains reserved except with those he really knows and loves. Because the puppies are so very appealing, prospective buyers should be careful to know the line well. Charming puppies do not always turn out to be splendid dogs.

Sealyham Terrier

Land of origin: Wales

Original purpose: Gaming and hunting vermin

Recent popularity ranking by K.C. registration: Moderate

HEIGHT: To 12 inches

WEIGHT: Dogs to 20 pounds, bitches to 18 pounds

COAT: Soft, dense undercoat and wiry outer coat. Never silky or curly

COLOUR: All white. Lemon, tan or pale badger markings allowed on head and ears

Amount of care coat requires: 1 2 3 4 5 6 7 8 9 10
                                     * * * * * *

Amount of exercise required: 1 2 3 4 5 6 7 8 9 10
                                     * * * * *

Suitability for urban/flat life: 1 2 3 4 5 6 7 8 9 10
                                     * * * * * * * * * *

The Sealyham was developed between 1850 and 1890 in Haverfordwest, Wales. The breed's benefactor – really its designer – was Captain John Edwardes. The ancestral stock used by Captain Edwardes is not known. After the Sealyham's first show appearance in 1903, it caught on. By 1908 a club had been formed in Wales to further interest in the breed. Although it has never been a terribly popular dog, it has been admired, and some fine specimens have appeared.

The K.C. standards sum up the breed well: 'Alert and fearless but of friendly disposition'.

Like most terriers, perhaps all, the Sealyham is a natural watchdog, and a stranger is unlikely to approach unannounced. Extremely loyal to his family, the Sealyham is likely to be cautious with strangers, animals included. He is fast, tough, determined and hardy. He needs exercise and loves a good romp. He has a proud carriage and looks just splendid ploughing on ahead at the bottom end of a leash. The Sealyham does not shed much and makes an almost ideal house and flat dog. However, his coat needs care, and the dog looks fine only when properly groomed. The Sealyham is easily trained, although if he detects weakness he will play up to it and be stubborn. He recognizes a master once his worth is demonstrated.

With our enormous urban population and the desire of people in flats for watchdogs who are also trouble-free pets, it is predictable that the Sealyham

will continue to grow in popularity. His character and qualities are so ideally suited to the urban life-style that he will surely take off and move up on the charts. People thinking seriously of this dog, however, should remember his need for plenty of exercise. The occasional visit to the country will be appreciated.

Shar-Pei

(CHINESE FIGHTING DOG)

Land of origin: China

Original purpose: Hunting, herding, fighting, food

Recent popularity ranking by K.C. registration: Rare (world's rarest breed)

HEIGHT: To 20 inches

WEIGHT: To 50 pounds

COAT: Ultra-short

COLOUR: N.S.G.

Amount of care coat requires: 1 2 3 4 5 6 7 8 9 10

Amount of exercise required: 1 2 3 4 5 6 7 8 9 10

Suitability for urban/flat life: 1 2 3 4 5 6 7 8 9 10

This most interesting and ancient breed dates from the Han Dynasty in China, and only one or two are in Great Britain. At the time of writing, the Kennel Club is considering whether this breed is to be registrable; no decision has yet been reached. The breed is highly intelligent (successful in U.S.A. obedience trials) and these animals are said to make good, affectionate family dogs while remaining sound guard-dogs. The skin appears outsized – like a Bloodhound – and forms wrinkles over the head and entire body. This gives rise to fears that the Shar-Pei may be prone to skin ailments; as a breed, they are susceptible to entropion (inturned eyelids). The bitches are said to have irregular and untypical seasons, in that they do not attract 'non-Shar-Pei' dogs and only 'some' of their own breed. This may well explain their reputation as difficult breeders.

The Shar-Pei, though described as a breed developed for dog-fighting, makes an amiable companion. Originally a general-purpose working dog, most of the Chinese stock were probably eaten, following the swingeing increase in dog tax levied by the authorities after the Chinese Cultural Revolution in 1947. Hopefully, breeding in Canada, America and eventually Britain will ensure the survival of a breed snatched from the jaws of extinction.

Shetland Sheepdog

Land of origin: Scotland and Shetland Islands

Original purpose: Shepherding and as watchdog

Recent popularity ranking by K.C. registration: 10th

HEIGHT: Dogs to 14½ inches, bitches to 14 inches

WEIGHT: N.S.G.

COAT: Double – outer coat is long, straight and harsh; undercoat is short, furry and very dense. Hair on face, feet and ear tips smooth. Mane and frill abundant and impressive

COLOUR: Black, blue merle and sable ranging from golden through mahogany. White or tan markings. More than 50 per cent white disqualifies. Brindle also not allowed

Amount of care coat requires: 1 2 3 4 5 6 7 8 9 10
                                                * * * * * * *

Amount of exercise required: 1 2 3 4 5 6 7 8 9 10
                                                * * * * * * * *

Suitability for urban/flat life: 1 2 3 4 5 6 7 8 9 10
                                                * * * * * * * * *

The Shetland Sheepdog, or 'Sheltie', is more than a very small Collie, although the two breeds have some ancestry in common and do resemble each other in conformation. The Sheltie has qualities of his own and very great charm. The ancestral stock carried to the islands from mainland Scotland was the Hill Collie, a smaller animal than the one we know as the Collie today. Various small breeds were crossed in over the years, including some Spaniels and a small herding dog from Iceland. Eventually Collies were used again to give the dog a final shape and proper coat. There has been more than a little controversy as to what this breed should look like and how big it should be.

The Shetland Sheepdog, despite his diminutive size, is a clever working animal and was, and would be again, good with sheep. He also works well with pigs and goats. He is fast and alert and responds well to training. He is responsive to human moods and demands and always strives to fit himself in. He was used at the outset as a watchdog, and that is a quality he has not lost. A Shetland today, reserved with strangers but not snappy, is a dog who can be depended upon to give the alarm. He has a loud and insistent bark. Some Shetlands, in fact, tend to overdo it!

The Shetland Sheepdog requires grooming; that resplendent dog we see in the show-ring will not be apparent in the casual owner's living room unless he is brushed regularly and kept in fine trim. It is not a hard job or a long one, since this is a small and obedient dog, but it is a job that should be seen to every day. The Shetland also requires exercise. He is a delightful flat dog, fine with children, small, neat and easily trained, but he has descended from working dogs of harsh country and harsh weather, and that part of him must be seen to as well. Long daily walks are in order and, whenever possible, good country romps.

The superior little Shetland Sheepdog can live anywhere as long as he has love and a reasonable amount of attention. He should be trained early and well – something he naturally loves anyway – and taught not to be unnecessarily yappy. A good watchdog is one thing, a noisy nuisance is another. Beware of the mass-production breeders, for the Shetland Sheepdog is one of the most popular breeds in the country, and terrible examples abound. Seek sound advice and do your homework if you intend to add a Shetland Sheepdog to your family. Avoid obviously shy specimens. That can mean poor breeding or bad early handling.

Shih Tzu

(CHRYSANTHEMUM DOG)

Land of origin: China since the seventh century; unknown before that

Original purpose: Companionship

Recent popularity ranking by K.C. registration: 24th

HEIGHT: To 10½ inches

WEIGHT: To 18 pounds

COAT: Luxurious, long and dense. May be slightly wavy but never curly. Woolly undercoat

COLOUR: All colours allowed

Amount of care coat requires:	1	2	3	4	5	6	7	8	9	10
		*	*	*	*	*	*	*	*	
Amount of exercise required:	1	2	3	4	5	6	7	8	9	10
	*	*								
Suitability for urban/flat life:	1	2	3	4	5	6	7	8	9	10
	*	*	*	*	*	*	*	*		*

The Shih Tzu (pronounced 'sheed-zoo') is a legendary creature who also just happens to exist as a flesh-and-blood companion animal in our own time. We do not know where he came from originally, although the Byzantine Empire, Tibet and other areas of Asia and the Middle East have been proposed. What we do know is that by the seventh century A.D. the breed was the rage in the royal courts of China. The breed does have the typical Asian dog pushed face and curled tail, but it is clear that his true origins will never be known, so the legends do nicely and add to the character of the beast.

The Shih Tzu was probably always bred for exactly what he is used for today: companionship. It is unlikely that he was ever a guard-dog or a hunting animal, although he most likely was once a little larger than his present nine to eighteen pounds. His popularity as a companion of kings and queens a thousand years ago is easy to understand when you get to know a few good examples of the breed today.

The Shih Tzu, whose name means 'lion' in Chinese, is a perfect companion animal for the city-dweller who enjoys having something to fuss over. A sprightly little character with great charm and personality, the little chrysanthemum-faced dog prefers the quiet dignity of a well-appointed flat to

the longest dog run in the world. If you gave an adult Shih Tzu an entire national park for a playground, he wouldn't use an acre. For the Shih Tzu, home is where his human family is and where the goodies, the comfort and the security he demands are.

Enormously appealing to fanciers of the toy breeds, the Shih Tzu has been known here only since 1908.

The Shih Tzu, needless to say, has a coat that demands attention. This is a dog to cherish and fuss over and enjoy for his great charm, his unfaltering loyalty, his beauty and his exotic and romantic past.

Siberian Husky

Land of origin: North-east Asia

Original purpose: Pulling sleds

Recent popularity ranking by K.C. registration: Moderate

HEIGHT: Dogs to 23½ inches, bitches to 22 inches

WEIGHT: Dogs to 60 pounds, bitches to 50 pounds

COAT: Double, and medium in length. Generally smooth-lying and not harsh to the touch. Not to be trimmed or clipped. Undercoat sheds out in summer

COLOUR: All colours are allowed, from black to white. Interesting and very handsome face markings are usual. Eyes may be brown or blue or even one of each

Amount of care coat requires: 1 2 3 4 5 6 7 8 9 10
Amount of exercise required: 1 2 3 4 5 6 7 8 9 10
Suitability for urban/flat life: 1 2 3 4 5 6 7 8 9 10

The Husky is a striking dog – handsome and solid – and a devoted pet. He is naturally friendly and usually does not make the best watchdog despite his fine size and 'wolf-like' appearance.

The Husky is seldom quarrelsome with people and is usually very good with other animals in the family. He can return to being a hunter, and some will take to molesting stock. This can be a difficult habit to break; it is obviously most undesirable.

The Husky is not the easiest dog in the world to train, and anyone contemplating this active, outdoor breed should plan on intensive obedience-training. It is particularly important that a Husky be taught to come when called. They are often tramps at heart and will look at their owner beguilingly and then take off with tail held high while the owner fumes and rages helplessly. It is not wise to allow Huskies to roam, any more than it is any other dog, for it is then that they get into trouble.

Huskies are so intent on human companionship and so openly affectionate that many people have taken to keeping them in flats and small, restrictive suburban homes. Locked up alone during the day, a Husky can become destructive. He isn't by nature that kind of dog, and although human relationships are more important to a Husky than anything else, he is better off

in cooler climates and in open country – after he has had intensive obedience-training. From the very beginning the Husky will try to test the pecking order, and if an owner is indecisive or unassertive, the Husky will be very pleased to be on top. From there on, it is straight downhill until the dog is a first-rate nuisance to everyone.

Huskies are excellent family dogs and generally fine with children. Most Huskies love snow and harsh weather, but, believe it or not, there are individual animals who hate to get their feet wet or spend much time in the snow (it is not hard to tell how many generations *that* strain has been out of Siberia). But for the typical Husky there is no temperature that is too low. He can tolerate anything from the Arctic to the Antarctic.

In the spring it is wise to have as much of the Husky's undercoat pulled as possible. It will come away by the handful. The shedding is constant until that coat is gone.

The Husky is to be recommended only to the owner or family that will work with their dog, teach and maintain his manners, and keep the animal from wandering too far afield. A Husky is more than a casual pet. He may be enchanting, but he can also be a destructive pest. The difference lies more with the owner than with the dog.

Skye Terrier

Land of origin: Isle of Skye, Scotland

Original purpose: Sporting, hunting

Recent popularity ranking by K.C. registration: Moderate

HEIGHT: To 10 inches

WEIGHT: Dogs to 25 pounds, bitches to 23 pounds

COAT: Double – undercoat soft, woolly and short; outer coat hard, straight, flat and very long

COLOUR: Black, blue, grey (dark or light), silver platinum, cream or fawn

Amount of care coat requires: | 1* | 2* | 3* | 4* | 5* | 6* | 7* | 8* | 9 | 10 |
Amount of exercise required: | 1* | 2* | 3* | 4* | 5* | 6* | 7 | 8 | 9 | 10 |
Suitability for urban/flat life: | 1* | 2* | 3* | 4* | 5* | 6* | 7* | 8* | 9* | 10* |

The terriers generally are not particularly old, but the Skye goes back at least four hundred years, making him one of the oldest. He was the product of the rough, harsh islands off Scotland, particularly the Isle of Skye in the north-west, where he reached the form we know long, long ago.

By the middle 1500s the Skye was known in London, where he quickly became a favourite at court and, quite naturally, down through the ranks of nobility until even commoners recognized him as fashionable. For two hundred years at least, he ranked as a kind of king among terriers, but then newer breeds began to take over. Perhaps the short-haired terrier coat of the younger breeds was more attractive because it meant less work. Still, the Skye, less popular now than in the past, has his fanciers, and they are tenacious in their devotion.

The Skye Terrier was almost certainly developed to fight tough vermin and run them to ground. How much of that original purpose was based on necessity and how much on sport is hard to say, for man has always claimed much of his sport as necessary. However that may have been, the Skye was a tough roughneck of a go-to-ground dog, and that original terrier fire and determination is still in him.

The Skye's coat requires care, and anyone considering this handsome, stylish

dog should keep that in mind. They are not self-keepers; they need help to look their best.

The Skye Terrier is a devoted pet and needs a great deal of attention. Reassurance and the opportunity to interact with human family members must come frequently. An ignored Skye Terrier is an unhappy dog. Because of his devotion to family and his stylish appearance, the Skye is a fine city dog – but only if long walks are provided. That is a commitment the new Skye owner must make and keep.

Because he ranks rather far down in popularity, the Skye is generally available from only a few specialty breeders. That is a good thing, too, for this is a dog with a long history and a heritage worth preserving.

Sloughi

Land of origin: North Africa

Original purpose: Hunting

Recent popularity ranking by K.C. registration: Rare

HEIGHT: To 30 inches

WEIGHT: N.S.G.

COAT: Smooth, short hair

COLOUR: N.S.G.

Amount of care coat requires: 1 2 3 4 5 6 7 8 9 10
                               *

Amount of exercise required: 1 2 3 4 5 6 7 8 9 10
                              * * * * * * * * * *

Suitability for urban/flat life: Unsuited

This breed is extremely rare and looks like a smooth-coated Saluki, although it is heavier in build. Like the Saluki, it has the distinction of being the only other breed recognized by Arabs as pure-bred, and its name means 'The Aristocrat'.

It is well camouflaged for desert hunting, particularly in pursuit of the gazelle, and it is a variety of hound that hunts only by sight. It is an extremely fast and active dog which requires, therefore, a very great deal of exercise or a vast garden area. Although reputed to be a good family companion, it must, as with all hounds, be treated with some degree of caution unless it can be guaranteed to have adequate exercise.

The dog has characteristic black marks round its eyes.

Soft-coated Wheaten Terrier

Land of origin: Ireland

Original purpose: All-purpose farm work

Recent popularity ranking by K.C. registration: Moderate

HEIGHT: Dogs to 19 inches, bitches to 18 inches

WEIGHT: Dogs to 45 pounds, bitches to 40 pounds

COAT: Abundant, soft and wavy. Should appear natural and not overtrimmed or styled

COLOUR: Clear wheaten; may be shaded on ears and muzzle

Amount of care coat requires: 1 2 3 4 5 6 7 8 9 10
                                 * * * * *

Amount of exercise required: 1 2 3 4 5 6 7 8 9 10
                                 * * * * * * * * *

Suitability for urban/flat life: 1 2 3 4 5 6 7 8 9 10
                                 * * * * * * * * * *

The Soft-coated Wheaten Terrier has been known in Ireland for centuries. Here is a breed that is about to catch on.

No one knows the ancestry of this Irish farm terrier. He has just 'always been there'. He *may* be an ancestral form of the Kerry Blue Terrier, but that is not known for sure. Whether it is true that the dogs who swam ashore from the ill-fated Spanish Armada are part of this dog's past is not known either.

The Soft-coated Wheaten Terrier is an all-purpose farm-dog, a fine companion for children, and a first-rate watchdog. He is also adept at herding, hunting and chasing any vermin to ground and dispatching them. He is spry, resilient and intelligent. He will take any training and remember what he has been taught. He is willing, positive in his approach and extremely responsive to his master and his family.

Although the Soft-coated Wheaten Terrier is a good working dog, he is a flawless companion animal as well, and will settle down in the suburbs and city as long as his family is at hand. Wheatens should be exercised religiously so that they don't become hyperactive from confinement. They love to interact with other living things and should not be left for long periods of time without companionship, or else they will pine. Soft-coated Wheaten Terriers need to belong and to share.

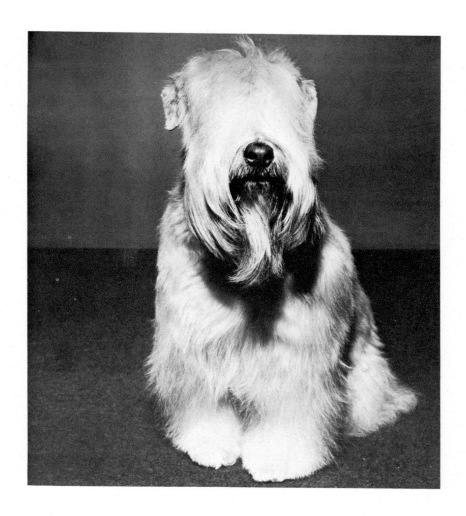

There should be nothing exaggerated about the Wheaten. His coat is a lovely shade of ripening wheat. It doesn't really settle down until the dog is almost two years old; then coat condition and colour are final. Extreme clipping and trimming spoil the look of the dog.

It is likely that the Soft-coated Wheaten Terrier will become popular in this country. When purchasing, care must be taken to find examples that properly represent the fine qualities of this dog; mass-production should not be encouraged.

Spaniel (American Cocker)

Land of origin: England

Original purpose: Hunting

Recent popularity ranking by K.C. registration: Moderate

HEIGHT: Dogs to 15 inches, bitches to 14 inches

WEIGHT: N.S.G.

COAT: Flat or slightly wavy but *never* curly. Silky in texture and of medium length. Good undercoating. Well feathered on ears, chest, abdomen and legs, but never to be excessive or deny sporting-dog character of breed

COLOUR: Black, white, tan, liver and other solids with white on chest only – no white is better on coloured dogs. Parti-colours definite and primary colour to be less than 90 per cent. Good distribution required. Tan markings must be less than 10 per cent

Amount of care coat requires: 1 2 3 4 5 6 7 8 9 10
   * * * *

Amount of exercise required: 1 2 3 4 5 6 7 8 9 10
   * * * * *

Suitability for urban/flat life: 1 2 3 4 5 6 7 8 9 10
   * * * * * * * * * *

The American Cocker Spaniel is not only one of the handsomest dogs ever bred, he also has a long record as a fine sporting animal. He is a true gentleman of the field. Without doubt this Cocker Spaniel comes down from a Spanish dog and has the same ancestry as the setters and larger spaniels of our time. Long ago, he was reduced in size, with one branch going off into the toy spaniels – strictly companion animals – and one branch developing towards the smallest of the true sporting dogs. The Cocker got his name from 'cocking' dog, being especially adept with woodcocks.

Over the years the great beauty of this little gem of a dog began taking precedence over his ability in the field. More and more he was bred for the bench, while his intelligence was ignored or subordinated. Breeders strove to outdo each other in the feathery glory of their champions. When several truly magnificent American Cockers began chalking up spectacular show careers, the fad was on, and everybody had to own one of these dogs. The mass-producers had their day, and the American Cocker Spaniel as a field-dog all but disappeared.

Through it all, however, much of the true character of the original Cocker Spaniel has remained. It wants only for enough breeders to show enthusiasm for this breed's intelligence. It will not necessarily require breeders to sacrifice much of the animal's admitted beauty to resume breeding for character, sense and intelligence.

Anyone availing themselves of a spaniel today is getting a dog not only of enormous style and class but also of noble field lineage. If they intend to breed, they are also investing in an opportunity to help reconstruct one of the truly great breeds. The true American Cocker Spaniel is a steady, even dog, affectionate and fine with children. He is also a dog who should be able to accept training. Unfortunately, there is a better than even chance that a careless buyer will get a snappy, yappy brat without the strength of canine character to do anything but pose, if that. The prospective owner should buy with care and only from breeders of reputation.

Spaniel (Clumber)

Land of origin: England and France

Original purpose: Flushing game and retrieving

Recent popularity ranking by K.C. registration: Moderate

HEIGHT: N.S.G.

WEIGHT: Dogs to 70 pounds, bitches to 60 pounds

COAT: Straight, silky, very dense, but not too long. Feathers long and abundant

COLOUR: Lemon and white or orange and white. Better if there are fewer markings on body. Ideal has lemon or orange ears, even head and face markings, and ticked legs

Amount of care coat requires: 1 2 3 4 5 6 7 8 9 10
                               * * * *

Amount of exercise required: 1 2 3 4 5 6 7 8 9 10
                               * * * * * *

Suitability for urban/flat life: 1 2 3 4 5 6 7 8 9 10
                                 * * * * * * *

One of the least spaniel-like of all spaniels, the Clumber has a mysterious background. The long, low and rather heavy-set body suggests Basset Hound blood (and many people insist this is true), and the heavy, Saint Bernard-like head suggests an old Alpine spaniel we no longer know. It is a matter that will never be resolved, as is true for many breeds. Animals were bred for a need of the time, and apparently no one felt that anyone in the future would be interested in how shapes and forms were arrived at.

The name of this breed is derived, it is believed, from Clumber Park, the seat of the Dukes of Newcastle in Nottingham. The records indicate that the Duc de Noailles sent several dogs over from France in the nineteenth century, dogs of a type he had been perfecting for years. No doubt they figured heavily in the development of the breed, so the listing of England as the home of the breed may be only partly true.

The Clumber is a large, slow and very deliberate worker in the field. He has enormous strength and is hardy enough to withstand almost any weather and almost any work regimen. He is a great retriever and very willing.

The Clumber is, or at least can be, devoted to his master, but once again we encounter a breed that may not be everybody's ideal pet. He prefers one master

and can be temperamental – some people even say sullen – when placed in a position of working with other people or animals. He is a highly polished professional at his work and goes about it in a stolid, purposeful, no-nonsense way. He does not readily express great joy and does not want to bother with anyone but his master – that is, after his master has established his right to that position. The Clumber should be trained early and well, and only then will that excellence in performance be evident.

People selecting a fine, steady field-dog without enormous social grace may want to consider this somewhat dour character. Those wanting the excitement of a canine friend and fellow socializer may find this breed less than ideal.

Spaniel (Cocker)

Land of origin: England

Original purpose: Hunting

Recent popularity ranking by K.C. registration: 6th

HEIGHT: Dogs to 16 inches, bitches to 15½ inches

WEIGHT: To 32 pounds

COAT: Medium length with good undercoating. Hair flat or slightly wavy and silky in texture. Well feathered but not too profuse

COLOUR: Broken and evenly distributed – white, roan, blue, liver-red, orange, lemon, black, tan and others; should be attractive in balance and placement

Amount of care coat requires:	1 2 3 4 5 6 7 8 9 10
	* * * * *
Amount of exercise required:	1 2 3 4 5 6 7 8 9 10
	* * * * * * *
Suitability for urban/flat life:	1 2 3 4 5 6 7 8 9 10
	* * * * * * * * * *

The English Cocker Spaniel is a perfectly splendid-looking dog with the same background as the American Cocker Spaniel. He is, though, a little larger. It wasn't until 1892 that the Kennel Club recognized that the English Cocker Spaniel and the English Springer Spaniel were different breeds. Up to that time they appeared in the same litter, separated only by size.

There is no doubt that the Sussex, Cocker, Field and Springer Spaniels have been closely associated and that all manner of interbreeding occurred even after they were acknowledged as different breeds and set upon their own courses of development. Interbreeding is no longer permitted. Fanciers of these handsome breeds feel each spaniel has its own character and desirable qualities.

The Cocker Spaniel is one of the finest of the small field-dogs and is both intelligent and responsive. If kept in the city or suburbs, he should be exercised regularly; the more often he is taken into the country, the better. His coat does need care, but it is not a long and arduous task if the dog receives proper attention. In show specimens we often see an exaggeration of the elaborate feathering on the legs and ears. This can be overdone, and the feathering should not be so profuse as to hide the true field-dog character of this breed.

Spaniel (English Springer)

Land of origin: England

Original purpose: Hunting

Recent popularity ranking by K.C. registration: 7th

HEIGHT: To 20 inches

WEIGHT: To 50 pounds

COAT: Flat or wavy, medium length. Waterproof, weatherproof and thornproof. Fine and glossy. Never rough or curly

COLOUR: Liver or black with white markings, liver or black and white with tan markings. No lemon, red or orange

Amount of care coat requires: 1 2 3 4 5 6 7 8 9 10
                                         * * * *

Amount of exercise required: 1 2 3 4 5 6 7 8 9 10
                                         * * * * * * *

Suitability for urban/flat life: 1 2 3 4 5 6 7 8 9 10
                                         * * * * * * * * * *

The English Springer Spaniel carries in him all the best qualities of the English land spaniels. As a breed, he was separated from the English Cocker Spaniel at the turn of the century and is considerably larger.

The English Springer by nature is affectionate and loyal. This is a wonderful breed for children. He may be slow to take up with strangers, but he is not snappy or silly about it. He just likes to be sure of his ground. He therefore can make a first-rate watchdog.

The English Springer Spaniel is still a splendid field-dog, although he will take well to a quieter and less active life. In city and suburban settings he should be given very long walks. It is a great kindness to get him out into the country as often as possible. He loves water and loves to retrieve. Most of all, he loves to belong to a family and will return affection pound for pound.

The Springer coat, like that of all spaniels, must be seen to if the dog is to remain handsome and regal. That does require some care, although the task need not be difficult. It is quite different, however, if a Springer is allowed to go long periods without attention. The feathering on the ears, chest and legs will become matted, and he becomes a case for a professional. Things should not be allowed to go that far.

The English Springer Spaniel is one of those dogs who is as nice in character as he looks. The standards call for him to be friendly, eager to please, quick to learn and willing to obey. One cannot ask for much more than that in a dog who already has refined beauty in his favour in addition to a fine tradition of service and companionship!

Spaniel (Field)

Land of origin: England

Original purpose: Hunting

Recent popularity ranking by K.C. registration: Moderate

HEIGHT: To 18 inches

WEIGHT: To 50 pounds

COAT: Flat or slightly wavy. Never curly. Dense, silky, glossy. Feathering setter-like

COLOUR: Usually black but also liver, golden liver, mahogany red, roan – or any of these with tan markings. Should not be so coloured and marked as to resemble a Springer Spaniel

Amount of care coat requires:	1	2	3	4	5	6 7 8 9 10			
	*	*	*	*	*				
Amount of exercise required:	1	2	3	4	5	6	7	8	9 10
	*	*	*	*	*	*	*	*	
Suitability for urban/flat life:	1	2	3	4	5	6	7	8	9 10
	*	*	*	*	*	*	*	*	

The Field Spaniel, probably the least-known spaniel in this country, was badly hurt by some rather bizarre breeding experiments that for a long time kept this dog from being as appealing as his spaniel kin. He is thought to have been derived from the Cocker and Sussex Spaniels, with the Cocker strain being largely Welsh. Much of that may be conjecture.

In an effort to improve the look of the breed, both Cocker and Springer Spaniels were bred in, and eventually the present-day Field Spaniel emerged.

By nature the Field Spaniel is steady and determined although essentially good-natured. He is not fast and flashy, but he is reliable. He will probably never be a popular gun-dog in this country but, if he does in fact become popular in the future, it will be as a pet.

The Field Spaniel is fine in the suburbs and even in flats if properly exercised – he is, after all, a sporting dog designed for the field – and his coat, although rather more setter-like than exaggerated as in some Cockers, does require a reasonable amount of attention. It is not the sort of task that need be oppressive, just acknowledged and taken care of regularly.

Anyone seriously interested in this potentially very fine breed of companion animal may want to think about importing specimens to combine with the

finest available examples here. It would be a kind of 'ground-floor' venture that could pay off in satisfaction not generally available from coming into a breed after it has already become a fad. The Field Spaniel may be a dog of the future.

Spaniel (Irish Water)

Land of origin: Ireland

Original purpose: Water retrieving and other hunting uses

Recent popularity ranking by K.C. registration: Moderate

HEIGHT: Dogs to 23 inches, bitches to 22 inches

WEIGHT: N.S.G.

COAT: Extremely important point. Dense, tight ringlets without any woolliness. Longer on legs, wavy and abundant

COLOUR: Solid liver. No white markings

Amount of care coat requires:	1	2	3	4	5	6	7	8	9	10
		*	*	*	*					

Amount of exercise required:	1	2	3	4	5	6	7	8	9	10
		*	*	*	*	*	*	*	*	*

Suitability for urban/flat life:	1	2	3	4	5	6	7	8	9	10
	*	*								

The Irish Water Spaniel is not everybody's dog. This is a special-purpose breed with excellent qualities and a superb record of performance. He is so ancient that we have no real information about his origin. He may go back six thousand years to Asia Minor; he may have inhabited the Iberian Peninsula when the Romans were there; and he may have arrived in Ireland with the earliest settlers of that land. All maybe, but we do know that he reached his present state of excellence in Ireland and that even Shakespeare wrote of his outstanding characteristics.

The excellence of this dog lies in his devotion to his master and his tolerance of his family. The Irish Water Spaniel is a great water-dog of endurance and skill. He is obedient if well trained early in life, and is a top-level performer in any field for which he is suited. He is not necessarily the best of general pets, since he is tricky with strangers. For that reason he makes a better watchdog than most sporting dogs, but he does have to be guided since his natural suspiciousness tends to be non-selective. He also must be well controlled when around other animals. He can be a scrapper.

None of this is to say that the Irish Water Spaniel is a vicious dog (that word does not properly apply to dogs unless they have been made that way by ill treatment or disease), but rather that he is an assertive, hard-headed animal

who is not approving of people he does not know well or see regularly. This can be a problem, particularly in an urban environment.

The distinctive ringleted coat of the Irish Water Spaniel does not require much heavy grooming unless it is badly neglected, and there's the rub. The coat does tend to mat and retain dirt unless it is brushed every three or four days at least. Although not a long or arduous process, it is an essential one that should always be performed.

The Irish Water Spaniel is a breed with staunch devotees. They like the look of the animal, including the distinctly rat-like tail; they like the purposeful gait and stance and fiery willingness of the animal to work, to perform, to please. This, the tallest of the spaniels, despite his somewhat clownish appearance, is a special dog for special owners. Casual dog-owners who are not accomplished at the art of being a master may be disappointed. Real dog people who are attracted to the dog for his antiquity, his skill in the field and his aloof independence will be delighted.

Spaniel (Sussex)

Land of origin: England

Original purpose: Hunting

Recent popularity ranking by K.C. registration: Moderate

HEIGHT: To 16 inches

WEIGHT: Dogs to 45 pounds, bitches to 40 pounds

COAT: Abundant and either flat or slightly waved. No curl allowed. Moderate feathering on legs and stern

COLOUR: Rich golden liver

Amount of care coat requires: 1 2 3 4 5 6 7 8 9 10
                         * * * * *

Amount of exercise required: 1 2 3 4 5 6 7 8 9 10
                         * * * * * *

Suitability for urban/flat life: 1 2 3 4 5 6 7 8 9 10
                         * * * * *

This breed apparently originated – or at least was perfected – in the county of Sussex. When it was developed, hunting was still done on foot, and there was plenty of game around. What was needed was a slow and steady dog who was at the same time companionable. These developments all took place in an area and a period of what was called rough shooting.

The Sussex Spaniel is a slow, not terribly elegant animal, who is intelligent and deliberate in everything he does. He has a massive appearance, although even a big male will be under fifty pounds. He makes a good pet and will do well in any normal family situation. He has not really caught on in this country because he is not stylish-looking enough to fascinate the show enthusiast, and he is really not well suited to modern hunting needs and habits.

Because he is slow and steady, neither mean nor silly, and because he is loyal and eminently trainable, the Sussex Spaniel holds real promise as a companion animal. It is a moot point as to whether the breed will ever be given an opportunity to show its worth. All it takes, really, is a few determined enthusiasts to take the breed on.

The Sussex Spaniel is a reasonably good watchdog; he is usually calm and gentle, and gets along well with other animals.

Anyone seriously interested in this breed will probably find it difficult to locate puppies for sale. Anyone looking for a cause as well as a pet might want

to think about this gentleman from Sussex. There is a lot of quality built into the breed, and a little public relations could launch it on a whole new and unexpected career.

Spaniel (Welsh Springer)

Land of origin: Wales

Original purpose: Hunting

Recent popularity ranking by K.C. registration: Moderate

HEIGHT: Dogs to 19 inches, bitches to 18 inches

WEIGHT: N.S.G.

COAT: Straight, flat, thick and silky. Not wiry or wavy; curliness considered especially bad

COLOUR: Red and white; colours clear, strong and rich

Amount of care coat requires:	1 2 3 4 5 6 7 8 9 10
	* * * * *
Amount of exercise required:	1 2 3 4 5 6 7 8 9 10
	* * * * * * *
Suitability for urban/flat life:	1 2 3 4 5 6 7 8 9 10
	* * * * * * * *

The Welsh Springer is not as well known in this country as its cousin the English Springer Spaniel. They are different breeds with very similar qualities. The Welsh Springer developed in Wales over six centuries ago and has always been quite distinctive. There are some major differences between the breeds, and the English is the larger dog.

The Welsh Springer Spaniel is a tireless hunting dog and is easily trained for a variety of tasks. The breed is intelligent, steady, and responsive to approval. It is as fine a companion as it is a hunting breed.

In the home the Welsh Springer shows his other and equally desirable side. He is sensible and steady and not quarrelsome or foolish. He loves to play and will be the wise old dog or the clown, depending on age and the demands of the moment. He loves to participate in all group activities and does not take well to being left behind. He is naturally good with children and will adjust to any reasonable family situation. He needs a lot of exercise, though, as might be expected of a sporting animal, and no one should attempt to maintain one in the suburbs or the city unless a good exercise regimen can be developed and adhered to. No weather is too tough for this Welshman, and he will not understand why you find any condition not perfect for a long walk or a romp. He needs that exercise not only for his peace of mind but also for body conditioning.

A certain amount of brushing is required if that fine and elegant spaniel look is to be maintained. It isn't much of a chore if it is performed faithfully as part of a regular weekly schedule.

Staffordshire Bull Terrier

Land of origin: England

Original purpose: Sport fighting, bull- and bear-baiting

Recent popularity ranking by K.C. registration: 15th

HEIGHT: To 16 inches

WEIGHT: Dogs to 38 pounds, bitches to 34 pounds

COAT: Smooth and short; close and not trimmed at all

COLOUR: Red, white, fawn, blue or black, or any of these colours with white. Any shade of brindle with or without white. Black and tan or liver not allowed

Amount of care coat requires: 1 2 3 4 5 6 7 8 9 10
                                             * *

Amount of exercise required: 1 2 3 4 5 6 7 8 9 10
                                           * * * * * * *

Suitability for urban/flat life: 1 2 3 4 5 6 7 8 9 10
                                           * * * * * * *

In the England of Elizabeth I, bear- and bull-baiting were major pastimes. Large mastiff-like dogs were developed for these brutal contests, and from them have descended a variety of smaller breeds. One of these is the Staffordshire Bull Terrier. He is descended from dogs known variously as Bulldog Terrier and Bull-and-Terrier, and he became known in time as the Old Pit Bull Terrier. He is probably ancestral to the English Bull Terrier we know today.

To say that the Staffordshire Bull Terrier has had all of his history bred out of him is wishful thinking. He is still a tough, tenacious and intelligent dog who will probably continue to be aggressive towards other animals for many generations to come. In fact, aggression may never be bred out of him.

The Staffordshire Bull Terrier has common ancestry with and was bred for the same purpose as other fighting dogs, but he has not been used for that purpose for some time. He is now a companion animal who shows great affection toward his human family. He is said by his fanciers to have special fondness for children.

Because he is a robust, if not large, and certainly a powerful and athletic dog, he should be exercised regularly and well. He will keep his condition and certainly be less tense if allowed to work off steam every day on a reliable schedule.

The Staffordshire Bull Terrier is an easy dog to maintain because he is short-coated and clean. His ferocious background has not made him untrustworthy with people, but he is a potential fighter, and therefore is a dog who should be leashed and controlled at all times.

Swedish Vallhund

Land of origin: Sweden

Original purpose: Herding

Recent popularity ranking by K.C. registration: Moderate

HEIGHT: Dogs to 13 inches, bitches to $12\frac{1}{4}$ inches

WEIGHT: To 28 pounds

COAT: Medium length, harsh and close; undercoat soft and woolly

COLOUR: Slate grey, grey-brown, grey-yellow, red-yellow, red-brown. Should have darker hairs on the back, neck and sides

Amount of care coat requires: 1 2 3 4 5 6 7 8 9 10

Amount of exercise required: 1 2 3 4 5 6 7 8 9 10

Suitability for urban/flat life: 1 2 3 4 5 6 7 8 9 10

The Vallhund is a magnificent little dog, still becoming popular in Great Britain. It is similar in appearance to the Corgi, but possibly has a more reliable temperament. The tail is docked. It may well be that the origin of this dog was the importation by the Vikings of Corgis to Sweden. As with Corgis, the original purpose seems to have been one of cattle-herding, but it is most adaptable from every point of view, and will cope with unlimited exercise as well as with rather restricted walks. It is a perky little dog, being intelligent and loyal and affectionate, and will make an impressive guard-dog for the home.

Swiss Laufhund

(SCHWEITZER LAUFHUND)

Land of origin: Originally Egypt/Greece; eventually Switzerland

Original purpose: Hare-hunting

Recent popularity ranking by K.C. registration: Rare

HEIGHT: To $17\frac{1}{2}$ inches

WEIGHT: N.S.G.

COAT: Short-coated

COLOUR: N.S.G.

Amount of care coat requires:	1*	2	3	4	5	6	7	8	9	10
Amount of exercise required:	1*	2*	3*	4*	5*	6*	7*	8*	9*	10*
Suitability for urban/flat life:	1*	2	3	4	5	6	7	8	9	10

This is a breed little known in the U.K. They are strong, but happy, friendly dogs which will bay when on a scent. They are particularly good trackers. As with all hounds, their tendency is to hunt in packs, either with their own kind or indeed with any canine varieties. Their very strong hunting instincts really preclude their suitability as house dogs, and they can only really be managed in outdoor kennels, especially if more than one is kept.

Another point to consider is their inclination to bay – for even kept out of doors in custom-built kennels the noise factor may result in complaints from neighbours and even a charge of nuisance in the local court. Furthermore, unless kept well under control when exercising, such dogs will regard as fair game any small animals, such as cats, pet rabbits and even smaller dogs, which they are likely to pursue, catch and kill, with resulting complaints and financial penalties from their justifiably aggrieved owners.

Tibetan Mastiff

Land of origin: Asia

Original purpose: Flock-guarding

Recent popularity ranking by K.C. registration: Rare

HEIGHT: Dogs to 27 inches, bitches to 24 inches

WEIGHT: N.S.G.

COAT: Long, dense coat

COLOUR: N.S.G.

Amount of care coat requires:	1*	2*	3*	4*	5*	6*	7*	8*	9* 10
Amount of exercise required:	1*	2*	3*	4*	5*	6	7	8	9 10
Suitability for urban/flat life:	1*	2*	3	4	5	6	7	8	9 10

The Tibetan Mastiff closely resembles the St Bernard. It is supposedly a reliable companion and guard-dog. However, its temperament may be regarded with a degree of concern. The Mastiff breeds are renowned for gentleness with their own families, but they are also daunting guard-animals who tend to be unselective in their aggression towards visitors, including youngsters. As a result, they can be a liability rather than a pleasure for all but a minority of households, and because of their vast size and weight can cause a lot of damage to any person falling foul of them.

As with many large dogs, the breed can be expected to show a number of orthopaedic problems, especially affecting the back and hind-legs, and particularly as they age. Also bear in mind the cost of feeding, for a dog of the Mastiff size can be expected to eat several pounds of food per day.

Tibetan Spaniel

Land of origin: Tibet

Original purpose: Companion dog

Recent popularity ranking by K.C. registration: Moderate

HEIGHT: To 10 inches

WEIGHT: To 15 pounds

COAT: Silky in texture, lying flat, feathers on ears, tail, forelegs and buttocks

COLOUR: All colours and mixtures permissible

Amount of care coat requires: 1 2 3 4 5 6 7 8 9 10
                   * * * * *

Amount of exercise required: 1 2 3 4 5 6 7 8 9 10
                   * *

Suitability for urban/flat life: 1 2 3 4 5 6 7 8 9 10
                   * * * * * * * * * *

The Tibetan Spaniel is an attractive small dog. It fits in well with many family patterns, and is mistaken by many for a Pekingese. It may well be slightly snappy with strangers or impulsive visitors, and may also be somewhat yappy.

It has been documented that the breed was at one stage supposed to turn the Tibetan prayer wheels in monasteries in bygone days, and the dog was introduced to the U.K. nearly eighty years ago. It is a close relation of the Lhasa Apso and Tibetan Terrier which, also being of Tibetan origin, would suggest some cross-breeding.

Tibetan Terrier

Land of origin: Tibet

Original purpose: Farm work

Recent popularity ranking by K.C. registration: Moderate

HEIGHT: To 16 inches

WEIGHT: N.S.G.

COAT: Double – undercoat is a fine wool; outer coat profuse and fine but not silky or woolly. Long and either straight or waved

COLOUR: Any colour, including white, or any combination of colours. Nose must be black

Amount of care coat requires: 1 2 3 4 5 6 7 8 9 10
                                  * * * * * * * *

Amount of exercise required: 1 2 3 4 5 6 7 8 9 10
                                 * * * * *

Suitability for urban/flat life: 1 2 3 4 5 6 7 8 9 10
                                * * * * * * * * * *

The Tibetan Terrier is another of those Asian breeds that come down to us from ancient times loaded with legend, romance and tradition. The Tibetan Terrier was said to have been bred exclusively by monks in a hidden valley and only given as gifts to honoured friends (usually visiting monks), never sold. Only males were ever given, and these sometimes were crossed with the so-called Tibetan Spaniels. The dog was slow in reaching the outside world, and is now attracting a great deal of attention.

The Tibetan Terrier is distinctly *not* a terrier. He was named that years ago when all large dogs were called guard-dogs, all medium-sized dogs hunting dogs and all small breeds terriers. It is doubtful that there is a trace of terrier in the breed; a more likely choice would be a spaniel-like dog and some small form of mastiff. Misnamed or not, the Tibetan Terrier is a fine, solid little character and one treasured by those lucky enough to own examples. They are good watchdogs, being slow to take up with strangers. They are busybodies and participators. In the city they can tolerate limited exercise, but they love a good romp, particularly in the country.

The look of the Tibetan Terrier is solid and square. He moves well, and although not 'hyperactive' and silly, he is very playful. He is fetching as a

puppy and should become popular fairly quickly. Tibetan Terriers still vary in size, and no doubt a preference will be shown in the years ahead and the standards altered accordingly.

There is a studied ragamuffin look about the Tibetan Terrier, but the coat does require some attention every day or it can become tangled.

The real popularity days of the Tibetan terrier may be just ahead.

Weimaraner

Land of origin: Germany

Original purpose: Big-game hunting

Recent popularity ranking by K.C. registration: Moderate

HEIGHT: Dogs to 27 inches, bitches to 25 inches

WEIGHT: N.S.G.

COAT: Short, smooth, sleek

COLOUR: Solid – shades of mouse grey to silver grey. Small white spot on chest alone allowed. A distinctly blue or black coat is grounds for disqualification

Amount of care coat requires: 1 2 3 4 5 6 7 8 9 10
                                     *

Amount of exercise required: 1 2 3 4 5 6 7 8 9 10
                  * * * * * * * * * *

Suitability for urban/flat life: 1 2 3 4 5 6 7 8 9 10
                  * *

The Weimaraner is an all-purpose hunting dog developed in Germany from the Bloodhound. He is a large, assertive, intelligent animal of unmistakable quality. He is also a dog who requires special qualities in his master.

The Weimaraner makes a better watchdog than almost any other breed of sporting dog because he is aggressive and quite fearless. He is a dog of great character, and he spends much of his time telling everyone about it. If allowed to have the upper hand, there is no worse pest than this breed. He should not be a person's first dog.

This is a breed that simply must be given a full course of obedience-training at the professional level. If the owner is competent, that is fine; if not, then the cost of taking your Weimaraner to a top obedience school should be considered a part of the acquisition price. An untrained Weimaraner is going to walk all over his owner, his family and their friends. While not dangerous, he can be pushy and extremely unpleasant to have around. Conversely, a well-trained Weimaraner is one of the most splendid-looking and gentlemanly of all breeds, sporting or otherwise.

The Germans were almost neurotic in the severity with which they governed the breeding of Weimaraners. Poor specimens were destroyed, and good specimens were bred only after the most careful consideration. Predictably,

when the breed became known here around 1950, it caught on. Equally predictable was the slipping in breeding standards. Weimaraners bred in this country today range from the really excellent to the utterly hopeless. Retail all-breed puppy outlets often feature these dogs, but they should never be obtained from this source. Be suspicious of the inexpensive Weimaraner: only the finest show and field-trial stock should be accepted, and only after a visit with the breeder and a chance to see and meet the puppy's parents.

The only real problem with the Weimaraner as a breed is that he is often more intelligent than the person who owns him. When this happens, it is not the happiest of man–dog relationships. The owner should always be cleverer and should always be in command. Any person clever enough and strong-willed enough to properly select, train and manage a Weimaraner is in for an unparalleled dog-owning experience. The owner who overrates himself or underrates his Weimaraner is in for an ordeal.

Welsh Corgi (Cardigan)

Land of origin: Wales

Original purpose: Herding cattle

Recent popularity ranking by K.C. registration: Moderate

HEIGHT: To 12 inches

WEIGHT: Dogs to 26 pounds, bitches to 24 pounds

COAT: Medium length, dense, slightly harsh, but never wiry or silky. Weather-resistant

COLOUR: Red, sable, red brindle, black brindle, black tri-colour, blue merle. White markings on neck, chest, face, feet and tail tip usual. Pure white disqualifies, and predominant white heavily faulted

Amount of care coat requires: 1 2 3 4 5 6 7 8 9 10
                                                  * *

Amount of exercise required: 1 2 3 4 5 6 7 8 9 10
                                                   * * * * *

Suitability for urban/flat life: 1 2 3 4 5 6 7 8 9 10
                                             * * * * * * * * * *

The Cardigan Welsh Corgi is a very ancient breed said to have come to southern Wales as early as A.D. 1200 He is believed to have arrived there in the company of central European Celts and to have had common ancestry with the Dachshund. The breed was used for everything a pastoral people might need – rushing small game, herding, guard work, chasing away neighbours' cattle, ratting and general vermin work. This dog has enough fire and stamina to handle all these assignments, and he is intelligent enough to take any training required to excel at each task in turn.

The Cardigan Welsh Corgi, 'the Corgi with the tail', is a tough little animal who can raise havoc with other animals. He is utterly fearless and quick and sharp in his movements, despite his short legs. He is territorial and protective of his master's property, and that can lead to confrontations. The Cardigan Welsh Corgi should be trained early and well. He is a long-lived dog and should be reminded of his training regularly. He has a natural desire to please his master and wants to fit in with everything that is going on around him. He tends to be careful with strangers and even a little too suspicious at times. It is to the owner's advantage to keep that characteristic in check. Being a watchdog, which the Cardigan surely is, is enough. Barking is all that is needed.

The Cardigan Welsh Corgi is above all things intelligent. He watches his master, constantly seeking clues as to what is expected and what will win praise. He responds instantly in his own flashy way, without being excessive or silly. Not quite as soft in nature as the Pembroke Welsh Corgi – there are inevitably many exceptions to that, however – he is a bit one-personish, but the owner who has that friendship has a loyalty that cannot be beaten. The love of a Cardigan Welsh Corgi is a special privilege.

The Cardigan Welsh Corgi is not as well known in this country as the Pembroke Welsh Corgi, a very different dog. Fewer K.C. registrations generally mean less interest on the part of the mass-production breeders, but care is still advised so that a satisfying example of the breed may grow up in your home.

Welsh Corgi (Pembroke)

Land of origin: Wales

Original purpose: As general farm-dog – cattle-herding

Recent popularity ranking by K.C. registration: 25th

HEIGHT: To 12 inches

WEIGHT: Dogs to 24 pounds, bitches to 22 pounds

COAT: Short, thick, weather-resistant undercoat with a longer, more coarse outer coat. Wiry, marcelled or thin coat is very serious fault

COLOUR: Red, sable, fawn, black or tan, with or without white markings. White allowed on legs, chest, neck, muzzle, underparts and as blaze on head only. Blue or smoky cast very serious fault

Amount of care coat requires: 1 2 3 4 5 6 7 8 9 10
                                * *

Amount of exercise required: 1 2 3 4 5 6 7 8 9 10
                              * * * * *

Suitability for urban/flat life: 1 2 3 4 5 6 7 8 9 10
                                  * * * * * * * *

The Pembroke Welsh Corgi has a wholly different ancestry from the Cardigan Corgi. He came to the British Isles with the Flemish weavers brought over by Henry I in 1107. The weavers settled in Wales, and the little Schipperke-like dog they brought with them evolved into a cattle dog. The Pembroke Welsh Corgi, then, is descended from Spitz-type dogs and is not as old as the other Corgi. There was a great deal of interbreeding, but that is not done today. Fanciers of each breed want to keep their favourite distinct, as it should be. Any similarity noted today is a result of interbreeding in Wales up to the last century.

There are easy distinctions to be made between the two Corgis: the Cardigan has rounded ear tips and a good tail, while the Pembroke has pointed ear tips and a very short tail, no more than two inches. The two are quite similar in size and outline, however.

The Pembroke Welsh Corgi is a gentle, sensible and even-tempered dog. He is a dog for the farm, the suburbs and the city flat. He is affectionate, and although he can be a good little watchdog, he is not quarrelsome or foolish and is never mean. It is stated in the standards of the breed that shyness or

viciousness are grounds for immediate disqualification, and judges are admonished to dismiss any dog showing these undesirable characteristics.

Corgis travel well and are fine with children. They are, in fact, as close to being ideal pets as can be found. They have spunk and fire and enormous charm. Naturally obedient, they take training well and are very hardy. They are naturally healthy but should be exercised well to maintain both health and condition. They are so pleasant that you can take them anywhere, and it would be the unusual Pembroke Welsh Corgi who could not fit in with other animals. They are very often owned in pairs and are especially pleasant that way.

Be careful in buying a Corgi, and rely only on the best breeders to provide you with a satisfactory example of this marvellous companion animal.

Welsh Terrier

Land of origin: Wales

Original purpose: Hunting and sporting

Recent popularity ranking by K.C. registration: Moderate

HEIGHT: To 15½ inches

WEIGHT: To 21 pounds

COAT: Wiry, hard, abundant and very close

COLOUR: Black and tan or black grizzle and tan. No black marks (pencilling) on toes

Amount of care coat requires:	1	2	3	4	5	6	7	8	9	10
	*	*	*	*	*					

Amount of exercise required:	1	2	3	4	5	6	7	8	9	10
	*	*	*	*	*	*	*	*	*	*

Suitability for urban/flat life:	1	2	3	4	5	6	7	8	9	10
	*	*	*	*	*	*	*	*	*	*

The Welsh is one of the oldest of terrier breeds and almost certainly figured in the modelling of many of the other terriers we know today. He has had a number of names down through history, including Old English Terrier, Black-and-tan Wire-haired Terrier and various combinations of those names with the designation Welsh. The origin of the breed was undoubtedly old England, but it was in Wales that the Welsh Terrier evolved as a tough sporting dog to hunt foxes, otters, badgers and anything else that offered a chase and a fight. He was bred to take on all comers and do all the dirty work necessary. He can handle any terrain and just about any temperature – on land or in the water. Give him something to tackle, and nothing will deter him.

This muscular, well-boned little roughneck needs plenty of exercise. He is a dog that needs to run and needs to play, and for that reason he is great with children. He is good with his family but may be a little slow warming to strangers. He is a natural watchdog and can be relied upon to announce strangers day or night. He isn't yappy or silly, however, and serves well the family with whom he agrees to live.

These tough terriers vary in their adaptability to other animals. Some are fine and never quarrel unless challenged. Others will be holy terrors wanting to dissect every four-footed creature they meet. One person's experience with

the breed may not be a fair indication of what the next owner's will be. You have to watch and wait, and if you do have a scrapper, he must be controlled and trained to behave.

The Welsh Terrier is a first-rate family dog in the country or the city. He is half human most of the time, and fun and games all of the time. It helps for you to be young and vigorous at the same time that your Welsh Terrier is. He demands that you participate in his high-stepping style of life.

West Highland White Terrier

Land of origin: Scotland

Original purpose: Companionship

Recent popularity ranking by K.C. registration: 14th

HEIGHT: To 11 inches

WEIGHT: N.S.G.

COAT: Double. Outer coat straight and hard, to 2 inches, shorter on neck and shoulders. Never silky or curly

COLOUR: Pure white with a jet black nose

Amount of care coat requires: 1 2 3 4 5 6 7 8 9 10
                                     * * * * * *

Amount of exercise required: 1 2 3 4 5 6 7 8 9 10
                                     * * * * *

Suitability for urban/flat life: 1 2 3 4 5 6 7 8 9 10
                                     * * * * * * * * * *

This marvellous little dog shares a common ancestry with the Scottie, the Cairn and the Dandie Dinmont, as well as with the other rough-haired terriers of southern Scotland. Some of those breeds, unfortunately, are now extinct. The West Highland White Terrier may have the best of all of them bred into his spirited little body. This is a dog who is an individual. He knows exactly who and what he is and never fails to exhibit the true terrier style and temperament. Never shy, he should not be really aggressive – assertive, certainly, but not snappy. He is courageous if a challenge is ever offered, and he is fine with strangers once he has done the usual terrier check-out.

West Highland White Terriers like games, toys, their own well-defined position in the house, treats, travel and the undiluted attention of their master. They like to chase cats, but usually for the chase and not with any real intention to do harm (they will live with a cat peacefully). They are adaptable and settle down in new situations as long as their family is with them. I have had friends visit us for weekends with their West Highland White Terrier without any problem, and that required the dog, a mature male, to settle down immediately into a household of six other dogs and ten cats. The Westie managed to check everybody out and get checked out by everybody in the first half-hour. Relatively few dogs can handle that kind of situation so well.

Without giving the West Highland human qualities (which one is prone to do), it can be said that this breed has such a strong sense of himself that much of the nonsense some other breeds have to go through in order to establish identity is unnecessary. A West Highland White Terrier walks into a room with self-assurance and an easy grace that seems to put other animals at ease.

West Highlands do shed and their white hair does show, but most owners don't complain. They feel it is worth it. I have known West Highland White Terriers to settle well into a family with children, but once again, if we were to seek a perfect situation, it would be where the West Highland White Terrier could be the child himself. He is certainly ideal for the couple without children or for the couple whose children have grown and left home.

A lot of poor-quality West Highlands are being bred and sold, and a prospective owner should proceed with caution. It is difficult to find an example with a perfect coat, and it is only with a coat at least near perfection that the true style of the West Highland White Terrier really shines through. People seeking this breed should stick with the specialty breeder and hold out for the ideal dog. It is a commitment that they will live with for a long time.

Whippet

Land of origin: England

Original purpose: Rabbit-coursing and racing

Recent popularity ranking by K.C. registration: 27th

HEIGHT: Dogs to 18½ inches, bitches to 17½ inches

WEIGHT: N.S.G.

COAT: Smooth, close-lying and firm. Doesn't shed much

COLOUR: Given in the K.C. standards as 'immaterial'. Very often seen in greys and tans, brindles and white

Amount of care coat requires: 1 2 3 4 5 6 7 8 9 10
                                                *

Amount of exercise required: 1 2 3 4 5 6 7 8 9 10
                                                * * * * * * * * *

Suitability for urban/flat life: 1 2 3 4 5 6 7 8 9 10
                                                * * * * * * * * * *

The Whippet is, in many people's opinion, one of the loveliest of all dogs. It is impossible for one of these small slight hounds, the fastest dog in the world in his weight category, to assume an awkward position. He always looks as if he has just stepped out of an Aubusson tapestry or off the shelf as a piece of Sèvres porcelain. He is as elegant as any dog can be.

The Whippet was developed for gaming and for the 'sport' of gambling as he raced around small enclosures killing rabbits that had no chance to escape. The more rabbits the 'Miniature English Greyhound' could kill or snap up (they were also called snap hounds) the better. The Whippet today has not lost that old taste for coursing, and he should be carefully watched. He can take off like an arrow and hit a stride of thirty-five miles an hour almost instantly. A dog moving at that speed may be assumed to be short on road sense. When anywhere near traffic, a Whippet is best kept on a lead.

There are few dogs that make better all-round family pets. Because a Whippet doesn't shed much and is neat and clean, he is a pleasure to maintain; he is also easy to house-train. For people who want to show a dog, the Whippet is excellent in the ring, a born ham, and because of his small size he is easy to transport. He is, essentially, a family dog, and won't really show his quality when kept in a kennel. This is a foot-of-the-bed dog for sure. He also likes to

curl up in a blanket or its equivalent when he sleeps, so unless an owner wants all the beds in the household unmade, it is a good idea to leave the Whippet his own blanket. And don't step or lean on that blanket without checking – your Whippet won't make much of a lump inside it.

A Whippet is fine in a flat – he is fine anywhere as long as the family is at hand – but he should be exercised. Long walks are needed every day, and periodically the dog should be taken to a wide open area – an empty beach is right – and allowed to run. You have never seen anything quite like a Whippet enjoying the power of his incredible body at full tilt. Despite what some people feel is a somewhat fragile appearance, the Whippet is hardy and durable. He is not at all keen on cold weather, however.

Whippets take to children naturally and are seldom mean. They are not yappy, although they can make good watchdogs. In a home where the Whippet is allowed to be *the* child, or at least one of the children, this dog will flourish. Whippets don't like being left out. Given his attractive looks, that is about the last thing the Whippet has to fear.

Yorkshire Terrier

Land of origin: England

Original purpose: Companionship

Recent popularity ranking by K.C. registration: 2nd

HEIGHT: N.S.G.

WEIGHT: To 7 pounds

COAT: Very important – glossy, fine, silky and long; straight, highly styled

COLOUR: Steel blue and golden tan

Amount of care coat requires: 1 2 3 4 5 6 7 8 9 10
                                              * * * * * * * * * *

Amount of exercise required: 1 2 3 4 5 6 7 8 9 10
                                                *

Suitability for urban/flat life: 1 2 3 4 5 6 7 8 9 10
                                                * * * * * * * * * *

The Yorkshire Terrier is a fantastic bundle of assertiveness. This cross of perhaps several different terriers with a few toys is a creature of dignity and character. The Yorkie is without question a dominant animal. Other dogs usually back off when he gives warning of temper.

The Yorkie is a delightful little animal, ideally suited for a flat and unstinting in his display of affection. He is a participator and expects to be taken along, even if only in a handbag. He couldn't care less about walks and exercise, and many city people simply train him to a cat litter-box with fresh newspapers several times a day.

What a Yorkshire Terrier saves the owner in long walks in bad weather he makes up in the care his coat demands. It must be seen to, preferably at least once a day. The marvellous little Yorkshire becomes, then, a perfect dog for people who want to fuss. As it happens, many Yorkshire Terrier owners do not brush their pets once a week, much less once or twice a day. Their pets look it. Because his hair does hang to the floor when in its full splendour, the Yorkie quickly is in a first-class mess in the country. Most people keep their Yorkshire Terriers at home.

No matter what the owner does, the Yorkshire Terrier is going to run the show. People and animals all get in line, and the little tyrant of the dog world, the marvellously well-organized Yorkshire Terrier, takes over. He spends his

every waking hour seeing to the matter of his household. He is a fussbudget, busybody, watchdog and knockabout dictator. He is among the most lovable and most clever of all dogs. Beware of mass-producers and retailers, for there are *many* poor examples of the breed around. Some are passed off as Australian Silky Terriers, and vice versa. Fine examples of the Yorkshire Terrier are a work of art, and they will both look and act the part.